THE ETHICS OF OPTING OUT

The Ethics of Opting Out

QUEER THEORY'S DEFIANT SUBJECTS

Mari Ruti

Columbia University Press
New York

Columbia University Press
Publishers Since 1893
New York   Chichester, West Sussex
cup.columbia.edu
Copyright © 2017 Mari Ruti
All rights reserved

Library of Congress Cataloging-in-Publication Data
Names: Ruti, Mari, author.
Title: The ethics of opting out : queer theory's defiant subjects / Mari Ruti.
Description: New York : Columbia University Press, [2017] | Includes
bibliographical references and index.
Identifiers: LCCN 2016033452 | ISBN 9780231180900
(cloth : alk. paper) | ISBN 9780231180917
(pbk. : alk. paper) | ISBN 9780231543354 (e-book)
Subjects: LCSH: Queer theory.
Classification: LCC HQ76.25 .R88 2016 | DDC 306.7601—dc23
LC record available at https://lccn.loc.gov/2016033452

Columbia University Press books are printed on permanent
and durable acid-free paper.
Printed in the United States of America

Cover design: Kimberly Glyder

CONTENTS

CONTENTS

Conclusion
A Dialogue on Silence with Jordan Mulder   215

AUTHOR'S NOTE

In this book, I use the lowercase *other* to refer to the intersubjective other (the other person). When the word is capitalized, it refers to the Lacanian big Other (the symbolic order). When these concepts are impossible to untangle, I resort to the capital letter. Many of the authors I quote do not adhere to the same practice, but their meaning should be clear from the context. I have opted for the pronoun *it* when referring to the human subject in order to avoid unnecessary gendering. Otherwise, *he* and *she* are used randomly.

ACKNOWLEDGMENTS

I thank Wendy Lochner at Columbia University Press for wanting this book; Todd McGowan for supporting it; the anonymous peer reviewer for not ripping it apart; Steph and Jess Gauchel for being a rock to hang onto in a sea of isolation; and Alex Gillespie, Michael Cobb, and Andrew Dubois for being what colleagues should be. My heartfelt gratitude goes to Elizabeth Evans for her loyalty over the years: I will miss working with you. My incredible research assistants Julia Cooper and Philip Sayers are also important intellectual allies: thank you for thinking with me. Thanks also to Brenda Cossman, David Rayside, and Scott Rayter at the University of Toronto Mark S. Bonham Centre for Sexual Diversity Studies for indulging my wish to teach queer theory on the graduate level. A special thanks to the Harvard Program for the Study of Women, Gender, and Sexuality— particularly Alice Jardine, Caroline Light, Christianna Morgan, Afsaneh Najmabadi, Amy Parker, and Linda Schlossberg—for housing me during the final stages of this project: you truly are a treasure. Finally, I thank the students of my queer theory seminars for having over the years given me a good sense of what fascinates them, confuses them, irritates them, and challenges them about the field. I can only hope that this book gives back some of what I have gotten.

There is some overlap between chapters 1 and 2 of this book and chapter 4 of my 2015 book *Between Levinas and Lacan: Self, Other, Ethics.* The borrowed materials have been recontextualized and expanded upon to meet the demands of this book. I thank Bloomsbury Press for its gracious permission to reuse the materials. Some of the same materials can also be

x

ACKNOWLEDGMENTS

found in an essay I published in 2014: "In Search of Defiant Subjects: Resistance, Rebellion, and Political Agency in Lacan and Marcuse," *Psychoanalysis, Culture and Society* 19, no. 3 (2014): 297–314. A rudimentary version of chapter 3 was published as "Why There Is Always a Future in the Future: The Antisocial Thesis in Queer Theory," *Angelaki: Journal of the Theoretical Humanities* 13, no. 1 (2008): 113–126. I thank both journals for being able to reuse aspects of these essays in this book.

THE ETHICS OF OPTING OUT

INTRODUCTION

The invitation to join the mainstream is an invitation to jettison gay identity and its accreted historical meanings. Insofar as that identity is produced out of shame and stigma, it might seem like a good idea to leave it behind. It may in fact seem shaming to hold onto an identity that cannot be uncoupled from violence, suffering, and loss. I insist on the importance of clinging to ruined identities and to histories of injury. Resisting the call of gay normalization means refusing to write off the vulnerable, the least presentable, and all the dead.

—HEATHER LOVE, *FEELING BACKWARD: LOSS AND THE POLITICS OF QUEER HISTORY*

Heteronormative common sense leads to the equation of success with advancement, capital accumulation, family, ethical conduct, and hope. Other subordinate, queer, or counterhegemonic modes of common sense lead to the association of failure with nonconformity, anticapitalist practices, nonreproductive life styles, negativity, and critique.

—JACK HALBERSTAM, *THE QUEER ART OF FAILURE*

"Resisting the call of gay normalization," as Heather Love puts it, has been one of the main goals of recent queer theory. Although the rhetoric of opting out of normative society—of defying the cultural status quo, refusing to play along, and living by an alternative set of rules—has always been an important trope of queer theory, the dawn of the twenty-first century has witnessed an escalation of the queer theoretical idiom of opting out, driving a wedge between mainstream lgbtq activists fighting for full social inclusion and radicalized queer critics who see gay and lesbian normalization as a betrayal of queer politics. On one side of this divide stand lgbtq activists who are trying to escape painful histories of pathologization, who want to be considered "normal," and who are demanding the equal civil rights that such normalcy, in their view, entails. On the other side stand queer critics who, in the spirit of Michael Warner's *The Trouble with Normal* (1999), are asking: Why would we want to be normal? Isn't the normal what has always oppressed us?

One might sum up the matter as follows: while many lgbtq activists are embracing an ethos of positivity—succinctly expressed in the popular "It Gets Better" campaign—many queer critics are advocating queer negativity, crystallized in accounts of self-destruction, failure, melancholia, loneliness, isolation, abjection, despair, regret, shame, and bitterness. It is not an exaggeration to say that "bad feelings," broadly speaking, have become the "good feelings" (or at least the useful feelings) of contemporary queer theory in the sense that they provide—whether through psychoanalysis, affect theory, or Foucauldian genealogies—a way to convey something about the contours of queer negativity. Queer negativity, in turn, underpins the various discourses of opting out that I outline in this book.

The degree to which different queer critics adopt the stance of negativity varies, as does the type of negativity they emphasize, but it seems safe to say that, for many, this stance represents an antidote to the valorization of success, achievement, performance, and self-actualization that characterizes today's neoliberal society. From a queer theoretical perspective, this society is premised on false cheerfulness, on the cult of positivity that Barbara Ehrenreich, in *Bright-Sided* (2009), analyzes as one of the cornerstones of American culture. Ehrenreich argues that many Americans are conditioned to be so optimistic that they have an almost boundless faith in their ability to succeed, acquire wealth, bring about miraculous reversals of fortune, attract good things to their lives simply by imagining them, and beat the odds of illness even when their chances of doing so are extremely slim. Ehrenreich specifies that, according to this mentality, success arises from having a positive attitude, which, unfortunately for those who fall short of success, implies that "there is no excuse for failure": the flipside of positivity is "a harsh insistence on personal responsibility, meaning that while capitalism produces some people's success through other people's failures, the ideology of positive thinking insists that success depends upon working hard and failure is always your own doing" (2009, 8).

The neoliberal culture of positivity assures us that personal fulfillment is attainable through ambition, striving, and calculated risks; that there is no obstacle that cannot be overcome by perseverance; that effort will invariably be rewarded; and that dissatisfaction is merely a temporary state, often just a stepping-stone to satisfaction. By selling us the fantasy of eventual happiness—happiness that seems to await us just around the corner but that repeatedly eludes us—it causes us to pursue one goal after another, one consumer item after another, in the hope that we will one day arrive at the end of frustration. Neoliberal capitalism is psychically appealing, and hence economically lucrative, because it plays into the basic structure of human desire by promising that it can replace a state of scarcity by a state of satiated abundance; like religions of yesteryear, it implies that (the right kind of) exertion leads right to paradise.

What may be harder to discern is that the system produces the very scarcity that it proffers to help us transcend. Indeed, without this production of lack—without this ability to make us feel like something is missing from our lives (yet surely attainable in the future)—the system would quickly collapse, for if we ever reached a state of complete contentment, our desire would come to an end, and with it, our conviction that the new products we see advertised might add something to the quality of our lives; we would stop consuming beyond what we actually need. This is why, despite appearances, neoliberal capitalism thrives on the perpetuation of lack—frequently experienced as a vague anxiety about losing what we already have—more than on the generation of excess even as its excesses threaten to drown us in waste. Moreover, as Ehrenreich suggests, within this system, problems of social inequality have individual rather than collective solutions, so that if you are not making a living wage, you need to work harder rather than to agitate for higher pay. Queer theory's stance of negativity offers a resounding *No!* to this mentality, essentially rebelling against the sugarcoating and depoliticization of life, including queer life, in contemporary American society.

Those familiar with the history of queer theory know that negativity has until recently been most strongly affiliated with the field's so-called antisocial (or antirelational) school. The vanguard of this approach consists of prominent Lacanians such as Leo Bersani (1995) and Lee Edelman (2004). But it also includes antipsychoanalytic scholars such as David Halperin (2007), who seeks to flee the terrain of depth psychology to the more historically grounded methodology offered by Foucault. What unifies these otherwise divergent approaches is, precisely, the valorization of queer negativity, which Bersani and Edelman theorize through the Lacanian notion of death-driven jouissance and which Halperin theorizes through abjection as the hallmark of gay male subjectivity.

Halperin perhaps offers us the clearest snapshot of the contours of antisocial queer negativity. Using Jean Genet as his antihero, Halperin posits that Genet's magnificence (his "sainthood") can be located "not in an ascent to heaven but in the 'abjection' of being driven down into the darkness of crime and perversion" (2007, 73). Such abjection in turn offers a coveted break from ordinary life, a means of transcending the boundaries of normative sociality: through his abjection, Genet becomes a pariah who, "like the saint, is no longer subject to all the usual rules" (74). Abjection, in short, leads to the possibility of "opting out" in the sense that antisocial queer theory (sometimes) defines the concept: by embracing his abjection, his utter humiliation, the gay antihero attains a paradoxical freedom from social constraint, including the sexual norms of "polite" society.

A great deal has been said about the extent to which this thrill of "being naughty, disobedient, sinful, bad" (2007, 57), as Halperin describes it, represents a specifically white gay male approach to social transgression. This is a topic I will return to in the pages that follow. In addition, I will pay special attention to Edelman's Lacanian approach, for one of my main aims in this book is to counter Edelman's Lacan of destruction and antirelationality with a Lacan of creativity and relationality. My hope is that my alternative interpretation will open up new ways of bringing Lacan into conversation with queer theory, thereby, among other things, bridging the gulf that separates the field's Lacanians from its Foucauldians.

Lacan and Foucault represent two powerful precursors to contemporary queer theory. Judith Butler's (1990, 1997) early efforts to combine these two thinkers notwithstanding, the queer theoretical community appears fairly starkly divided between those who have chosen to follow Lacan (Bersani, Edelman, and Tim Dean) and those who have chosen to follow Foucault (Halperin, Lynne Huffer, and a whole host of scholars who are "vaguely Foucauldian" without overtly proclaiming themselves as such). As a thinker who specializes in Lacan—but who also has a great deal of admiration for Foucault—I have always found this rift unfortunate.

It seems to arise from three causes. First, Lacan has been hijacked by antirelational hardliners, such as Edelman, to such an extent that critics who advocate a more relational approach—critics who comprise queer theory's so-called social (relational) school—have found it difficult to find a palatable entry point to Lacanian theory. Second, many queer theorists have interpreted Foucault's (1961) early critique of psychoanalysis as a normalizing discourse to mean that Foucault and psychoanalysis are incompatible. This perspective overlooks the ways in which Foucault's (entirely justified) attack on the conservative tendencies of psychoanalysis does not apply to Lacan, who, as I will show, was just as critical of these tendencies as Foucault was. Indeed, in *The Hermeneutics of the Subject* (1981–1982), Foucault explicitly "exempted" Lacan from his critique of psychoanalysis, recognizing that Lacan not only shared his preoccupation with antinormativity but also offered a psychoanalytic version of what he, toward the end of his life, came to theorize as the care of the self.

I will return to the parallels between Lacan and Foucault in chapter 4. In the present context, I want to mention that one of the seeds of this book was my realization, in reading the scathing critique of psychoanalysis that Lynne Huffer offers in *Mad for Foucault* (2010), that Huffer's Foucault really is not very different from "my" Lacan, that ironically enough, if there is a divergence between Huffer's thinking and mine, it is that I feel that Huffer's Foucault is too close to Edelman's antisocial Lacan. As I will illustrate, Huffer's Foucault of desubjectivization is, despite her vehement protestations to the contrary, virtually identical to Edelman's Lacan of self-shattering jouissance. Still, because Huffer appreciates the Foucault of the care of the self as well as the Foucault of desubjectivation, her Foucault also ends up converging in important ways with my Lacan, with the result that, at the end of the day, I agree with Huffer more than I disagree with her.

The third reason for the rift between those who gravitate toward Lacan and those who gravitate toward Foucault is the rapid rise of affect theory. Affect theory—which resides at the core of queer theory's relational approach—draws many of its insights about the collectively generated ("public") nature of bad feelings from Foucault's account of biopolitics, from Foucault's account of the intangible ways in which social hegemonies infiltrate the deepest recesses of our bodily and psychic being. Because affect theory often focuses on the visceral impact of structural forces such as poverty, racism, sexism, and homophobia, it is sometimes contrasted with the tendency of psychoanalysis to emphasize the enduring imprint of intimate relationships, such as early Oedipal scenarios. Yet those well versed in both discourses know that this distinction is largely arbitrary, that there are plenty of psychoanalytic theorists who are invested in understanding the bodily and psychic consequences of unequal social realities, and that there are plenty of affect theorists who are invested in understanding the wounding effects of personal histories.

This may explain why the attitude of affect theorists toward psychoanalysis is usually less hostile than it is simply just ambivalent. Unlike Halperin, queer affect theorists such as Sara Ahmed (2004, 2006, 2010, 2014), Lauren Berlant (2008, 2011), and Ann Cvetkovich (2003, 2012) recognize the usefulness of psychoanalytic paradigms, often even supplementing their analyses with such paradigms. Their work has been among the most exciting in recent queer theory, intersecting in rewarding ways with the work of more psychoanalytically oriented queer critics, such as David Eng (2010). One reason for my aspiration to present a Lacan that cannot be reduced to Edelman's antisocial thesis (which is deeply antithetical to affect theory's more relational ethos) is that I wish to contribute to this dialogue between affect theory and psychoanalysis.

Historically, the antirelational strand of queer theory has been promoted mostly by white gay men interested in the subversive potential of radical negativity, particularly the connection between jouissance and self-undoing, whereas the relational strand has been promoted by "the rest of us," by those who have been interested in the complex entanglements of sexuality with class, race, gender, nationality, and other collective identity markers. In chapters 3 and 4, I will return to the details of this division, including José Muñoz's notorious contention that the antisocial thesis represents "the white gay man's last stance" (2006, 825). Here I merely want to note that the diversification of the rhetoric of negativity in recent queer theory has begun to erode the split between the antirelational and relational schools, so that these days even a critic such as Jack Halberstam (2011)—who in the past has condemned Edelman's antisociality for the same reason as Muñoz does—speaks a language that courts antisociality, as is evident from the epigram that I placed at the head of this preface. By this I do not mean to say that the antisocial–social divide has entirely disappeared, and even less that Halberstam's version of negativity (or "failure") is the same as that of Edelman, for much of my analysis in this book consists of teasing out the different frequencies of negativity circulating in contemporary queer theory. Yet it seems undeniable that a convergence of visions has been taking place even if the critics in question are not fully aware of this development.

The main reason for this convergence is the hostility of queer theory to neoliberal capitalism that I have flagged. That is, queer critics on both sides of the antisocial–social divide have come to see queer negativity as a means of countering neoliberalism's insidious hold over the bodily and psychic lives of its subjects. This is why the target of recent relational critiques has been the same as that of Edelman's antirelational stance: capitalist accumulation, normative ethical paradigms, the cultural ethos of good performance and productivity, narcissistic models of self-actualization, the heteronormative family, and related reproductive lifestyles. What is noteworthy in this context is that both the antisocial and social factions take aim not only at heteronormativity but also at homonormative gays and lesbians seeking to join the ranks of "model citizens" by accepting mainstream society's definition of the good life, including its valorization of the reproductive nuclear family; the critique of homonormativity represents an important point of agreement between the antirelational and relational schools, which in turn explains why the schism between mainstream lgbtq activists and progressive queer theorists has leaped into such prominence during the opening decades of the twenty-first century.

This critique of homonormativity is the main preoccupation of chapter 1. I enter the topic through the by now paradigmatic case of gay marriage. What I have to say about this contested issue is not new to readers familiar with recent queer theory, but I scrutinize it because I know from teaching queer theory on the graduate level that the field's adamant rejection of gay marriage tends to come as a shock to many students. In my experience, students often find it counterintuitive that many of the most prominent queer critics of the last two decades—and let me add Lisa Duggan (2003), Jasbir Puar (2007), and Michael Cobb (2012) to the names I have already mentioned—have been massively critical of the lgbtq movement's attempts to secure marriage rights. Even a cursory familiarity with the reasons for this condemnation tends to lift the bewilderment, even if it does not always lift the resistance, of students who are used to thinking of gay marriage as an essential civil right.

I use the marriage debate to launch my analysis of the queer ethics of opting out because it provides a concrete backdrop for the more abstract arguments that follow. After a brief foray into queer critiques of gay marriage, chapter 1 opens to a more general examination of the stance of opting out, drawing examples from Edelman, Dean, Puar, and Halberstam. This chapter is largely expository, designed to provide an accessible introduction to queer theory to those—including graduate students—who are relatively new to the field. Expert readers might wish to skip or skim it. That said, the final sections of chapter 1 offer a critique of Judith Butler's model of queer performativity that functions as a segue to the concerns of chapter 2.

Chapter 2 is where my own arguments start to gather momentum. I outline the radical potential of Lacanian ethics, positing that Lacan offers a stronger account of both personal and political agency than Butler's performative ethics. My goal is not to replace Butler by Lacan as much as it is to bring into focus aspects of Lacanian theory that I believe overlap productively with many of the main preoccupations of recent queer theory. Chapter 3 remains on the Lacanian terrain, illustrating that Edelman is not quite as wrong as his relational critics have accused him of being even if his account of Lacan is not the only possible account. On the one hand, I defend aspects of Edelman's approach by translating some of his Lacanese into vocabulary that non-Lacanians might be able to appreciate; on the other, I present the aforementioned reinterpretation of Lacan that emphasizes creativity and relationality—including "reparation" in Eve Sedgwick's (2003) sense—in ways that are attuned with relational versions of queer theory.

There are three major components to my reinterpretation of Lacan. First, if Edelman reads Lacanian negativity as a matter of self-annihilation, I read it as the foundation of many of the things that make our lives worthwhile: our psychic complexity; our ability to wield the signifier, often in creative ways; our capacity to be interested in the surrounding world; our desire to interact with others; and our tendency to form meaningful bonds with those we love. Second, though I admit that exiting the normative social order (the symbolic Other) through a destructive act of plunging into the jouissance of the real—which is what Edelman advocates—is a significant component of Lacanian ethics, I develop an alternative version of this ethics by focusing on our fierce loyalty to our most cherished objects of desire, arguing that this loyalty can, under some circumstances, trump the Other's demand that we relinquish such objects. That is, Lacan offers us a way to understand the ethical valences of the fact that we experience some of our objects as utterly irreplaceable, with the result that we may be willing to sacrifice some of our well-being for the sake of these objects. Third, if Edelman celebrates the subversive potential of jouissance, I am more interested in the kind of pleasure that we obtain from objects we find compelling, proposing that whether or not we actually attain such objects is less important than their capacity to mesmerize us; I am, in short, interested in the kind of pleasure that we are able to experience for longer than a fleeting (orgasmic) moment.

Though the rest of the book does not leave Lacan behind, it opens to a broader examination of queer theory, particularly the contributions of affect theory, queer of color critique, Huffer's Foucauldian perspective, and the rich vocabulary of bad feelings that has animated the field. Chapter 4 begins with a critical assessment of the debate between Berlant and Edelman in *Sex, or the Unbearable* (2014), siding with Berlant's nuanced understanding of the various ways in which the (queer) subject can be negated beyond the foundational lack-in-being that Edelman fixates on. I posit that Edelman's stubborn refusal to admit the importance of forms of wounding that transcend the constitutive wounding of subject formation is not merely politically suspect but theoretically unsound. This chapter also stages a conversation between Huffer's Foucault and my Lacan to convey why I think that the divide between Lacan and Foucault is misleading. These detailed readings are framed by larger questions about subjectivity, autonomy, and ethics that push queer theory in directions that it has not (usually) chosen to pursue, expressing, among other things, my fatigue with the field's by now entirely habitual attempts to slay the sovereign subject of Enlightenment philosophy. While I agree with the reasons for which French poststructuralists undertook the deconstruction of this subject, I believe that it is all too easy to forget that it is a theoretical abstraction that has historically eluded the grasp of most flesh-and-blood subjects. As a result, queer theory's repeated efforts to reiterate its hatred of this subject generate the kinds of ethical dilemmas that the field has not been able to resolve, including the tendency to call for the downfall of subjects who are already leading overly precarious lives.

Chapter 5 highlights the work of Muñoz, Eng, and Love in order to showcase the dynamic "use" that queer theory has made of bad feelings. I explain that because Muñoz's queer utopianism relies on a complex temporality that reaches to the past for a glimmer of future possibility—for what Muñoz calls "anticipatory illuminations"—it is surprisingly compatible with Eng's analysis of racial melancholia and Love's analysis of "backward feelings." Yet I also interrogate the tendency of some queer critics—particularly those who have been influenced by Foucault's analysis of biopolitics—to adopt a hyperbolic rhetoric of bad feelings. Such misuse of bad feelings, I propose, leads critics to overlook the distinction between bad feelings as a banal reality of contemporary biopolitics on the one hand and more acute forms of traumatization and marginalization on the other, sometimes even giving the (questionable) impression that subjectivity as such is a matter of deep victimization. This chapter also contains a tough critique of queer theory's chronic denigration of femininity as well as of Halberstam's equally denigrating endeavor to redefine feminism as a function of "feminine" masochism. The chapter ends with a sympathetic assessment of the efforts of Dean and Bersani to devise an "impersonal" ethics with universalist aspirations.

I have introduced, in rapid succession, a number of schisms that split queer theory into semiantagonistic factions: Lacan vs. Foucault; psychoanalysis vs. affect theory; the antisocial vs. social schools; white gay men vs. "the rest of us." These schisms blur in various ways in the work of most critics, with the consequence that it is frequently impossible to slot any given critic neatly on one side or the other of these oppositions (though some, like Edelman, do not leave much space for ambiguity). The analysis that follows will further explicate the theoretico-political complexities of these rifts.

In this context, I want to emphasize that this book has a pedagogical as well as a critical aim. Over the years, I have written books in different voices: some are strictly academic; others are a matter of me thinking out loud without citations or footnotes. Though this book contains no footnotes, it is academic in tone and contains a wealth of citations. I made a conscious effort to quote generously so as to give those new to queer theory a "feel" for how the field sounds; I wanted to create a cacophony of voices in order to provide a map of sorts for the current state of the field. This is obviously an idiosyncratic map in the sense that its borders have been drawn on the basis of my own preoccupations. But I hope it is a usable one. At the same time, I have also attempted to offer the expert reader some new critical tools, not just through my interpretations of Lacan in chapters 2 and 3 but also through my intermittent questioning of the foundational assumptions of queer theory (most strongly expressed in chapters 4 and 5). The book ends on a dialogue between myself and one of my graduate students, Jordan Mulder, on silence as one possible—but this far undertheorized— modality of the ethics of opting out.

There is more Lacan in this book than is customary in queer theory (even among the field's Lacanians). As I have mentioned, one of my goals is to demonstrate Lacan's relevance to relational queer theory, including affect theory, and the only way I can accomplish this goal is by going into detail about aspects of Lacanian theory that I know are unfamiliar to most scholars and students in the field. Because my Lacan is very different from that of Edelman, it is also very different from the Lacan that queer theory, broadly speaking, is used to: the bad news is that illustrating how this is the case takes some explaining; the good news is that, for reasons that remain somewhat enigmatic, I have always found it easy to convey Lacan in lucid (yet sufficiently complex) terms. It is precisely in part because I knew that I could give queer theory a fresh—and I hope inspiring—version of Lacan without drowning the reader in jargon that I undertook the challenge of writing this book.

Chapter One

QUEER THEORY AND THE ETHICS OF OPTING OUT

Lesbian and gay people see the opportunity for an identification with the institution of marriage and so, by extension, common community with straight people who inhabit that institution. And with whom do they break alliance? They break alliance with people who are on their own without sexual relationships, single mothers or single fathers, people who have undergone divorce, people who are in relationships that are not marital in kind or in status, other lesbian, gay, and transgender people whose sexual relations are multiple (which does not mean unsafe), whose lives are not monogamous, whose sexuality and desire do not have the conjugal home as their (primary) venue, whose lives are considered less real or less legitimate, who inhabit the more shadowy regions of social reality.

—JUDITH BUTLER, "COMPETING UNIVERSALITIES"

Given that marriage provides the principal mechanism whereby nation-states regulate their citizens' intimate lives, nonheterosexual people might have been expected to express more skepticism about the wisdom of entangling themselves in this institution. . . . Queers confront a kind of Faustian bargain, whereby we tacitly agree to renounce public sex—or to sell downriver those who find value in it—in return for the legitimacy afforded by the right to marry.

—TIM DEAN, *UNLIMITED INTIMACY*

1

Though the Supreme Court's 2015 decision of legalize gay marriage constitutes a considerable victory for the lgbtq movement, and though queer critics understand why many lgbtq activists view gay marriage as an important civil right, the pronouncements of Butler and Dean are representative of queer theory's adverse attitude toward the issue. Butler's statement is taken from a book—*Contingency, Hegemony, Universality* (Butler, Laclau, and Žižek 2000)—where she is debating her Lacanian nemesis: Slavoj Žižek. Dean, in contrast, has a track record as a Lacanian. But when it comes to gay marriage, Butler and Dean find themselves on the same page: marriage, according to both, represents a narrow political agenda that merely reproduces the core values of normative society, including its privileging of one relational modality (marriage) over all others.

The problem with a marriage-based organization of intimacy is not only that social benefits—including access to one's partner's hospital room—remain tied to a marriage certificate but also that it automatically vilifies those who reject monogamy, thereby threatening to wipe out queer subcultures that have historically been organized around promiscuous, anonymous, and fleeting sexual encounters. For many queer critics, the disappearance of such subcultures equals the death of queer culture as such. As Dean notes, "the mainstream gay movement [has] achieved considerable institutional success only by desexualizing queers" (2009, 19). Ironically, it is because the lgbtq movement has managed to make gays and lesbians seem "just like" straight people, eager to endorse the family values of married monogamy, that it has made such tremendous political strides. Essentially, the gay and lesbian subject has been sanitized, stripped of its disturbing "otherness," in order to make it more palatable to straight society. For many queer critics, this is a shortsighted victory that undermines more radical efforts to gain social justice.

More specifically, queer critics accuse the lgbtq movement of pandering to the desires of the most domesticated—and usually the most privileged—members of the gay, lesbian, and queer community. From their perspective, relatively affluent, mostly white gays and lesbians are using marriage as a way to purchase their way into "normalcy" at the expense of those who cannot be so easily assimilated: poor queers, racialized queers, gendervariant queers, immigrant queers, and so on. As Heather Love argues, "the increasing media visibility of well-heeled gays and lesbians" threatens to obscure the fact that one may enter the mainstream only "on the condition that one breaks ties with all those who cannot make it" (2007, 10). Simply put, from a queer theoretical viewpoint, gay and lesbian mainstreaming—or homonormativity—merely intensifies the problem of social marginalization, so that while some gays and lesbians now "make it" in dominant culture, others are all the more irrevocably excluded and exploited.

In addition, queer critics of homonormativity question the mainstream lgbtq movement's desire to "make it" in dominant culture in the first place. As David Eng explains:

While in prior decades gays and lesbians sustained a radical critique of family and marriage, today many members of these groups have largely abandoned such critical positions, demanding access to the heteronormative nuclear family and the rights, recognition, and privileges associated with it. Paradoxically, prior historical efforts to defy state oppression and to oppose state regulation of family and marriage have, to a striking extent, given way to the desire for state legitimacy, sanction, and authorization of same sex marriage. Once considered anathema to family and kinship, homosexuality in our current political moment is being legally and ideologically reconciled to its normative mandates, paving over alternative public worlds and social formations that previous generations of gays and lesbians have made.

(2010, 27–28)

Surely, Eng suggests, there is something problematic about gays and lesbians asking for legitimation, sanction, and authorization from the very entity—the state—that has historically excluded them, particularly as the plea for inclusion comes at the expense of the critical perspectives on family and marriage advanced by earlier generations of gays and lesbians. Along similar lines, José Muñoz chastises the lgbtq movement for seeking membership "in a corrupt and bankrupt social order," adding that such assimilationist politics only speaks to "queers with enough access to capital to imagine a life integrated within North American capitalist culture" (2009, 20). Jasbir Puar in turn links the pursuit of gay marriage to the rise of "homonationalism," to the attempts of mainstream gays and lesbians to align themselves with the state's security systems against the onslaught of undesirable "outsiders," particularly Muslim immigrants. According to Puar, gay marriage amounts to a ploy to differentiate between Muslims— coded as "sexually lascivious and excessive, yet perversely repressed"—who refuse to assimilate on the one hand and "upright homosexuals engaged in sanctioned kinship norms" on the other; in essence, it is a means of insisting on "the distance between barbarism and civilization" (2007, 20).

Such arguments are so common in queer theory that it would be hard to find a text published in the field since 2000 that does not at least caution us against the easy acceptance of gay marriage as a political goal. In many ways we are dealing with a rift that has always complicated progressive politics, namely, the battle between those who want to improve the existing system by making it more inclusive and those who want to blow this system into smithereens and replace it with something completely different. That is, we are dealing with a tension between rights-based political approaches on the one hand and more revolutionary approaches on the other: the supporters of gay marriage want equal rights within the system whereas queer critics of gay marriage see marriage as the rotten foundation of a thoroughly rotten system.

In this context, I want to reemphasize that the system under critique is fairly well defined: when queer theorists condemn the so-called system, it is neoliberal capitalism—and its biopolitical tools of control, such as marriage—specifically that they are attacking. As I explained in the introduction, they question the ideals of success that neoliberal capitalism promotes as the route to happiness, pointing out that these ideals blind us to structural inequalities such as poverty, racism, sexism, and homophobia which make it impossible for some people to succeed no matter how hard they try. Basically, if the neoliberal creed tells people that their individual efforts can surmount any and all obstacles, queer critics of neoliberalism stress that this creed is just a convenient way to gloss over the fact that some people will never attain the American dream. From a queer theoretical perspective, gays and lesbians who hang their political hopes on marriage rights are caught up in the tentacles of what Lauren Berlant (2011) calls "cruel optimism," hoping against hope that the heteronormative, patriarchal, and state-controlled institution of marriage will somehow make up for the legacies of gay and lesbian abjection.

2

Berlant defines "cruel optimism" as the stubborn, irrational belief that social arrangements and ways of life that hurt us will eventually pay off and make us happy, specifying that "a relation of cruel optimism" exists when something we desire is in reality an impediment to our flourishing (2011, 1). That is, cruel optimism entails the hope that our relentless efforts (say, our efforts to fit into neoliberal society) will bring us the love, intimacy, success, security, harmony, or financial reward—in sum, the good life—we crave even when they are extremely unlikely to do so. Berlant explains that what is cruel about such hope, and about the fantasies it spawns, is that we might not be able to endure the loss of such fantasies even when they threaten our well-being. This is because the continuity of our fantasies—of our psychic and affective attachment to various scenes of desire—sustains our sense of subjective continuity, our sense of "what it means to keep on living on and to look forward to being in the world" (24).

To the extent that our fantasies underpin our understanding of ourselves as beings who can somehow, however precariously, carve out a place in the universe we inhabit, they can be virtually impossible to leave behind. As Butler (1997) also suggests, optimistic attachments to wounding modalities of life often arise from the desire to feel like we are a part of something familiar, like we belong to—and are recognized by—the world in which we live, with the result that we go along with the expectations that render this world comprehensible to us. In Berlant's terms, our investment in the notion of a "dependable life," "a life that does not have to keep being reinvented" (2011, 170), can be so strong that we remain faithful to specific fantasies of satisfaction even after they have repeatedly disappointed us. We, in short, endorse forms of life that are not in the least bit good for us, coming, as it were, "to misrecognize the bad life as a good one" (174).

The hope that effort will eventually pay off, that things will eventually get better, keeps many of us loyal to ways of life that demoralize us; we are so seduced by the mirage of happiness that shimmers on the horizon that we stay patient even when we should not. On the one hand, Berlant is critical of this dynamic, of "the 'technologies of patience' that enable a concept of the *later* to suspend questions about the cruelty of the *now*" (2011, 28). On the other, she is careful not to pathologize cruel optimism because she recognizes that a degree of hopefulness about the future can be a precondition of surviving the harshness of the present. Precisely because optimistic attachments can feel life-sustaining even as they cause pain, because they provide the kinds of fantasies of flourishing that allow injured subjects to keep on living despite the obstacles they face, it would be misleading to interpret them as a mistake: "optimism is, instead, a scene of negotiated sustenance that makes life bearable as it presents itself ambivalently, unevenly, incoherently" (14). For those experiencing a drastic attrition of the quality of life, cruel optimism, as Berlant succinctly puts it, may be "better than none at all" (16).

One can see how marriage can come to function—for queers just as much as for straights—as an enabling crutch of this type. In *The Promise of Happiness* (2010), Sara Ahmed in fact admits that the desire for marriage among queers may be a legitimate response to a history of suffering, including the suffering caused by intimate lives that have been systematically rendered invisible by a lack of collective recognition. Yet Ahmed, like most queer critics, also acknowledges the pitfalls of gay marriage, including the fact that it implies the willingness to become "the right kind of queer by depositing your hope for happiness in the right place," in the place that heteronormative society has determined as "right": the price of being acceptable is to "*become* acceptable to a world that has already decided what *is* acceptable" (2010, 106). In the context of such a bargain, Ahmed concludes, it might be better to opt out rather than to blend in.

Opting out—the ability to defeat cruel optimism, as it were—presupposes the capacity to resist what Ahmed calls the dominant "happiness scripts" (2010, 91) of our society, such as the marriage script. However, developing this capacity is not easy, for happiness is more or less an unquestioned value in our culture: something that everyone is supposed to want. In addition, our society's happiness scripts direct us to a very particular vision of the good life, blocking other possible visions so that large swaths of life are deemed either undesirable or untenable before we even get a chance to imagine what it would be like to pursue them. And, sadly, we are often not even aware of what it is that we are giving up. Ahmed explains that it is not only social prohibitions ("don't do that") that lead us to sacrifice alternative life paths but, equally importantly, the affirmations we receive ("yes, that's good"). As a matter of fact, the latter are more difficult to resist because it is harder to see them as instruments of social conditioning: while prohibitions overtly guide us to conformist ways of desiring, affirmations occlude the machinery of disciplining, making it harder for us to discern that we are getting an education in how to desire. As Ahmed observes, "We can hear the 'no' in part as it asks us to stop doing something. It might be harder to hear the 'yes words' . . . because the words seem to 'go along' with or affirm what we are already doing" (48).

3

Our commitment to dominant happiness scripts can be so strong that when a given script does not deliver what it promises, when it makes us unhappy rather than happy, we do not think of questioning the script (say, the marriage script) itself but instead assume that somehow we have failed to live out the script correctly. When we have been invested in the notion that a certain kind of life is the happy life, it can be very difficult for us to admit that this life has not made us happy; it can be difficult to admit that our faith in a particular happiness script has led us astray. As Ahmed notes,

"It is hard labor just to recognize sadness and disappointment, when you are living a life that is meant to be happy but just isn't, which is meant to be full, but feels empty" (2010, 75). Importantly, Ahmed maintains that deviating from dominant happiness scripts does not necessarily mean that we discard the ideal of a meaningful life; it merely means that we conceptualize such a life differently: "If we do not assume that happiness is what we must defend, if we start questioning the happiness we are defending, then we can ask other questions about life, about what we want from life, or what we want life to become. Possibilities have to be recognized as possibilities to become possible" (218).

Against this backdrop, the defiant subject—the subject who opts out of the system—is one who is able and willing to turn away from the promise of happiness (as conceptualized by the normative order). Ahmed asserts that the emergence of such a subject entails becoming aware of "how one's being has been stolen" (2010, 167). Ahmed presents four figures of rebellion—the feminist killjoy, the unhappy queer, the melancholy migrant, and the radical revolutionary—whose capacity to resist the happiness scripts of the social establishment depends on their ability to desire differently. For instance, in the context of the feminist killjoy, Ahmed revisits Betty Friedan's unsatisfied suburban housewife as a figure whose politicization was directly linked to her recognition that the truth of her desire deviated from the happiness script that she was being asked to accept. We all know that this figure has been problematized—taken to task for the white middle-class privilege she represents—and Ahmed does not ignore these complexities. But ultimately she is interested in the fact that this woman, who had been taught to desire the comforts of heteropatriarchal domesticity, came to see that what was supposed to make her happy made her despondent.

For many women in the 1960s, the realization that they did not actually want what they had been told to want was the spark of feminist consciousness. From this viewpoint, Ahmed explains, "Feminist genealogies can be described as genealogies of women who not only do not place their hopes for happiness in the right things but who speak out about their unhappiness with the very obligation to be made happy by such things. The history of feminism is thus a history of making trouble" (2010, 59–60). The feminist killjoy, Ahmed posits, is a woman who kills the joy of others because she refuses to desire in the way that others would like her to desire. Feminists, Ahmed concludes, kill joy because they "disturb the very fantasy that happiness can be found in certain places": "it is not just that feminists might not be happily affected by the objects that are supposed to cause happiness but that their failure to be happy is read as sabotaging the happiness of others" (66).

Along related lines, Ahmed argues that queers are a political irritant in mainstream society not because they themselves are unhappy but because their refusal to desire in the expected way makes *others*—more normative subjects—unhappy, often to the point that they seek to convince queers that, deep down, they cannot really be happy. "Even the happy queer might become unhappy at this point" (2010, 94), Ahmed states, for "the unhappy queer is here the queer who is judged to be unhappy" (93). Likewise, the melancholy migrant—the immigrant who is unable to discard his attachment to lost modalities of life—frustrates those who would (for example) like to align the pursuit of happiness with the pursuit of the American dream, so that it is incomprehensible to them why anyone who has been lucky enough to get a foothold in this dream is not perfectly happy, why such a person might have desires other than those condoned by this dream.

Finally, the revolutionary is obviously a figure who refuses to bring her desire in line with the desire of the collective order. This is one way to understand what I will, in the next chapter, strive to express more fully from a specifically Lacanian perspective, namely, that social change demands subjects who are able to mobilize behind desires other than those dictated by the normative social order. In Ahmed's words, "It is no accident that revolutionary consciousness means feeling at odds with the world, or feeling that the world is odd. You become estranged from the world as it has been given: the world of good habits and manners, which promises your comfort in return for obedience and good will. As a structure of feeling, alienation is an intense burning presence" (2010, 168).

4

In every society, the promise of happiness clings to particular goals—goals that are deemed necessary for the attainment of the good life—so that those who are perceived as falling short of such goals are also perceived as falling short of happiness. In our society, marriage, with its expectation of life-long monogamy and reproductive aims, is foremost among such privileged goals. As Michael Cobb posits, our culture depicts singleness as a transitory state, "a conundrum to be solved by coupling off, and as soon as possible," whereas marriage is seen to end "our tragic twists and turns, nullifying all the bad feelings of misunderstanding and misconnection that preceded it" (2012, 4, 13). As a result, "no one is *really* supposed to be single": "there are no *real* single people out there—they're all just waiting for the chance to find that special someone, sometime soon" (5). Essentially, as Cobb astutely remarks, "you're not allowed to be without love"; love is "not merely an activity one adds to a list of things that have to get done in this life . . . but life itself" (18).

No wonder, then, that social critics have long interpreted marriage as a tool of social normalization, including the fashioning of diligent workers. Back in the early twentieth century, Antonio Gramsci observed that Henry Ford was among those who recognized the socioeconomic benefits of marriage. When Ford updated the technology of his car factories in the 1920s— shifting to an assembly line process that hugely increased the productivity of his workers (while arguably eroding the quality of the hours they spent at work)—he capitalized on the (presumed) link between marriage and industriousness by demanding proof of marital status as a precondition of higher wages. He even had a cadre of investigators who conducted spot-checks at the homes of his workers to verify that their domestic arrangements were what they had reported. This is because he thought that stable domestic arrangements would produce more stable, and therefore more efficient, workers. As Gramsci states:

The new industrialism wants monogamy: it wants the man as worker not to squander his nervous energies in the disorderly and stimulating pursuit of occasional sexual satisfaction. The employee who goes to work after a night of "excess" is no good for his work. The exaltation of passion cannot be reconciled with the timed movements of productive motions connected with the most perfected automatism.

(2012, 304–305)

The precision of industrial labor thus benefits from an ideology of family values; from the perspective of capitalism, it is better that you are married, no matter how miserably, than that you cruise sex clubs until 4 AM, ending up at the conveyor belt (or desk) at 8 AM hungover and bleary-eyed. Though it is not necessarily actually true that married people are more productive than unmarried ones—I can think of many reasons, including the responsibilities of child care, that might make them less so—the social perception that they are is one reason that capitalism and marriage seem so compatible.

Herbert Marcuse agrees with Gramsci in *Eros and Civilization* (1955), noting that our society—like perhaps all societies—seeks to channel sexual desire into specific pathways in order to generate the necessary discipline for a well-oiled economic order. Marcuse argues that Western societies are governed by what he calls "the performance principle": an ideal of productivity and efficiency for the sake of which we are asked to sacrifice a big portion of our pleasure, particularly of our sexual pleasure. The performance principle asks us to perform on higher and higher levels of productivity and efficiency even though our (Western) societies are already generating an excess of goods, services, and commodities. In addition, to compensate for the pressures of keeping up with the system—the fact that we are working much harder than our survival would, strictly speaking, require—the system produces substitute pleasures in the form of consumables and luxury items as well as in the form of an extensive entertainment system that keeps us glued to our television sets (and, increasingly, our computers) at night.

Such socially condoned pleasures do not detract from the performance principle but instead feed it by making sure that our bodies and minds get to recharge at night so that we are ready to tackle the task of productivity and efficiency the next morning. But the system is much less tolerant of pleasures that do not bolster its needs, which is precisely why it seeks to control sexuality by restricting it to the confines of marriage. As Marcuse specifies, in the context of the performance principle, sexuality outside of marriage is a "useless" pleasure: beyond reproduction it doesn't "lead" to anything. In Marcuse's words, in "a repressive order, which enforces the equation between normal, socially useful, and good, the manifestations of pleasure for its own sake must appear as *fleurs du mal*" (1955, 50). Marriage, in short, is how man's "erotic performance is brought in line with his societal performance" (46).

Foucault (1978–1979) also views marriage as a biopolitical mechanism that allows social power to penetrate the most intimate corners of our being. Most people in our society believe that their decision to marry is a "choice." But from a biopolitical perspective, it is a means of disciplining the unruliness of desire, of producing a population that acts in a relatively predictable, relatively responsible manner. It of course routinely fails at this task, as is obvious from the prevalence of infidelity. As much as our society may try to tell us that the durability of marriage is its own reward—and even a sign of our moral fiber—this narrative cannot always stifle the fact that there is something deeply antithetical about marriage as a long-term intimate arrangement and the realities of human desire. As social critics have long argued, desire in its unshackled form—eros as the kind of drive that resists collective control—is one of the most antinormative forces under the sun. To put the matter bluntly, this type of desire is not in the least bit interested in the viability of the cultural order. It could not care less about tax breaks, joint bank accounts, or our children's welfare. When it overflows the restrictions that are designed to contain it, it wreaks havoc with everything that is organized and well established about our lives. Still, even desire is not impervious to biopolitical manipulation. In the same way that capitalism knows how to shape, intensify, and perpetuate our desire in order to sell us an array of commodities that we do not need, the ideal of marriage—which, not coincidentally, feeds an enormously profitable industry of costly engagement rings, sumptuous dresses, lavish banquets, ostentatious limousines, and other accouterments of true love—ensures that the desire of all but the most cynical gets channeled toward reproductive (and productive) ends.

5

Biopolitical conditioning is evident, for instance, in the fact that many people in our culture are willing to conscientiously "work at" their marriages even when these marriages make them utterly wretched. As Laura Kipnis remarks in her piercing critique of marriage in *Against Love* (2003), the notion that marriage takes hard work has become so widely accepted that it is these days almost impossible to talk about marriage without immediately conjuring up the language of mines, factories, sweatshops, and chain gangs. "Yes, we all know that Good Marriages Take Work," Kipnis quips: "we've been well tutored in the catechism of labor-intensive intimacy" (2003, 18). As a consequence, when married couples are not bickering or screaming at each other, they often spend countless hours negotiating, adjusting, and resolving their "issues," frequently even paying therapists to play umpire to their domestic dramas.

Sometimes the mere tone of a mate's voice demands countless therapy sessions to work through, for even a hint of disapproval can open the floodgates of a long history of bruised egos, callous rejections, painful letdowns, and stinging disenchantments. Sniping, sarcasm, resentment, the silent treatment, and other forms of psychological warfare seem to be among the standard devices of this mode of relationality, which is why Kipnis notes that it is difficult to imagine "a modern middle-class marriage not syncopated by rage" (2003, 35). Those who have moments of yearning for something different often do not act on these yearnings because they have already invested so much of themselves in their marriages that they cannot bear the thought of losing it all. So they work even harder. They even work at sex. As Kipnis poignantly asks, "When did sex get to be so boring? When did it turn into this thing you're supposed to 'work at?'" (5–6).

In a way, having to work at sex, let alone love, means that something has already gone astray. Yet our society elevates this type of labor-intensive relationality—relationality that demands constant exertion—over less permanent sexual arrangements, and this is the case regardless of how vitalizing or uplifting the latter might be. One of the incredible feats of our social order is that it has managed to make "working for love" sound admirable—as the "noble," "mature," and "grown-up" thing to do. Those who question this logic are told to become more realistic, lower their expectations, and ask less from their marriages. Yet are the rewards of marriage really worth the repetition of arguments, the monotony of overfamiliarity, the tedium of routines, the aggravation of daily torments, and the emotional deep freeze that characterizes so many marriages? Can they hide the degree to which some people experience their marriages as stifling, deadening, frustrating, and sometimes even frightening? Can they compensate for the sacrifice of libido that seems so often to accompany married life, for sex lives that have shriveled into a hushed, insipid, slightly embarrassing, and largely unappetizing task? In short, can the social glorification of marriage obscure the fact that, as Kipnis concludes, "toxic levels of everyday dissatisfaction, boredom, unhappiness, and not-enoughness are the functional norms in millions of lives and marriages" (2003, 90)?

Apparently it can—or at least it has been able to until recently. What is more, the social glorification of marriage arguably determines the very parameters of our being. Drawing on Foucault's account of biopolitics, Kipnis proposes that the ideology of romantic love that underpins our culture's vision of marriage not merely infiltrates our interiority but actually brings this interiority into being, creating "the modern notion of a soul—one which experiences itself as empty without love" (2003, 26). Like Cobb, Kipnis thus emphasizes that the ideology of romantic love is so powerful that it manages to convince us that without love our lives are more or less worthless.

At the same time, the private rituals of domesticity regulate the contours of our daily life down to the minute details of where and how we spend our time. Foucault already argued that societies invent institutions such as factories, schools, prisons, and asylums to guarantee that people can be disciplined into predictable routines, which is why they tend to regulate both mobility and timetables, forcing people's lives to conform to enclosed spaces and the ticking of the clock. Kipnis is only half-joking when she asserts that no modern social institution besides married domesticity "offers greater regulation of movement and time, or more precise surveillance of the body and thought to a greater number of individuals" (2003, 93).

Kipnis's scrutiny of marriage is frankly polemical, unapologetically leaving out of the picture the potential benefits of marriage; it excludes the various ways in which marriage might enrich the lives of those who manage to be happily coupled up. Kipnis also ignores the fact that many modern marriages do not fit her caricature, that the institution of marriage can be revised to accommodate people who do not wish to replicate its suffocating traditions, such as the tradition of gender specific roles. Yet Kipnis's critique—along with the other critiques I have outlined—offers a context within which we can understand queer theory's repeated attacks on gay marriage, and more generally, on neoliberal capitalism: if marriage has drawn so much critical energy, it is because it represents the very cornerstone of the system of biopolitical control—a system that valorizes productivity, good performance, achievement, and self-actualization—that queer theory has been so keen to destabilize.

In this context, it is worth adding that it is not merely the management of sexual pleasure, but of pleasure as such—of our various ways of enjoying ourselves—that marriage facilitates. As Žižek—whose hostility to queer theory can only be explained by assuming that he does not realize how close many of its arguments are to his own—proposes, contemporary Western culture is governed by the imperative to enjoy (rather than the more traditional imperative to curtail enjoyment). From "direct enjoyment in sexual performance to enjoyment in professional achievement or in spiritual awakening," Žižek notes, we are "bombarded from all sides by the different versions of the superego injunction 'Enjoy!'" (2005, 152). At the same time, because we understand that the profusion of the various "enjoyments" on offer in our culture—from drugs, alcohol, cigarettes, and French fries to unprotected sex—can harm us, we can become a bit paranoid about our satisfactions. This is why Žižek's fellow-Lacanian Alenka Zupančič characterizes the double-bind of contemporary life as follows: "on the one hand, the imperative 'Enjoy!,' and, on the other, the reminder that we are also constantly bombarded with: 'Enjoyment can kill you!,' 'Enjoy!—but be aware that enjoyment can kill you'" (2003, 68).

Our society is therefore terribly conflicted about the very enjoyment it advocates. Marriage seems to offer a solution to this predicament by providing a space within which we can enjoy prudently and moderately: not only does it direct us to the "right" kinds of enjoyment—family vacations, children's soccer games, Sunday brunches, and walking the dog—but it also promises to keep enjoyment within "reasonable" bounds ("Mommy can't have another drink because daddy wouldn't like it"). Marriage, in short, allows neoliberal subjects to enjoy without jeopardizing their ability to produce, perform, achieve, and actualize themselves. Among other things, it minimizes the lack of productivity that ensues from emotionally messy relationships: by creating predictable emotional routines that endure from year to year, it enables married partners to anticipate the trajectory of emotional tensions, as well as to gradually devise effective strategies—including indifference—for defusing these tensions, thereby making it possible for them to direct the bulk of their energies toward the socially useful goals that the system promotes, such as career advancement.

Again, I do not mean to suggest that married people are always more productive than unmarried ones. This probably depends on the individual in question. My point is merely that our society would like us to think that they are. This same motive of protecting productivity underlies other aspects of neoliberal culture as well. For instance, when catastrophe strikes, either on the collective or personal level, we are encouraged to mourn our losses as quickly as possible, to get back on our feet, to brush ourselves off, and to get "back to business." While ostentatious demonstrations of anguish are actively elicited as "proof" of our enduring humanness—of the goodness of our souls and the generosity of our spirits—prolonged periods of paralyzing grief are unacceptable because they render us incapable of participating in the life of the economy, either as producers or as consumers. The kind of depression that drives you to the mall may be worth something; but the kind of debilitating sadness that drives you to your darkened bedroom is not. If you are going to grieve, then at least you should do so efficiently (and preferably through some retail therapy).

It is not for nothing that one of the most enduring elements of American cultural mythology is the idea that Americans are a resilient people, capable of bouncing back from any obstacle, setback, or defeat. As this mythology would have it, hindrances are mere temporary impediments. Even better, they are blessings in disguise in the sense that they pay off in the long run by giving you more backbone, by strengthening your character, thereby making you more capable of leaping over the next barrier that appears on your path. Like singleness, they are to be overcome as expediently as possible (join an Internet dating site, pick yourself up by your bootstraps). Those who linger, who fall behind, are prodded to catch up, a bit like a chubby and clumsy army recruit is prodded to catch up with his team of lean and mean soldiers on a training run.

6

One of the strengths of recent queer theory is that it highlights our complicity with this cultural edifice and offers some tools for starting to think about how our failures (or refusals) to live up to its expectations might serve as a form of rebellion. The chapters that follow will explore some of the field's most pronounced trends in this regard. At this juncture—at this early stage in my argument—I merely want to offer a few schematic examples of the queer theoretical discourse of opting out, of rejecting the neocapitalist creed of success, including its various happiness scripts, such as the marriage script.

Perhaps the most obvious example is Lee Edelman's *No Future: Queer Theory and the Death Drive* (2004). In this text, Edelman utters a resounding *No!* to all fantasies of a better future, to the kinds of fantasies of progress that are upheld by both the neoliberal capitalist order and the mainstream lgbtq movement. Edelman claims that such fantasies—which imply that one day things will be better—merely obscure the fact that the day we are waiting for will never come. Edelman's main target is the innocent child as the sentimental emblem of hope that underpins what he calls "reproductive futurism," a social system that not only valorizes reproductive sexuality but also routinely sacrifices the present for the sake of an imagined future (essentially, for the sake of the child). This mentality, among other things, implies that the future of children is more important than the present well-being of adults. Edelman's antidote to this state of things—Edelman's version of what I am calling the ethics of opting out—is to propose that queers should stop chasing a more hospitable future and, instead, embrace the negativity that dominant culture routinely bestows upon them by casting them as death-driven, AIDS-ridden, self-hating, and dangerous to the social order. In other words, instead of fighting the damaging stereotypes that heteronormative culture imposes on queers, queers should accept the negative force of these stereotypes, thereby, as it were, raising the middle finger at the establishment.

I will examine Edelman's argument, including some of its problematic aspects, in greater detail in chapter 3. Here I merely want to stress that to grasp why his stance can be categorized as *ethical*—rather than, say, nihilistic—we need to move away from the usual understanding of ethics as what determines the parameters of right and wrong, just and unjust, behavior; we need to enter into a queer theoretical world within which what is antinormative almost automatically carries an ethical force. In the next chapter, we will see that Lacan already interpreted ethics in this manner, so that it is not a coincidence that Edelman's account is deeply indebted to Lacanian theory.

My second example of the ethics of opting out comes from Tim Dean's *Unlimited Intimacy* (2009), which analyzes gay male practices of bareback sex—which sometimes include the semi-intentional wish to contract HIV—as a means of countering the idea that all of us want to lead long, healthy, balanced, and reasonable lives. Dean remarks that our culture is so health-obsessed that we are constantly barraged by advice on how to increase our longevity. We are told that we can keep illness at bay through the meticulous management of our bodies: the avoidance of risk factors such as smoking, drinking, and sexual promiscuity, along with the promotion of a balanced diet and regular exercise, is supposed to prolong our lives. To a degree, this is obviously true. But it is also a way to moralize illness, to cast judgment on those who fail to adhere to the right regimen. Like marriage, this process of medicalization attempts to regulate pleasure, to tell us which kinds of pleasures are acceptable and which are not (so that eating a well-cooked meal that contains plenty of organic vegetables is an acceptable pleasure but anonymous, unprotected sex is not). This mentality is what bareback subcultures reject, thereby—as Dean explains—staging an "explicit critique of the value of safety as a governing principle" (2009, 191).

Dean connects our culture's preoccupation with safety to oppressive practices of exclusion: "This rhetoric of safety exploits our terror of the unfamiliar in the service of consolidating class hierarchies, maintaining racial segregation, and intensifying xenophobia. I might go so far as to say that the rhetoric of safety, by inducing such paralyzing fear, approaches a form of terrorism in its own right" (2009, 190). Moreover, in keeping with the individualistic principles of neoliberalism, the rhetoric of safety—and particularly the rhetoric of taking responsibility for our own well-being— turns the pursuit of health into a personal obligation. Not only does this absolve the collective order of any accountability for, say, food poisoned by chemicals, but it also turns health into a matter of vigilant self-surveillance, with the result that we spend so much time worrying about getting sick that we might become largely incapable of experiencing the comfort of times when we are actually healthy. If anything, such times come to function as ominous preludes to the dreaded moment when something goes wrong— when our efforts to stay healthy fail and we fall ill. In this manner, anxiety regarding all the "badness" that the future potentially holds becomes the status quo of our lives, so that, ironically, our quest for well-being produces a constant state of not feeling well. Barebackers, Dean posits, are saying *No!* to this way of going about the project of living, choosing instead to accept risk as an intrinsic (and even desirable) component of human existence.

7

My third example of the ethics of opting out is taken from Jasbir Puar's *Terrorist Assemblages*, which suggests that suicide bombing (terrorism) "is a modality of expression and communication for the subaltern" (2007, 218). Drawing on Gayatri Spivak's claim that "suicide resistance is a mes- sage inscribed on the body when no other means will get through" (quoted in Puar 2007, 218), Puar argues that suicide bombing is a way for the subal- tern, denied all other avenues of expression, to speak. Puar goes on to align suicide bombing with queerness, contrasting the rebellious queer/suicidal subject with the homonormative subject. In this manner, Puar, like Edelman and Dean—implicitly at least—relies on the dichotomy of the defiant queer subject and the homonormative subject, but she globalizes the field of analysis by illustrating how the Western homonormative subject comes to function as a homonationalist one so that the "good" gay or lesbian subject purchases his or her social assimilation at the expense of racialized "terrorist populations" which are seen to present a direct threat to the American or European nation-state, and which are therefore targeted for extinction.

Within this dynamic, the salvaging of (white, Western) gay and lesbian lives takes place in tandem with the designation of (brown, non-Western) subjects—queer or straight—as killable, as well as, in Butler's (2004) terms, unmournable. Western gay and lesbian bodies are here no longer equated with death, as they have historically been in the dominant cultural fantasy, but serve the "life" (viability) of Western imperialism by helping relegate non-Western subjects to the realm of death; biopolitics within the West serves to strengthen necropolitics outside the West. Furthermore, the Western nation-state's sudden benevolence toward the sanctioned (white) gay or lesbian subject depends on this subject's willingness to uphold kinship normativity by marrying and reproducing as well as on its willingness to endorse the rituals of consumer culture. Puar specifies that, for the homonormative subject, the promise of social inclusion can create a pattern of deferred gratification, of patiently "pining for national love": the nation-state "produces affective be/longing that never fully rewards its captives yet nonetheless fosters longing and yearning as affects of nationalism" (2007, 27, 32). As a result, the homonormative patriot—as opposed to the racialized terrorist—obediently (and sometimes ostentatiously) participates in the capitalist game of production and consumption.

What is more, the collective discourse of broadmindedness in relation to homonormative gays and lesbians allows the American nation-state to advertise its "exceptionalism," its incomparable degree of freedom. Americans, we are told, are "exceptionally" accepting of difference ("See how well we treat our gay and lesbian citizens!") whereas those outside the Western world are coded as "barbarically" undemocratic. As Puar maintains, in order to uphold its image as a bastion of tolerance, the United States "must temporarily suspend its heteronormative imagined community to consolidate national sentiment and consensus through the recognition and incorporation of some, though not all or most, homosexual subjects"

(2007, 3–4). Conversely, we are repeatedly reminded that non-Westerners, including non-Western immigrants to Western countries, are more homophobic, more prejudiced than Westerners. This differentiation between cultures of sexual expression (Western) and sexual repression (non-Western)—to borrow the vocabulary Wendy Brown develops in *Regulating Aversion* (2006)—conceals legacies of colonialism and economic exploitation, suggesting that non-Western cultures are intrinsically less tolerant than Western ones when in fact "intolerance" toward homosexuality is in some instances a direct result of the imposition of (neo)colonial views on indigenous populations.

Puar, like Brown, at times understates the degree to which non-Western cultures were homophobic (and misogynistic, and perhaps even racist) well before Western imperialism as well as the degree to which they remain so today, as if being "non-Western" automatically absolved a culture of all charges of bigotry; both critics tend to allow their (understandable) impulse to rescue non-Western cultures from the legacies of colonialism to overshadow their critical acumen in relation to non-Western cultural hegemonies, with the result that they, at times, make it sound like non-Western cultures are squeaky-clean—entirely devoid of the kinds of power imbalances that progressive critics have spent decades deconstructing in the Western context. One could even say that such withholding of critical acumen represents its own form of Western paternalism, whereby the non-Western "other" is either romanticized as beyond reproach or deemed to be too brittle to survive the full force of critical scrutiny. That said, I agree with Puar's problematization of the American discourse of exceptionalism, for this discourse incorrectly portrays non-Western cultures as static: forever mired in the swamp of tradition.

In the present context, the point to focus on is Puar's contention that one version of American exceptionalism is "queer exceptionalism": the conceptual alignment of American queer subjects with incomparable transgressiveness and subversiveness (precisely, with the capacity to "opt out"). Problematically, such queer exceptionalism relies on ideals of fluidity and endless self-transformation that converge effortlessly with neoliberal ideals of individual choice, agency, and self-fashioning. In this manner, American queerness comes to index liberation from all norms, customs, and constraints, functioning, as Puar puts it, as "an elite cosmopolitan formulation contingent upon various regimes of mobility" (2007, 22). As Ahmed also remarks, the fetishization of mobility characteristic of Western queer culture "depends on the exclusion of others who are already positioned as *not free in the same way*" (2004, 152).

Under the rubric of queer exceptionalism, access to material and social resources—resources that facilitate mobility—comes to define the queer in ways that may in part explain why the innovations of queer culture can be relatively easily co-opted by neoliberal capitalism. After all, mobility—in both the physical and the psychological sense—is not merely an ideal of queer culture but also of free market capitalism, which seeks to detach people from stable lifeworlds in order to better exploit them as producers and consumers. Likewise, the carrot held under the noses of homonormative gays and lesbians is the freedom to be whatever they "want to be," including married, in a society that offers the promise of a better future for those willing to participate in its ethos of flexibility, adaptability, accumulation, and consumption. This promise is of course usually precarious—predicated upon the successful emulation of dominant cultural ideals—which is why it can become coterminous with cruel optimism.

Puar's account of queer exceptionalism illustrates that she recognizes the downside of the trope of queer mobility. Yet ultimately even she cannot resist the siren song of this trope, for she ends her analysis with an enthusiastic celebration of Deleuzian–Guattarian fluidity, offering a rhizomal model of "assemblage" to counter the (presumed) rigidities of intersectional analysis. If intersectionality—in Puar's opinion—presupposes identities that can be named, discerned, understood, represented, and rendered meaningful, assemblage pulverizes identities, allowing us to envision "movements, intensities, emotions, energies, affectivities, and textures as they inhabit events, spatiality, and corporealities" (2007, 215). That is, if intersectionality freezes identities into legible entities, assemblage allows "for becoming beyond and without being" (216).

It would be possible to argue that Puar is creating a false dichotomy between intersectionality and assemblage, that intersectional analyses also often rely on a notion of identity as an open-ended process of becoming, that identity in the intersectional sense does not need to be fixed for all times to come (does not need to congeal into a stable state of "being"). But what is most relevant for our purposes is that Puar's allegiance to the Deleuzian–Guattarian ideal of the utter pulverization of subjectivity leads her to elevate the suicide bomber—whose "identity" is, literally, blown to pieces—to an icon of a "queer assemblage," to assert that "self-annihilation is the ultimate form of resistance" (2007, 216). Furthermore, Puar reads the fact that the suicide bomber gives his or her life in order to advance a political goal, to preserve "the 'highest cultural capital' of martyrdom," as a sign that the bomber is, somewhat paradoxically, interested "in living a meaningful life" (216). The suicide bomber, in short, opts out of the hegemonic order because of his or her fidelity to a higher cause, thereby enabling collective life—the symbolic life of a political struggle revitalized by martyrdom—to emerge from the very destruction of individual life.

Puar emphasizes the identity-dissolving effect of suicide bombing: "The dynamite strapped onto the body of a suicide bomber is not merely an appendage or prosthetic; the intimacy of weapon with body reorients the assumed spatial integrity (coherence and concreteness) and individuality of the body that is the mandate of intersectional identities" (2007, 217). In this way, Puar reads suicide bombing as the epitome of anti-individualist politics. The dissolution of subjectivity that poststructuralist, particularly Deleuzian–Guattarian, theory has for decades advocated as a politico-ethical goal becomes, in this vision, concretized in the image of splattered blood, muscle, tissue, and bone fragments. Indeed, by presenting the suicide bomber as a queer figure, Puar takes the queer rhetoric of opting out to a level that some might hesitate to embrace, for it is not merely unitary identities, narratives of progress, and other targets of posthumanist critique that get blown up with the body of the terrorist but also, arguably, any viable conception of queerness as anything but an all-purpose placeholder for whatever is destructive.

In this manner, Puar reveals one of the main limitations of queer theory's long-standing aspiration toward "subjectless" critique. On the one hand, this aspiration leads to capacious analyses that, by refusing to reduce queerness to sexual orientation, draw productive analogies between variously marginalized subjects, so that "queerness" comes to encompass anyone with a troubled, wounding, or antagonistic relationship to social processes of normativization. On the other, this aspiration can throw what Annamarie Jagose calls a "proprietary loop" (2007, 186) around an ever-widening array of subjects, so that there seems to be no limit to what queerness can accommodate. This not only threatens to dilute the meaning of queerness to the point that the concept becomes theoretically useless but it also arguably amounts to an imperialist gesture of interpellating subjects—such as the suicide bomber—who might well resent their induction to the queer nation. Puar, however, does not concern herself with such anxieties, unhesitatingly concluding that "queerness is constitutive of the suicide bomber" (2007, 221).

8

My final example of the queer ethics of opting out is less extreme: Halberstam's *The Queer Art of Failure* (2011). In this text, Halberstam promotes failure in its various forms—from stupidity, ignorance, and forgetfulness to the refusal to learn, slacking off, unemployment, and self-cutting—as a countercultural practice that rescues queers (and other marginalized subjects) from the cultural injunction to thrive. Tired of "the idealism of hope" that tells us that our success depends "upon 'trying and trying again,'" Halberstam posits that the queer art of failure capitalizes on the fact that failing "is something that queers do and have always done exceptionally well" (2011, 3). Success, Halberstam humorously notes, requires so much exertion that we might as well leave it "to the Republicans, to the corporate managers of the world, to the winners of reality TV shows, to married couples, to SUV drivers" (120). He summarizes his argument as follows:

Failure allows us to escape the punishing norms that discipline behavior and manage human development with the goal of delivering us from unruly childhoods to orderly and predictable adulthoods. Failure preserves some of the wondrous anarchy of childhood and disturbs the supposedly clean boundaries between adults and children, winners and losers. And while failure certainly comes accompanied by a host of negative affects, such as disappointment, disillusionment, and despair, it also provides the opportunity to use these negative affects to poke holes in the toxic positivity of contemporary life.

(3)

As a critique of linear life narratives and our culture's related ethos of positivity, Halberstam's argument is thought provoking. Though one could accuse Halberstam of a certain romanticization of childhood—surely childhood is not invariably characterized by a "wondrous anarchy"—there is undoubtedly something appealing about his conviction that "the queer art of failure turns on the impossible, the improbable, the unlikely, and the unremarkable; it quietly loses, and in losing it imagines other goals for life, for love, for art, and for being" (88).

Halberstam here echoes Muñoz's assertion that "to accept loss is to accept queerness—or more accurately, to accept the loss of heteronormativity, authorization, and entitlement" (2009, 73). Moreover, it is easy to see how many academics, particularly the overachievers among us, might be charmed (and even relieved) by Halberstam's claim that "the concept of practicing failure perhaps prompts us to discover our inner dweeb, to be underachievers, to fall short, to get distracted, to take a detour, to find a limit, to lose our way, to forget, to avoid mastery" (2011, 120–121). At the same time, the seductiveness of Halberstam's account of failure can cover over some of its contradictions, such as the fact that Halberstam denigrates "high theory" (as a discourse of mastery) without acknowledging that his own (presumably extensive) training in high theory is one of the preconditions of his ability to write *The Queer Art of Failure*. After all, Gramsci, Foucault, Stuart Hall, Walter Benjamin, Jacques Rancière, and other high theory luminaries crop up to support Halberstam's analysis on a regular basis. As a result, his flight from high theory seems a bit like the phenomenon of young women turning away from feminism even though they owe many of their current "privileges" to earlier feminist struggles.

For me at least, Halberstam's argument causes hesitation even as it compels. When Halberstam talks about "darkness" (as opposed to optimism) as a queer interpretive strategy—one that focuses on confusion, loneliness, alienation, negativity, and awkwardness—it is easy to nod in agreement. Likewise when he talks about forgetfulness as a survival technique of those who have been so deeply traumatized that dwelling in the past causes wave after wave of pain. Moreover, I am persuaded by Halberstam's claim that forgetfulness and other forms of failure can, under certain circumstances, give rise to alternative modalities of knowing and being in the world; I agree that forgetfulness and failure can sever our attachment to the success stories of heteronormative capitalism. Yet Halberstam's account generates discomfort insofar as it gives the impression of being articulated from the perspective of someone who has already succeeded.

I suspect that, unlike Halberstam—whose academic reputation has merely been solidified by the rapid entry of *The Queer Art of Failure* into the queer theoretical canon—those who have been severely marginalized are unlikely to experience their failures as anything other than failures and even more unlikely to be interested in further failure in the name of radical politics; those who have genuinely failed in relation to our society's dominant happiness scripts are unlikely to experience their failure as a sexy political stance. My sense is that the vast majority of those who "fail"—underperform in school, cannot secure employment, work at jobs that no one associates with success, or cut themselves in a desperate effort to bypass dominant beauty ideals, for instance—do so not out of choice but because they, precisely, feel like they do *not* have a choice. As a consequence, Halberstam's argument raises serious questions about who can afford to "opt out" in the ways that he advocates.

Consider, in this context, Halberstam's proud announcement that he has never been able to become fluent in a foreign language. Who can sustain such a failure? Certainly not immigrants who move to the United States from non-English-speaking countries. Along related lines, Halberstam's assertion that students are right to resist learning when what is being taught does not correspond to their interests can be problematic in some settings, as is the case when straight white men with some background in continental philosophy (particularly Hegel, Marx, and Žižek) show up in my graduate seminars convinced that they already know everything and can therefore move to critique without making much of an effort to understand what they are criticizing. In my experience, they are respectful of Adorno, Lacan, Foucault, and Derrida but relatively quick to dismiss female authors and authors of color without knowing the first thing about the arguments they are attacking. It may be one thing for Muslim youth in France to embrace hip-hop and soccer rather than the rigors of the French education system—as Halberstam approvingly notes—but the idea that learning, in some general sense, is "overrated" can easily become an arrogant strategy for avoiding engagement with ideas that one does not feel merit one's attention.

I was reminded of this problem recently when the one male student in my feminist and queer theory graduate seminar kept saying in relation to a book authored by a woman, "I admit that I didn't read this text very carefully, but isn't she wrong in arguing X?" I kept responding, "If you had read the text, you would know that she doesn't actually argue X. How about we try to understand the argument before we decide it's worthless?" I knew that this student would have been unlikely to say the same thing about a text authored by Foucault—which he would have made a considerable effort to comprehend—which is why I am more cautious than Halberstam is about singing the praises on unlearning. For the same reason, I cannot agree with Halberstam's conviction that ignorance is somehow intrinsically politically subversive. When placed in the context of the all-American complacency about the rest of the world that allows the US government to run over other nations without its population raising a protest, the argument sounds like an apology for American exceptionalism: Americans can afford to be uninformed because they do not need to worry about what the rest of the world thinks of them.

Paradoxically, arguing for the value of failure can, in the final analysis, amount to yet another iteration of positive thinking, as in, "I can totally blow things off, learn nothing, spend my days listening to hip-hop and playing soccer, and *somehow miraculously I'll still make it*." Alternatively, it can teach us to be content with very little. Consider the justification Halberstam offers for his queer art of failure: "A new kind of optimism is born. Not an optimism that relies on positive thinking as an explanatory engine for social order, nor one that insists upon the bright side at all costs; rather this is a little ray of sunshine that produces shade and light in equal measure and knows that the meaning of one always depends upon the meaning of the other" (2011, 5). On the one hand, the recognition that life is made of both shade and light is a valid assessment of the human condition. On the other, the idea that we should be content with the little ray of sunshine that we discover in our otherwise bleak existence can promote the notion that we should not expect very much from our lives, that we should be happy with whatever crumbs of satisfaction might fall in our lap. From this point of view, the valorization of failure results in depoliticization: if failure is just as good—nay, *better*—than success, then there does not seem to be much point to agitating for social change of any kind.

9

In Halberstam's world of queer failure, antinormativity has become a default politico-ethical stance to such an extent that what matters is not the practical viability but rather the sheer extremity (or rhetorical allure) of the arguments made. This is a problem that reaches well beyond Halberstam and that I will return to repeatedly in this book, namely, that the strand of queer theory that advocates various versions of the ethics of opting out often promotes the ideal of antinormativity so indiscriminately that one act of defiance seems just as good as any other, irrespective of the "content," let alone the outcome, of the act in question. I would say that this is, broadly speaking, one of the main shortcomings of contemporary progressive theory, including queer theory. In its eagerness to reach the next radical edge, the most hyperbolic position conceivable to stand on, this theory sometimes misses its aim, as I think Halberstam at points does, and as Edelman perhaps does in aligning queerness with the death drive and as Puar perhaps does in aligning queerness with suicide terrorism.

This is a politics of negativity devoid of any clear political or ethical vision: it wants to destroy what exists without giving us much of a sense of what *should* exist. It may of course be that offering an alternative politico-ethical vision is more or less impossible. Perhaps it is not the task of theory to define the future but merely to critique the present. In principle, I do not have a problem with the idea that the purpose of theory is to show us what is wrong rather than to tell us what to do. At the same time, I am more inclined to look for "real-life" referents for my theoretical paradigms than those who believe that theory is—or should be—an imaginative activity wholly divorced from the exigencies of lived reality. On the one hand, the latter attitude is freeing in the sense that suddenly anything is possible, including the idea that stupidity represents a radical politico-ethical project. But on the other, it can lead to what Lacan calls "empty" speech, speech devoid of any meaning (pure rhetoric). It is from this partly unconvinced perspective that I would like to start putting pressure on three interrelated tendencies within recent queer theory. I will return to each of these tendencies in greater detail in later chapters. Here let me merely name them briefly.

First, I do not think that the celebration of negativity for its own sake that characterizes some versions of queer theory amounts to much (besides explosive rhetoric). I prefer to *work with* negativity, to see what negativity can do for us. In the next two chapters, I will try to illustrate that this is what Lacan sought to do, despite Edelman's efforts to tell us otherwise. Second, I think that the semiautomatic—and therefore no longer honestly critical—attempt to annihilate "the subject" that runs through much of progressive theory, including queer theory, is a theoretical and politico-ethical dead end. Though I understand the historical reasons for the assault on the humanist subject, I wonder about the almost ritualistic manner in which the slaughter of "the subject" gets undertaken from text to text, as if thinkers such as Lacan, Derrida, Foucault, and Deleuze somehow botched the job back in the 1960s and 1970s. It seems to me that this all-too-predictable battering of the subject represents a theoretical repetition compulsion in the strictly Freudian sense, indicating, among other things, a traumatic fixation that keeps us from moving to new conceptual terrains, including the question of what it might mean to be a subject after the collapse of the unified, arrogant, and self-mastering subject of humanist metaphysics. Of all the recurring themes of queer theory, the assault on the subject is what, for me, gives the strongest impression of empty speech, for it seems to have virtually nothing to do with the personal realities of those who advocate it, most of whom live semicoherent, semicontinous lives in semiconsistent (usually tenured) lifeworlds.

Third, I think that queer theory's antinormativity can all too easily lose track of the continued need for normative justice: the kind of justice that makes judgments about the "right" or "wrong" of things. Though I am well aware of the ways in which traditional normative systems have been used violently to exclude, vilify, and mortify queer subjects, and though I have no wish to argue for "objective" foundations of justice, it seems to me that if we are to posit, say, that the dominance of heteropatriarchy represents a social injustice, then we have to have some normative grounds for making this claim, for pronouncing it "wrong." Antinormativity, in short, always retains an implicit normative content. I would say that queer theory's willful blindness to this fact—the attitude that says that "we" reject all norms as oppressive—represents the kind of theoretical bad faith that leads to various politico-ethical hypocrisies, such as a reliance on the much-maligned "liberals" to uphold the very principles of justice that queer theory likes to subject to a thorough (and again, ritualistic) trashing.

10

These objections will leap into prominence at various points of my analysis. The chapters that follow will reveal that my attitude toward the queer theoretical stance of opting out is conflicted in the sense that I see its shortcomings even as I find it conceptually engaging. But let me conclude the present chapter by foregrounding the main merit of the theoretical trend that I have outlined—and that I will connect to Lacanian ethics in the next chapter—which is that it offers a radical alternative to the Foucauldian–Butlerian paradigm of incremental social change. On the one hand—as I just noted—its vehement repudiation of the ideal of a better future can lead to a rejection of political and ethical agendas of all kinds, so that what matters is the rhetorical flourish of negativity rather than the politico-ethical vision that this negativity might usher into existence. On the other, whenever queer theory's negativity, however implicitly, manages to generate a politico-ethical vision, it is one of far-reaching—rather than piecemeal—social change. As a result, it challenges the Foucauldian–Butlerian paradigm of reperformance, resignification, and reiteration that has, since 1990 (since Butler's *Gender Trouble*), been the reigning model of politico-ethical intervention within North American progressive theory.

By this I do not mean that it is impossible to find a radical politics of negativity in Foucault. As I will show in chapter 4, Lynne Huffer discovers such a politics in Foucault's model of desubjectivation (which is, precisely, why her interpretation of Foucault is closer to Lacan than she realizes). Rather, my point is that Butler's more performative interpretation of Foucault—which suggests that the only way to counter hegemonic power is to deploy the terms of this power subversively—has cast such a long shadow over progressive theory, particularly feminist and queer theory, that it has become paradigmatic. Some Marxist Lacanians, such as Žižek, and some Lacanian queer theorists, such as Edelman, have offered resistance but, overall, Butler's model of performativity has enjoyed a remarkably strong run.

I myself have found the Butlerian approach persuasive. Yet one of its obvious limitations is that it remains remarkably respectful of hegemonic power in the sense that everything, including resistance, must be done *in relation to* power rather than in direct opposition to it: resistance, rather than being a matter of defiant insubordination, of opting out, is a matter of *negotiating* with power in the sense that every attempt to resist power requires a dialogue with this power. Take, for instance, Butler's claim that her theory of performativity emphasizes "the way in which the social world is made—and new social possibilities emerge—at various levels of social action through *a collaborative relation with power*" (Butler, Laclau, and Žižek 2000, 4; emphasis added). Butler's wording here is telling: we are asked to collaborate with power rather than to topple it. Butler in fact readily acknowledges her complicity with power when she asserts that "such complicity is, for me, the condition of agency rather than its destruction" (277).

The argument is familiar: agency is a function of power, of the "productive" (rather than disciplinary) side of power in the Foucauldian sense. We harness this productivity when we find new—parodic, playful, or otherwise innovative—ways of inhabiting power, thereby gradually altering the constitutive terms of power. Queer theory, like feminist theory, has gotten a great deal of mileage from this idea. After all, it has allowed us to theorize gender and sexuality as resignifiable entities that can be troubled and reinvented—reinvented because troubled—almost indefinitely. At the same time, there seems to be no way around the fact that every attempt to subvert norms presupposes the very norms it seeks to undermine, so that, for example, every reiteration of femininity on some level falls back on stereotypical notions of femininity. This is why the Butlerian performative subject is caught in an endless loop of collaborating with power.

The Butlerian performative subject does not revolt but merely reiterates with slight variation. A generous reading of Butler would assert that the subversive reiteration of norms can be a genuinely rebellious practice, not to mention all we are capable of. But a more critical reading would say that Butler's relationship to hegemonic power is too humble. And it would also point out that, like the related ideal of queer mobility, the performative reiteration of gender and sexuality is perhaps too seamlessly compatible with the spirit of consumer capitalism, which offers us an endless array of possibilities for self-reinvention. In other words, Žižek may be on the right track when he claims that today's "postmodern" politics of diverse subjectivities, which privileges hybridity, contingency, artificiality, and stylistics over more revolutionary alternatives, reflects "the specific ideologico-political constellation of Western late capitalism" (Butler, Laclau, and Žižek 2000, 107).

A related problem with the iconography of mobility (fluidity) is that sometimes it is merely another word for instability, and instability can cut two ways: its ability to hurt us is as marked as its ability to free us. Twenty-first-century queer theory is too cognizant of the suffering caused by instability, including compulsory mobility, in today's globalized world to be able to endorse it in any straightforward manner. This may be one reason that the field has undergone an important transformation: away from the politics of performativity toward the politics of opting out. If Lacanians such as Edelman and Leo Bersani have always pushed queer theory in the direction of opting out, it now seems that, in part because so many critics are analyzing the insidious effects of neoliberal capitalism, the entire field has to some extent shifted in that direction. In other words, critics now seem much less interested in negotiating with power in the Butlerian sense than they were at the end of the last century, instead calling for acts of defiance that undermine the entire worldview that hegemonic power—now often explicitly named as neoliberal capitalism—represents.

In the next chapter, in part in preparation for my detailed reading of Edelman in chapter 3, I will draw out the aspects of Lacanian theory that I believe support this new direction in queer theory. Among other things, I will focus on the Lacanian ethical "act": a destructive (or self-destructive) act through which the subject utters a categorical *No!* to the symbolic order (the Other). As Žižek explains, the act arises from "a principle for which, in clear and sometimes ridiculous contrast to its vulnerability and limitations, the subject is ready to put everything at stake" (2012, 829). In this sense, the act is a display of defiance that accomplishes what Butler has long told us is impossible: it breaks our psychic attachment to hegemonic power. This is why Lacan can, somewhat counterintuitively, offer queer theory a more robust theory of agency than Butler (and the rest of poststructuralist theory) has been able to devise.

However, ultimately, my aim in turning to Lacan is not only (or even primarily) to reproduce the narrative of defiance—of negativity, jouissance, and self-shattering—that queer theorists already know from Edelman and Bersani. I also wish to highlight elements of Lacanian theory that queer theory has not taken up but that I believe offer an affirmative alternative to Edelman's death-driven negativity. As I mentioned in the introduction, my Lacan is not Edelman's Lacan, even if I admire many components of Edelman's interpretation. I do not think that Lacan merely wishes to snuff out the subject in a frenzy of suicidal jouissance. Rather, I would say that he is primarily interested in resurrecting the subject from its humanist ashes, in trying to figure out what the subject could become in the aftermath of the Freudian revolution. Lacan certainly takes the radical decenteredness of the subject for granted. But this does not mean that he thinks that the subject *as such* is an obsolete notion.

In Lacanian terms, from the void where the humanist subject dies its agonizing death emerges a subject capable of taking a degree of critical distance from the Other. This should not be confused with Edelmanian antisociality, for the subject who challenges the Other may well remain capable of ethical fidelity to intersubjective others. That is, the defiant

Lacanian subject is not invariably a subject who severs its relational ties in order to exit the symbolic through a self-destructive act; often it is a subject who resists the hegemonic symbolic *in the name of* its relational ties, in the name of an other—or others—who is so deeply valued that the subject is willing to risk its own viability for their sake. The key point—one that both Žižek and Edelman tend to lose track of—here is that there is a difference between the Other as a hegemonic collective social formation and the universe of intersubjective others: the defiant subject may well wish to reject the Other without wishing to discard (all) intersubjective others, some of whom may be cherished rather than resented. This is why reading the Lacanian ethical act as one of "antisocial" (or "antirelational") rebellion can be somewhat misleading. As I will illustrate, the act is often undertaken in order to rescue antinormative versions of sociality and relationality from the pressure to *normativize* them.

Chapter Two

FROM BUTLERIAN REITERATION
TO LACANIAN DEFIANCE

It is because we know better than those who went before how to recognize the nature of desire . . . that a reconsideration of ethics is possible, that a form of ethical judgment is possible, of a kind that gives this question the force of a Last Judgment: Have you acted in conformity with the desire that is in you? . . . I propose then that, from an analytic point of view, the only thing of which one can be guilty is of having given ground relative to one's desire.

—JACQUES LACAN, *THE SEMINAR OF JACQUES LACAN, BOOK VII: THE ETHICS OF PSYCHOANALYSIS*

Lacan's position is thus that being exposed/overwhelmed, caught in a cobweb of preexisting conditions, is *not* incompatible with radical autonomy. Of course, I cannot undo the substantial weight of the context into which I am thrown; of course, I cannot penetrate the opaque background of my being; but what I can do is, in an act of negativity, "cleanse the plate," draw a line, exempt myself, step outside of the symbolic in a "suicidal" gesture of a radical act—what Freud called "death drive" and what German Idealism called "radical negativity."

—SLAVOJ ŽIŽEK, "NEIGHBORS AND OTHER MONSTERS"

1

Žižek is here reacting to Butler's claim, in *Giving an Account of Oneself* (2005), that the socially determined, partially opaque nature of our subjectivity robs us of autonomy. Butler believes that our inability to control the collective symbolic field into which we are inserted—along with our inability to access the murky history of our own formation—renders us partially incomprehensible to ourselves and therefore inherently incapable of giving a full account of ourselves. Žižek, in contrast, believes that being caught in a cobweb of preexisting social conditions is not incompatible with radical autonomy, including the kind of self-responsibility that allows us to give an account of ourselves. That we cannot master the collective context into which we thrown is a given, Žižek concedes, as is our inability to retrace the obscure, partially unconscious history of our own formation. But this does not consign us to an endless process of bargaining with power, for we always retain the freedom to reject our predicament. As Žižek elaborates:

"Even when the entire positive content of my psyche is ultimately impen-
etrable, the margin of my freedom is that I can say No! to any positive element that I encounter. This negativity of freedom provides the zero-level
from which every positive content can be questioned" (2005, 140).

The negativity of freedom—the *No!*—Žižek is referring to is crystallized
in the so-called Lacanian "act": a destructive (sometimes even suicidal) act
through which the subject, momentarily at least, extricates itself from the
demands of the big Other (the symbolic order) by plunging into the jouissance of the real. In other words, even when we feel overwhelmed by the
webs of power that surround us, we possess a degree of autonomy as long
as we are willing to surrender our symbolic supports, as long as we are
willing—even temporarily—to genuinely not give a damn about what is
(socially) expected of us. In short, the Lacanian-Žižekian subject of the act
comes into being as an entity of autonomy (and even of freedom) because
it is willing to honor its inner directive even at the risk of losing its social
viability. This inner directive is what Lacan is getting at when he asks, in
the passage quoted earlier, "Have you acted in conformity with the desire
that is in you?"

In the seminar from which this statement is extracted—his 1959–1960
seminar on the ethics of psychoanalysis—Lacan asserts the centrality of
desire to his ethical vision by juxtaposing desire and what he calls "the
morality of power, of the service of goods":

What is Alexander's proclamation when he arrived in Persepolis or Hitler's when
he arrived in Paris? The preamble isn't important: "I have come to liberate you from
this or that." The essential point is "Carry on working. Work must go on." Which, of
course, means: "Let it be clear to everyone that this is on no account the moment
to express the least surge of desire." The morality of power, of the service of goods,
is as follows: "As far as desires are concerned, come back later. Make them wait."

(1959–1960, 315)

The morality of power, the service of goods, makes desire wait; it wants us
to carry on working. In contrast, the ethics of psychoanalysis is centered
on the rebellious insurgence of desire. I hope that it is already clear why
Lacan's ethical vision is so compatible with the queer theoretical critiques
of neoliberal capitalism that I outlined in the previous chapter. The vocabulary that queer theory uses to talk about neoliberal capitalism was not yet

available to him, but what he calls "the service of goods" is arguably just another name for the ethos of high productivity, good performance, and pragmatic efficiency that underpins neoliberalism. Likewise, what he calls "the morality of power" is just another name for hegemonic power in the Foucauldian sense.

That Lacan is building an ethical vision that is attuned to the concerns of contemporary queer theory is also clear from his condemnation of Aristotelian ethics. According to Lacan, Aristotle builds an idealized ethical model based on moderation and the "cleaning up of desire," a model that functions as a "morality of the master, created for the virtues of the master and linked to the order of powers" (1959–1960, 314–315). Lacan's ethics of psychoanalysis, in contrast, is an ethics of desire that opposes the master's morality. More specifically, Lacan believes that if the big Other seeks to secure its authority by forcing (or seducing) us to accept the parameters of its desire, then the only way to oppose it is to mobilize frequencies of desire that retain a measure of autonomy from this (hegemonic) desire. This is why "guilt," in the Lacanian model, is a matter of having given ground relative to one's desire: to cede on one's desire, Lacan suggests, is to betray oneself as an ethical creature.

This explains why Lacan regards Antigone as the quintessential ethical actor: Antigone would rather die than obey Creon's ban on burying her brother Polyneces, stubbornly insisting on her act of insubordination in the face of Creon's efforts to intimidate her; by defying Creon Antigone becomes an ethical heroine of quasi-sublime status, a heroine who manages to assert her radical autonomy vis-à-vis Creon's symbolic law. As Lacan states, "When she explains to Creon what she has done, Antigone affirms the advent of the absolute individual with the phrase 'That's how it is because that's how it is'" (1959–1960, 278). Essentially, Lacan suggests that Antigone as an "absolute individual"—as a subject whose desire is nonnegotiable—comes into being as a result of her willingness to forgo her symbolic viability for the sake of a "real" act (or act in the real).

I state the matter in this way in order to call attention to the intrinsically subversive status of the real in Lacanian theory. For Lacan, the unruly, chaotic drive energies of the real represent a kernel of rebelliousness that reveals the intrinsic instability of the Other, including the fact that there is no Other of the Other, no ultimate guarantee of symbolic power. The ideological edifice of the Other may work overtime to conceal its fissures, to posit a compelling origin for its fantasies of coherence, but this is a losing battle, for the real retains the power to interrupt the smooth façade of the symbolic. By this I do not mean that the symbolic subject can be converted into a subject of the real in any definitive manner but merely that symbolic subjectivity is always undermined by the energies of the real, sometimes to the extent that—as is the case with Antigone—its symbolic viability shatters altogether. This is why the moment when the subject "hits" the real through the act, as Antigone does when she defies Creon, represents a counterintuitive declaration of freedom. As Žižek observes, "The bar of the Real is Lacan's way of asserting the terrifying abyss of the subject's ultimate and radical *freedom*, the freedom whose space is sustained by the Other's inconsistency and lack" (2000, 258). The bar of the real thus designates the subject's "freedom" because it reveals the contingent status of social subjectivity; paradoxically, the subject is "free" to the extent that its symbolic edifice is precarious, prone to being undone in the act.

2

It is precisely the possibility of such "freedom" (freedom in the real) that Butler keeps rejecting, that she has rejected since *Bodies That Matter* (1993), with the consequence that she has had trouble theorizing the prospect of the kinds of insubordinate acts that allow subjects to override the normative dictates of the big Other. To be sure, in her most recent work, Butler has made attempts to conceptualize revolutionary politics. *Parting Ways* (2012) contains an analysis of Walter Benjamin's notion of divine violence that brings Butler within a striking distance of Lacanian ethics. *Dispossession*, written with Athena Athanasiou (2013), in turn, focuses on the ways in which the "dispossessed" around the world have taken to the streets to demand fundamental social change, including the demise of global capitalism. But Butler's analysis of rebellion in this text remains largely empirical, based on the recognition that people have (in reality) chosen to defy the establishment. The "how" of it remains obscure beyond the basic Marxist idea that dispossession causes so much discontent that it generates radical politics. From a Lacanian perspective—as I will illustrate later—the "how" (the capacity to revolt) can only be explained by assuming that disciplinary power cannot reach every crevice of human life, that something of this "life" remains untamed.

This is the line of reasoning that Butler has objected to throughout her work, especially in the course of her ongoing disagreements with Žižek. More specifically, Butler has insisted that because every part of the subject has been infiltrated by power in the Foucauldian sense, the real cannot be anything but a symbolic construct; for Butler, the very notion that there could be a kernel of being that resists the symbolic is itself symbolically produced—one ideological fantasy among others. Žižek, in contrast, insists that the real is an internal limit to the symbolic, a "bone in the throat" that makes the symbolic cough. This does not mean that the real has not been marked by the symbolic, for it is true that even our bodily drives—which are one way to concretely "locate" the jouissance of the real—have come in contact with the social world in ways that have to some degree shaped them. The Lacanian perspective is merely that such shaping has never been entirely successful, that the real—and the jouissance that represents one of its manifestations—has not been nearly as rigorously domesticated as other components of our being.

Biopolitical control goes a long way in submitting the bodily real to social regulation, as Foucault so eloquently illustrated. Lacan does not dispute this insight but merely proposes that something of the disobedience of the real persists in even the most normalized subject. Consider, for example, instances when the body "malfunctions," when its jouissance—its pain, pleasure, or moments of utter awkwardness—betrays the subject's symbolic consistency, undercutting its polished and protected public image. This is a simple way to understand what Lacan means when he argues that something of the real always escapes socialization: there are parts of our being that the symbolic order tries to discipline but that it can never completely colonize. These parts slide into view whenever the veneer of our social selves fractures, as happens when we are embarrassed by the unruliness of our bodies (think of getting a facial tic while giving a public lecture), or—to bring my analysis back to the Lacanian act—when we behave in ways that the normative symbolic order does not endorse (or even recognize).

Nonnormative forms of sexuality are an obvious example of such defiance, which is exactly why queer theorists—as well as progressive social theorists, such as Marcuse (whom I will discuss below)—have always seen sexuality as a site of mutiny. One might in fact wonder how Butler can deny the potentially counterhegemonic status of the real at the same time as she, like most queer theorists, believes that there is something about queer sexuality that is intrinsically rebellious. Where does this rebellious- ness come from, if not from the symbolic order's inability to fully discipline the bodily real, including its circuits of jouissance?

It is this Lacanian understanding of the real as a seat of rebellious energy that enables Žižek to define the ethical act as "a gesture which, by defini- tion, touches the dimension of some impossible Real" (Butler, Laclau, and Žižek 2000, 121). Žižek goes on to explain the act as follows: "In a situation of the forced choice, the subject makes the 'crazy,' impossible choice of, in a way, *striking at himself*, at what is most precious to himself" (122). In such a scenario, the subject seeks to alter the basic coordinates of its predicament by destroying what it most values; it purchases its freedom at the cost of cutting itself off from what it holds most dear. Žižek's (characteristically drastic) cinematic example of such an act is the hero of *The Usual Suspects* killing his wife and daughter in order to be at liberty to pursue the mem- bers of the gang who held them at gunpoint. But Žižek also offers a real-life example when he asks: "Did not Lacan himself accomplish a similar act of 'shooting at himself' when, in 1979, he dissolved the *École freudienne de Paris*, his *agalma*, his own organization, the very space of his collective life?" (123). Žižek specifies that, in deciding to dismantle his association, Lacan "was well aware that only such a 'self-destructive' act could clear the terrain for a new beginning" (123).

Žižek thus suggests that, in breaking up his *École freudienne*, Lacan cleared the ground for a fresh start, thereby giving us our first glimpse of what it might mean—as I expressed the matter at the end of the last chapter—to "work with negativity" rather than to merely celebrate it for its own sake. Equally importantly, Žižek views the seemingly insane gesture of "striking at oneself" as "constitutive of subjectivity as such" (Butler, Laclau, and Žižek 2000, 123). Along similar lines, Alenka Zupančič maintains that the subject only emerges as a subject as a result of the act, positing that "it is at this level that we must situate the ethical subject: at the level of some- thing which *becomes* what 'it is' only in the act" (2000, 103).

The idea here is that the subject as a subject of freedom—as a subject of ethical capacity—can only arise from the ashes of the symbolic sub- ject. That is, if Butler reads subjectivity as a function of social subjection (interpellation into the dominant order), Žižek and Zupančič read it as the very antithesis of interpellation; for the latter thinkers, the subject comes into being when interpellation *fails*. As Žižek states, "Not only does the subject never fully recognize itself in the interpellative call: its resistance to interpellation (to the symbolic identity provided by interpellation) *is* the subject" (Butler, Laclau, and Žižek 2000, 115).

This is the crux of the disagreement between Butler and Žižek (or between the Foucault of biopolitics and the Lacan of the real): if for Butler the subject arises when social interpellation succeeds, for Žižek the subject emerges when interpellation falters; if for Butler the subject consists of a nexus of internalized ideological forces, for Žižek the subject only becomes a "real" subject when it attains a degree of freedom from ideology. This explains why Butler views subjectivity as a site of subjection whereas Žižek views it as a site of autonomy. For Žižek, the subject represents a gap in the structure of ideology rather than an instance of ideological closure.

In the same way that the Lacanian real ruptures the complacency of the prevailing symbolic, rendering it less securely authoritative than it pretends to be, the subject—through an act "in the real"—ruptures the complacency of the ideology of what it means to be a person. This is why Žižek often asserts that even though Butler accuses Lacan of being an advocate of heteronormative phallocentrism, Lacan actually offers a much more radical theory of agency than Butler herself does, thereby making it possible to imagine alternatives, among other things, to heteronormative phallocentrism. If the Butlerian subject's resistance is limited to the subversion of hegemonic norms, Lacan, in Žižek's assessment, "allows for a much stronger subjective autonomy: insofar as the subject occupies the place of the lack in the Other (symbolic order), it can perform separation (the operation which is the opposite of alienation), and suspend the reign of the big Other, in other words, separate itself from it" (2005, 137).

3

At the core of Lacanian ethics is therefore the idea that the subject who steps into the real—the place of the lack in the Other—severs its ties to the symbolic order. Such a subject is no longer embarrassed by its inability to adhere to the rules of social behavior but instead embraces—feels compelled to embrace—the destructive energies of the real. This subject is not interested in trying to solve its problems within the parameters of the system but rather insists on changing the game entirely, on defying the very structuring principles of the system, which is why the act opens a gateway to what might, from the perspective of the established order, seem completely inconceivable (or even utterly insane).

However, what is perhaps most interesting about Žižek's statement about separation is the claim that the separation that the act accomplishes is "the opposite of alienation." This means that the subject who commits the act follows the pulse of its own desire rather than acquiescing to the normative expectations of the big Other; if the subject is usually alienated from its desire by the desire of the Other (by collective, hegemonic elaborations of desire), in the act, its abrupt separation from the Other breaks this alienation: suddenly, if only fleetingly, the subject is united with its desire rather than alienated from it. As Žižek observes, "alienation *in* the big Other is followed by the separation *from* the big Other" (Butler, Laclau, and Žižek 2000, 253). In this sense, "the big Other is unassailable only in so far as the subject entertains towards it a relationship of alienation, while separation precisely opens up the way for . . . an intervention" (255).

Admittedly, this formulation—which relies on the assumption that the subject can, under certain circumstances, differentiate between its "own" desire and the desire of the big Other—introduces a whole host of complications, for if we have learned anything from twentieth-century theory (from the Frankfurt School to Althusser, Foucault, and Butler), it is the difficulty of accomplishing such a differentiation: insofar as we have been interpellated into a specific sociosymbolic edifice, our desire has been molded to reflect the desires of this edifice. For instance, as I have conceded, neoliberal capitalism is versatile in generating the kinds of desires that fill its coffers with surplus value. Indeed, capitalism even knows how to turn our rebellious impulses against us, marketing to us various modalities of fighting the man, coloring outside the lines, finding our "true calling," and so on. In this sense, we are trained to be defiant subjects—swaggering mavericks—from the moment we are born.

Yet there is a crucial difference between such socially prescribed rebelliousness and the Lacanian notion of defiance I have been explicating, and this difference is what Žižek is getting at when he tells us that the genuinely defiant subject is willing to strike at itself, at what it most treasures in the world, for the sake of its cause (or because it is desperate for change). The rebelliousness promoted by neoliberal capitalism does not undermine our viability as productive (and consuming) subjects; we may be encouraged to be insubordinate in various ways but only to the extent that this insubordination remains compatible with what Lacan calls "the service of goods." The *No!* of the ethical act, in contrast, opens to a negativity beyond this service, beyond the master's morality, which is precisely why it—at least temporarily—destroys the subject's social viability.

Let me formulate the distinction between the Lacanian and Foucauldian–Butlerian visions in yet another way: unlike the latter, Lacanian theory asserts that we are *not* eternally beholden to the Other that rendered us socially intelligible—that there is a way out of our servitude to the Other (as well as to the multiple others who function as avatars of the Other). I recognize that this formulation may be alien to readers whose understanding of Lacan has been shaped primarily by his (early) account of subject formation. According to this account, we all start out as presymbolic creatures, dwelling in the realm of the bodily real (jouissance); our first inkling of identity takes place during the mirror stage, which gives rise to both narcissistic self-regard (the grandiose ego) and self-alienation (the misrecognition of the self as more coherent and omnipotent than it actually is); finally, the signifier interpellates us into the symbolic order, thereby producing subjectivity as a site of signification. The core idea of this account is that we acquire our social viability at the cost of our bodily jouissance: the signifiers that cut into our presymbolic constitution bestow upon us a semicoherent identity, yet they also interpellate us into the normative conventions of the Other, ensnaring us in structures of power and meaning that we have had no say in devising; because we receive the signifiers of our psychic life from the Other, this Other inhabits our being—including our unconscious—in ways that make it impossible for us to extricate ourselves from its hegemonic messages.

This account is accurate. But it is hardly Lacan's final word on subjectivity. Ironically enough, it is in part because of Butler's powerful appropriation of Lacanian theory during the 1990s that this version of Lacan has become entrenched within the American academy among those who have not chosen to read Lacan beyond the standard compilation of early (strongly structuralist) texts from the *Écrits* (1966), such as "The Mirror Stage," "The Subversion of the Subject," and "The Signification of the Phallus." This is how many have ended up with the mistaken notion that Lacan believes that we are subjects only to the degree that we are subjected to the Other. What this Butlerian version of Lacan leaves out is the fact that Lacan was also—and increasingly so toward the end of his career—interested in what it might mean for the subject to disentangle itself from the discourse of the Other. This was apparent not only in his theoretical musings about the act as a radical rejection of the symbolic establishment but also in his clinical aim of enabling the analysand to come to terms with the terror-inducing realization that there is no Other of the Other.

This explains why Lacan's ethics of psychoanalysis—like the queer theoretical discourse of opting out—has little to do with the normative distinction between right and wrong, with justice in the usual sense of the term. Because Lacan envisions ethics as a matter of defying the big Other, his conceptualization largely bypasses the terrain of normativity as a symbolic endeavor, focusing instead on the subject's relationship to itself. As Joan Copjec explains, "The ethics of psychoanalysis is concerned not with the other, as is the case with so much of the contemporary work on ethics, but rather with the subject, who metamorphoses herself at the moment of encounter with the real of an unexpected event" (2004, 44). Stated slightly differently, Lacan invites us to consider ethics as a matter of staying faithful to the "truth" of our desire. This "truth" operates on a plane below our symbolic identity, reaching all the way to the fundamental fantasies that operate on the level of jouissance (the real, the drives) and that, therefore, determine our being in the most basic sense.

The status of fundamental fantasies in Lacan is ambiguous in the same way as the status of the real: these fantasies have arisen in relation to the social world, particularly in relation to what is most traumatizing about this world, without thereby being categorizable as entirely social. Among other things, they often motivate our behavior in ways that counter our rational (fully socialized) wishes. An example of this is the power of the repetition compulsion to defeat our conscious efforts to master our erotic destinies. This is the frequency at which the act—which is perhaps the most extreme manifestation of our refusal to give ground on our desire—intervenes, for it alters the outlines of our fundamental fantasies at the same time as it, momentarily at least, liberates us from the repressive dictates of the symbolic order. As Žižek elaborates, "An act does not merely redraw the contours of our public symbolic identity, it also transforms the spectral dimension that sustains this identity, the undead ghosts that haunt the living subject, the secret history of traumatic fantasies transmitted 'between the lines,' through the lacks and distortions of the explicit symbolic texture of his or her identity" (Butler, Laclau, and Žižek 2000, 124).

Note how entirely different the Lacanian–Žižekian account of the act is from Butler's trademark assertion that there is no way for us to break our passionate attachment to our own subjection. Butler's resignation about the matter is obvious in statements such as this: "The salience of psychoanalysis comes into view when we consider how it is that those who are oppressed by certain operations of power also come to be invested in that oppression, and how, in fact, their very self-definition becomes bound up with the terms by which they are regulated, marginalized, or erased from the sphere of cultural life" (Butler, Laclau, and Žižek 2000, 149). As much as I appreciate the idea that disciplinary power infiltrates our psychic lives in ways we cannot control, I have never been convinced that those who are oppressed are invariably "invested in" their oppression. Some may be, but others surely are not. Many are able to take a degree of critical distance from their oppression—a distance that often leads them (deeply and quite consciously) to resent their oppressors even when they, out of self-preservation, "go along" with their oppression. And sometimes this critical distance even leads to overt acts of rebellion.

What I find useful about the Lacanian–Žižekian perspective is that it tries to explain how some subjects become defiant enough to stage such acts. On the most fundamental level, Lacanian ethics asks the subject to confront the consequences of its encounter with the real, with whatever throws it out of joint with symbolic law. As Zupančič proposes, Lacanian ethics forces the subject to ask the following question: "Will I act in conformity to what threw me out of joint, will I be ready to reformulate what has hitherto been the foundation of my existence" (2000, 353). This is another way of saying that the Lacanian ethical act—such as Antigone's act of defying Creon—demands the eclipse of symbolic subjectivity in order to bring into being a new kind of subject who is willing to transgress the limits of normative sociality.

Badiou (2001, 2005) chooses to put a positive spin on the matter through his concept of the truth event as a sudden bolt of insight that irrevocably alters the subject's basic coordinates of being. Žižek, in contrast, veers toward the negativity of jouissance as the ultimate manifestation of the subject's desire, as where desire meets the death drive. Edelman in turn follows the Žižekian approach to its limits by equating ethics with death-driven jouissance. But the one thing all four thinkers—Zupančič, Badiou, Žižek, and Edelman—have in common is their insistence on what Butler has found so difficult to envision: the subject's ability to break its "investment" in its own oppression.

4

Unsurprisingly, Butler's objection to the ethics of the act is that it contains "individualistic" undertones. The notion of an unwavering "decision," in Butler's opinion, "fortifies the deciding 'I,' sometimes at the expense of relationality itself" (2009, 183). "Maybe the 'act' in its singularity and heroism is overrated," Butler continues: "It loses sight of the iterable process in which a critical intervention is needed, and it can become the very means by which the 'subject' is produced at the expense of a relational social ontology" (184). Butler here privileges her iterative, incremental political approach over the singularity and heroism of the act, and by implication, over the subject that this act brings into being. Moreover, she seems to presume that the act produces the subject at the expense of other subjects or at the very least at the expense of the ethical obligations that arise from its social ontology.

Yet the example of Antigone already illustrates that there is no need to assume that the act is antithetical to relationality: Antigone, after all, defies Creon not for her own sake but for the sake of her dead brother Polyneces. She claims her "freedom"—which is simultaneously her undoing—not for "nothing" but in order to make a politico-ethical statement about the importance of relational ties, about the importance of staying faithful to such ties in the face of persecution. If anything, in placing the fate of Polyneces above her own, Antigone exhibits an almost Levinasian respect for the vulnerability of the other.

I have already suggested that Žižek and Edelman make the same mistake as Butler: all three thinkers equate Lacanian ethics with antirelationality. I will return to this problem in the context of Žižek and Edelman at the end of this chapter. For now, I want to note that Butler's rejection of the act as a viable political strategy relies on the same logic as her rejection of everything that even hints at agency, namely, that it could increase the arrogance of the self by downplaying its relational (and hence precarious) constitution. In part because the critique of the autonomous humanist subject is so central to Butler's outlook, she remains resistant to the idea that the notion of autonomy could ever be dissociated from this subject; for Butler, *any* mention of autonomy appears to automatically lead back to the fully rational and coherent subject of Western metaphysics (to the fortification of the "I," understood in the humanist sense).

This is where Lacan is helpful. As we all know, Lacan was at the forefront of twentieth-century efforts to deconstruct the subject of Western metaphysics. Yet, as we saw in the context of his account of Antigone, he also upheld the "the advent of the absolute individual" as an ethical ideal. Clearly, what he means by autonomy has little to do with the autonomy of the humanist subject that Butler believes lurks behind every mention of freedom. What is unique about Lacan is precisely that he theorizes autonomy (defiance) in the context of a conception of subjectivity that is *otherwise* completely antithetical to the ideals underpinning the sovereign humanist subject. Again, Antigone is a case in point: when Antigone acts, when she claims her "autonomy" in the sense that Lacan means it, she does not become a unitary humanist subject; quite the contrary, she loses everything, including her life. But this does not mean that her "autonomy" at the moment of her act has no meaning.

Butler is nothing but consistent in her suspicion that the subject might be too self-promoting and therefore in need of being humbled. Yet what exactly is so bad about the kind of "decision" that gives rise to a defiant act such as Antigone's? One of the most conflicted parts of *Dispossession* is Butler's effort to retheorize agency as a collective—relational—rather than an individual concept. This theoretical move is, once again, predictable. In order to explain political action in this text, Butler needs a concept of agency. But because she finds "individual" agency objectionable, she can only admit the concept of collective agency, as if rendering agency collective automatically purified it of any contamination with the humanist subject. Yet I am not sure that the distinction between individual and collective agency can be so easily maintained. Have not many political movements— such as the civil rights movement—been spurred by individual "decisions," such as the decision not to move to the back of the bus?

I have argued elsewhere (see Ruti 2015b) that there is something overly simplistic about Butler's efforts to construct a new definition of the subject solely from elements left out of the humanist definition, so that instead of being robustly agentic, the subject—at least the good subject—is now completely devoid of agency. I am here referring to Butler's recent Levinasian theories of precarity more than to her earlier theories of queer performativity, for the latter still contained a glimmer of agency. The former, in contrast, tend to demonize the subject at the expense of the other, as Levinas already did, to the extent that Butler now seems to believe that any attempt to recenter the self is intrinsically *evil*.

For example, in *Giving an Account of Oneself*, Butler posits that there is "no recentering of the subject without unleashing unacceptable sadism and cruelty" (2005, 77). According to Butler, the only remedy to such sadism and cruelty is to remain "decentered," "to remain implicated in the death of the other and so at a distance from the unbridled cruelty . . . in which the self seeks to separate from its constitutive sociality and annihilate the other" (77). I agree that self-assertion can take place at the expense of others. And I agree that the fantasy of sovereignty can promote contempt not only for others but also for alternative, more relational modalities of being. But I am not convinced that the subject who seeks to recenter itself is *automatically* sadistic and cruel, driven to annihilate the other. For disempowered subjects—subjects who have been forcefully robbed of autonomy, violated, abjected, humiliated, or otherwise traumatized—acts of recentering can be the only way to survive.

Butler's anxiety about the subject's possessive and aggressive tendencies is so excessive that it threatens to exclude the possibility of benign relationships altogether. On the one hand, she elevates relationality to the ultimate good. On the other, she implies that nonviolent relationality is more or less impossible because of the subject's narcissistic and colonizing inclinations. The result of this contradiction is that the only way to be an acceptable subject, in Butler's vision, is to adopt a stance of unmitigated masochism; the good subject, in Butlerian terms, accepts its violation by the other while meticulously safeguarding against its own violent tendencies. In other words, the subject is always already guilty whereas the other—even the brutally violent other—can never be so. Again, Levinasian phenomenology—which castigates the self and worships the other—hovers in the background of this line of thought. But it also represents the culmination of the kind of poststructuralist reasoning that deems the very notion of "subjectivity" to be ethically corrupt.

Even though Butler is an antiessentialist thinker, her antipathy to the subject is so pronounced—and so repetitively asserted—that it arguably gives rise to a form of poststructuralist "essentialism" that forecloses certain conceptual possibilities, such as the idea that autonomy might sometimes be a desirable component of human life. Moreover, Butler often talks as if the fact that we are not fully autonomous creatures meant (or should mean) that we have no capacity for autonomy whatsoever. Yet in the same way that having an unconscious does not erase the conscious mind but merely complicates its functioning, our lack of seamless autonomy does not render us entirely devoid of it. Nor is autonomy always the antithesis of relationality. Autonomy is not necessarily a matter of putting up walls around oneself—of claiming complete self-reliance—but can rather serve as the foundation for respectful relationships with others. This is why I think that Butler's attempt to portray autonomy as wholly bad—and relationality as wholly good—causes her to overlook important aspects of human life, including the fact that autonomy and relationality can coexist and interact in interesting ways in the subjective experience of one individual.

Butler is of course not alone in her almost theological condemnation of the subject (and its "sovereignty"). As we will see in the next two chapters, Edelman and Lynne Huffer—both of whom are otherwise deeply critical of Butler—share her revulsion toward the subject. Generally speaking, many poststructuralist scholars of Butler's generation seem obsessively fixated on the idea that the subject must be ground to dust. Admittedly, in her most recent work, Huffer arrives at the very conclusion I referred to earlier, and will elaborate in the next two chapters, namely, that this drive to annihilate the subject is difficult to reconcile with the lived realities of subjects whose lives are already precarious. To her credit, Butler herself recognizes this tension in *Dispossession*, where she strives to find a way to dispossess the arrogant subject while protecting the already dispossessed—vulnerable—subject. In this text, she grapples with the question of how to attack the empowered subject without thereby undermining the attempts of disempowered subjects to attain a greater degree of empowerment. But her efforts remain convoluted because she cannot find her way past the idea that "the subject" *as such* is Enemy #1 of progressive theory.

It seems to me that at some point "we" (progressive critics) have to admit that it is impossible to advocate the empowerment of disempowered subjects if we have determined—a priori—that subjective empowerment is (always and already) a bad thing. Incidentally, the categorical condemnation of the sovereign subject is one way in which progressive (particularly poststructuralist) theory remains deeply "moral" even as it explicitly rejects normative morality: its "morality" consists of insisting on the absolute immorality of the subject. In this sense, as much as Butler seems to pull in an opposite direction from critics such as Edelman— Butler defending sociality and Edelman defending antisociality—they in fact share the same moral preoccupation with the demise of the subject, a preoccupation that dictates that allowing the subject to survive in any shape or form would amount to an ethical failure.

In contrast, as I will demonstrate shortly, Lacan's aim was to transform the subject, to allow it to undergo a radical reorientation of self-definition. Though Lacan was critical of the humanist subject, his goal was not to destroy the subject per se but to introduce new possibilities of subjective experience. On some level, this may always be the objective of psychoanalysis as a clinical practice. Theorists such as Edelman who underplay the clinical side of Lacanian theory lose sight of this, which is precisely why they end up advocating the utter dissolution of the subject. Yet a moment's reflection reveals that even Lacan—the antihumanist thinker par excellence—could not have possibly wanted his patients to obliterate themselves.

5

Let me enter the explanation of how Lacan reinvents—rather than destroys—the subject through the backdoor, by way of Marcuse's analysis of the problematic I raised earlier, namely, that it is difficult to dissociate the subject's desire from the desire of the Other. I have admitted that neoliberal capitalism finds countless ways to mold the desire of its subjects in order to maximize profit. Indeed, one of its main victories has been to translate the master's "service of goods," the master's demand that "work must go on," into "a way of life"—a mode of living organized around ideals of productivity, good performance, achievement, and self-actualization—that many of us have internalized to such an extent that we do not even think to question it. This is the state of affairs that Marcuse diagnoses when he notes that contemporary Western society is organized around the performance principle (which he reads as a deeply capitalist version of the Freudian reality principle).

Productivity, Marcuse notes, is one of the most sacrosanct values of modern culture in the sense that it "expresses perhaps more than any other the existential attitude in industrial civilization"; it permeates the very definition of the subject, so that man "is evaluated according to his ability to make, augment, and improve socially useful things" (1955, 155). More broadly speaking, the performance principle dictates that we strive for ever-higher levels of productivity; that we take it for granted that efficiency is not only a social good but a personal virtue; that we understand that progress cannot be made without a degree of pain (or at least boredom); that we are willing to accept the idea that pleasure, gratification, and moments of happiness belong to the realm of leisure rather than of work; and that we are consequently willing to delay our satisfaction until our work for the day is done.

Marcuse concedes that those who are privileged enough to work in creative professions—artists, writers, artisans, inventors, and professors, among others—may experience enclaves of satisfaction within their working lives. But for the majority of people performing various forms of "alienated labor," such as routine office work or tending the assembly line, there is a strict division of affective registers between work (pain) and leisure (pleasure). Yet even alienated workers do not usually interrogate the value of productivity and good performance. As I have underscored, our society asks them to approach their tasks with a positive attitude, even cheerfulness, as is the case with service workers, particularly women, who are expected to smile their way through the tedium of their jobs. For such workers, faking happiness is a precondition of keeping their jobs, a bit like faking orgasms is the precondition of some women's ability to keep their relationships.

As I emphasized in the previous chapter, even the leisure hours of contemporary workers can become a means of buttressing the productivity and good performance of their working hours. This is one reason passive forms of entertainment—what Marcuse's Frankfurt School colleague Adorno associated with "the culture industry"—have become so dominant in late capitalist consumer society. That leisure is often epitomized by the remote control of the television set in the privacy of one's living room is symptomatic of the fact that the high levels of activity demanded by the performance principle can only be sustained (replenished) by stretches of absolute passivity.

Add to this the fact that productivity has reached such a high level in Western societies that the workers themselves reap some of the benefits of the production process in the form of consumer comforts and commodities, and we have a situation where the desires of even the least privileged tend to coincide quite seamlessly with the desires of the big Other. Indeed, there is arguably something about the very nature of desire—which tends to restlessly seek new objects for its satisfaction—that accords extremely well with capitalism's alignment of enjoyment with consumption. In this sense, nothing stifles the revolutionary impulse more effectively than the ideal of conspicuous consumption (and the advertising industry that beautifies this ideal). As a matter of fact, even those who fall short of this ideal live in its shadow in the sense that they keep hoping that they might one day be able to attain it.

As we have seen, Berlant characterizes this predicament as one of cruel optimism. And we have also learned that Ahmed makes a parallel point about our culture's dominant happiness scripts, which can block our capacity to envision alternatives modes of life. Marcuse expresses the matter in more strictly psychoanalytic terms, arguing that workers often come to desire the performance principle even though it is predicated on a severe repression of their libidinal impulses. Simply put, social authority is internalized to the extent that the individual comes to live "his repression 'freely' as his own life: he desires what he is supposed to desire" (1955, 46). Indeed—and this is important for my purposes—Marcuse stresses that the repressiveness of the performance principle far exceeds the parameters of the kind of repression that Freud saw as the foundation of civilization.

Although social existence always requires a degree of repression, what we are witnessing in modern Western society is what Marcuse calls "surplus-repression": the kind of repression that meets the demands of a society organized by the unequal distribution of resources. "Within the total structure of the repressed personality," Marcuse explains, "surplus-repression is that portion which is the result of specific societal conditions sustained in the specific interest of domination" (1955, 87–88). Surplus-repression is therefore a historically specific form of suffering that is added, for the benefit of those who hold power, to the mutilation of the drives demanded by social life as such. And because our desires have become so neatly aligned with what Lacan calls the "order of powers" (or the "service of goods"), we willingly participate in this arrangement, earnestly believing that it serves our most fundamental needs.

In this context, I want to stress that even though Marcuse equated surplus-repression with the moralistic disciplining of sexuality character-istic of Western societies in the 1950s, there is no need to assume that this is the only form it can take. In the contemporary world, where, as I argued in chapter 1, it is the injunction to enjoy ourselves rather than the injunction to curtail our enjoyment that dominates, surplus-repression may be less a matter of suppressing our sexuality than of learning to be sexual in ways that feed the performance principle. Earlier I mentioned that Adorno recognized that entertainment plays a significant role in increasing our productivity. It is interesting to note, then, that contem-porary entertainment is saturated by overt forms of sexuality that would have been unthinkable in the 1950s: more or less any sexual predilection can find instant satisfaction on the Internet; every form of sexual "trans-gression" has been commodified, advertised through some of the most powerful machines of the culture industry. In a universe where even the most vanilla of straight bedrooms has been infiltrated by various shades of gray, it seems increasingly difficult to think about sexual transgression outside of the capitalist injunction to enjoy.

As a result, it would be impossible to argue that the current perfor-mance principle relies on the suppression of the libido in the sense that Marcuse depicts the matter. Instead, it relies on a meticulous *manipulation* of the libido. Consider the common practice of using online pornography to take a "break" from work, to recharge one's ability to tackle the next task, or to endure the dullness of the day. From this perspective, pornog-raphy is an efficient tool of biopolitical conditioning, perhaps even the epitome of neoliberal efficiency: you take your break, there is no emotional mess—the mess being limited to the physical surfaces of your immediate surroundings—and then you go back to work, back to the performance principle. The libido, in this scenario, is not repressed but instrumentalized in the service of increased productivity.

This is one reason that—as I will discuss in greater detail in chapter 4— I am not entirely convinced by queer theoretical attempts to view sexual-ity as intrinsically rebellious. I think that, like desire, it has the *potential* to be rebellious but that, like desire, it can be made to serve the performance principle. In other words, it seems to me that, in present-day Western societies, sex—including sex that used to be considered "perverse"—is more often a way to facilitate our capacity to successfully participate in the neoliberal game of keeping up with a multitude of psychic, emotional, and work-related pressures.

Moreover, the very fact that we are being trained to think that sex is (and should be) available to us at all times with a mere click of the mouse seems part and parcel of the capitalist mentality that presents consumerism as a solution to all of our problems; it explicitly promotes the idea that it is our inalienable right to "enjoy" the offerings of our affluent societies. The sad fact is that, at the very moment when we experience ourselves as sexually "free" (better off than earlier generations), we are getting a very precise tutoring in how to desire; we are being taught to desire in accordance to the desire of the big Other, including its desire to make money off our desire, whether directly through pornography or indirectly through our improved productivity.

I grant, then, that it is extremely difficult to differentiate our desire from the desire of the Other. Undoubtedly Lacan understood this better than most. This makes it all the more noteworthy that he conceptualized ethics in terms of the subject's unwillingness to give ground on its desire. Lacan knew perfectly well how challenging it is to shatter the spell of biopolitical conditioning, yet his ethics demands precisely the capacity to do so. This is why Lacanian ethics offers such a powerful point of contrast to Butler's conviction that there is no way to rupture the subject's psychic attachment to hegemonic power. Lacan admits that such a rupture is hard to accomplish, but he insists that it is the task of psychoanalysis as a clinical practice—as a practice of ethics specifically—to produce the kind of subject who might be able to carry out such a feat of defiance.

The ethical act that I have discussed is a radical example of such a feat of defiance. But we should not underestimate the importance of the moment when the analysand, perhaps after years of analysis, finally manages to say *Enough!* to whoever or whatever is causing her to suffer. If the goal of Lacanian analysis is to enable the analysand to dissociate herself from the desire of the Other, or from the desire of those who, in her life, embody this desire, it is because this is the only way for her to destroy her (cruelly) optimistic allegiance to power structures that oppress her. There may still be an enormous distance between such tiny acts of individual defiance and radical politics, yet there is arguably also a conceptual link between the analysand who is able to utter her *Enough!* with a degree of conviction and the politicized subject who utters the same *Enough!* in the context of collective social mobilization. That is, collective social mobilization relies on subjects who have the ability to stick to their desire in the face of the demand that they capitulate to the desire of the Other.

6

I will return to this connection between individual and collective acts of defiance toward the end of this chapter. But first I want to explore in greater detail how, from a Lacanian perspective, it might be possible to talk about desire as something that can be detached from the master's morality. To get started, let me restate the problem at hand as a question: If social subjectivity is a function of being interpellated into the symbolic order, then how can we even begin to conceptualize forms of desire that have not been completely overrun by the desire of the Other?

This is where I find Marcuse helpful, for his analysis of surplus-repression implies that if we were able to somehow peel off this excess of repression—or what we might, in the contemporary context, conceptualize as an excess of manipulation—we would be left with what Lacan calls the truth of desire: the kind of desire that has certainly come into existence as a result of repression, but not as a result of the expectations of the performance principle. Indeed, though Lacan does not share Marcuse's Marxist platform, he in many ways operates with a similar distinction between repression and surplus-repression: though he understands that there is no such thing as desire divorced from its social environment, he believes that there are degrees of freedom and unfreedom, that some of our desires are more primary than the desires driven by the performance principle. Such primary desires—desires that touch the subject's fundamental fantasies— reach toward the rebellious drive energies (jouissance) of the real rather than the conformist symbolic, which is why the subject's capacity to animate them is essential for its ability to defy the hegemonic decrees of the latter. Or, to put the matter slightly differently, the idea that the truth of desire might lurk beneath the performance principle explains why one of the objectives of Lacanian analysis is to allow the subject to break its allegiance to this principle.

On the one hand, Lacan—like Marcuse—believes that a degree of repression, of biopolitical manipulation, is necessary for the emergence of socially intelligible subjectivity. On the other, Lacan—again, like Marcuse—recognizes that the symbolic order is repressive (or manipulative) beyond the demands of subject formation, that it includes forms of violence that exceed the ubiquitous violence of the signifier. Indeed, even the violence of the signifier is not equally distributed, so that some of us are much more vulnerable to its injurious effects than others (consider, for instance, hate speech). This point is one of Butler's blind spots about Lacanian theory, for she believes that Lacan's concept of constitutive lack undermines our ability to comprehend the socially and historically specific ways in which individuals are rendered lacking: traumatized, wounded, injured, and so on. As she states, "I agree with the notion that every subject emerges on the condition of foreclosure, but do not share the conviction that these foreclosures are prior to the social," adding that, in Lacan, the trauma that inaugurated the subject is "prior to any and all social and historical reality" (Butler, Laclau, and Žižek 2000, 140–141).

This is simply not true. Though Lacan does suggest that we are all wounded by language, it does not follow that we are all wounded in the same (ahistorical) manner. This is why Žižek writes in response to Butler's criticism of Lacan's ahistorical "formalism": "when Lacan emphatically asserts that 'there is no big Other [*il n'y a pas de grand Autre*],' his point is precisely that there is no a priori formal structural scheme exempt from historical contingencies—there are only contingent, fragile, inconsistent configurations" (Butler, Laclau, and Žižek 2000, 310). In other words, the Lacanian subject, like any subject, is constituted in relation to context-specific collective forces, including socioeconomic and political inequalities. This is precisely why there is no Other of the Other, no "ultimate" big Other whose hegemony is secured (uncontested) for all times to come; it is why the symbolic field remains a battleground for ever-shifting political antagonisms.

Lacan does not talk about the unequal distribution of resources in the manner Marcuse does, but there is no doubt that his analysis of symbolic law as the Law of the Father refers to a historically specific, deeply heteropatriarchal and hierarchical organization of social life. In point of fact, one reason I have taken a detour through Marcuse is to illustrate the obvious ways in which Lacan's portraiture of the symbolic mirrors

Marcuse's more explicitly historical account: what Marcuse calls "the performance principle," Lacan calls the "service of goods." Both thinkers identify the biopolitical underpinnings of a social order dominated by the ideal of productivity. Both emphasize that the dominant morality of this symbolic—what Lacan calls "the morality of the master"—measures the merit of lives based on largely pragmatic criteria. And both acknowledge that the model citizen of this symbolic is a subject who shows up at work reliably every morning, performs its duties with a degree of diligence, does not let its desires get the better of its productivity, and seeks satisfaction ("enjoys") in moderate or at least efficiency-augmenting ways. As Lacan states, "Part of the world has resolutely turned in the direction of the service of goods, thereby rejecting everything that has to do with the relationship of man to desire" (1959–1960, 318). This, he adds, "is what is known as the postrevolutionary perspective" (318). That is, the service of goods, the performance principle that instrumentalizes desire, reflects the mindset of the levelheaded utilitarian subject who has deemed revolutionary change to be unrealistic.

Oddly enough, Butler seems to believe that Lacan had a personal investment in the heteropatriarchal Law of the Father. Yet if my analysis this far reveals anything, it is that Lacan was intensely critical of the morality of the master and the service of goods that this Law perpetuates. This is why Lacan mocked men who conflate the penis with the phallus—with patriarchal symbolic power (the Law of the Father)—and who therefore believe that their possession of the penis should automatically translate into heteropatriarchal privilege. Indeed, one of Lacan's innovations—the radicalness of which feminists have perhaps not yet fully recognized—was to "universalize" castration, to argue that castration was not a mark of female subjectivity specifically but rather of the human condition. "Castration," for Lacan, is just another term for being cut by the signifier, which is precisely why it applies to men just as much as to women, the result being that men who aspire to heteropatriarchal power are fooling themselves, are striving to deny their wounded—fragile, vulnerable, and precarious—status. Given that Lacan could not have been more scornful of this charade, I am inclined to read his commentary on the Law of the Father as an explanation of how heteropatriarchy manages to sustain itself rather than as a pronouncement on how our social order *should* be organized. In short, I read as descriptive what Butler reads as prescriptive.

The stakes of this disagreement become obvious when Butler asserts that Žižek—and by implication, Lacan—posits "a transcultural structure of social reality that presupposes a sociality based in fictive and idealized kinship positions that presume the heterosexual family as constituting the defining social bond for all humans" (Butler, Laclau, and Žižek 2000, 141–142). Though I find Žižek's anachronistic approach to feminist and queer theory as vexing as Butler does, in this instance I have to defend him by pointing out that heteronormative "sociality based in fictive and idealized kinship positions" is not Žižek's private invention but rather the edifice that has historically governed the collective reality of many, perhaps most, societies, and certainly of Western societies. Lacan never claimed that this type of sociality was the only way, or the most desirable way, to organize societies but merely that it was how heteropatriarchal societies had been organized. Lacan's argument is by no means, as Butler suggests, that a different kind of symbolic is intrinsically impossible but rather that the type of subjectivity that Western modernity has produced—a subjectivity that has been subjected to a particular form of surplus-repression (the heteropatriarchal performance principle, the service of goods)—makes it virtually impossible for us to entertain the idea that the symbolic could be organized differently, that it could be centered on a different version of the reality principle. This is precisely why he, like Marcuse, believed that subject formation is unnecessarily coercive, why he sought to enable the subject to dissociate itself from the desire of the Other.

7

I hope to have illustrated some of the ways in which Lacanian ethics is compatible with the queer theoretical discourse of opting out. Like queer theory, Lacan is deeply distrustful of hegemonic sociality. This distrust extends to normative ethics (the master's morality) so that, like queer theory, Lacan tends to focus on the oppressive rather than justice-producing aspects of collective ethical paradigms. This is exactly why Lacan was just as bothered as Foucault was by the normalizing tendencies of mid-twentieth-century psychoanalysis, railing against American ego-psychology in particular. According to Lacan, psychoanalysis has no normative goal; it does not seek to tell us how we should desire but merely to explore the idiosyncratic contours of our desire. Normalizing forms of clinical practice violate this principle, thereby undermining the nonprescriptive spirit of psychoanalysis that Freud developed.

We of course know that Freud himself was not always able to honor this spirit. We know that he sometimes lapsed in relation to women and homosexuals. Nevertheless, all things considered, Freud was well ahead of his cultural context in recognizing the "polymorphous" character of human desire (and in analyzing the tools—such as the Oedipus complex—that dominant culture uses to channel this polymorphosity toward normative heterosexuality). Even his infamous statements about women's "penis envy" are not necessarily antithetical to progressive aims, for they can be read as a critique of a social environment that bestowed upon the possessor of the penis a number of privileges that it denied those who lacked the organ.

Freud may not have been sufficiently precise about exactly what was envied, conflating the envy of social prestige with the envy of the organ. Yet his analysis, implicitly at least, reveals that there was nothing strange about women coveting the power conferred by the penis. If anything, if having a penis gave men access to cultural, political, and economic benefits—and even legal rights—that women were deprived of, then any woman who did *not* envy it could be accused of being a little obtuse. From this point of view, penis envy was a sign that women had not been fully interpellated into normative femininity, that they retained an awareness of the ways in which femininity was a socially denigrated category (and therefore "a bad deal"). Penis envy, in this sense, was an indication that the Oedipus complex had not entirely managed to accomplish its normalizing goal. As a result, what some critics have taken as an insult against women—Freud's notion of penis envy—might be reinterpreted as an embryonic indicator of female dissatisfaction; it might be reinterpreted as a precursor of feminist political consciousness.

It is unfortunate that the nonprescriptive spirit of psychoanalysis became compromised in mid-twentieth-century clinical practice. But it would be difficult to argue that Lacan participated in this trend. If anything, Lacan—like queer theory—could be criticized for elevating antinormativity to a new norm. Surely there are many other things besides having ceded on our desire that we could feel guilty about. And what if our desire is hurtful to others? What if it clashes with the desires of others, generating the kinds of power struggles that end violently?

I have addressed some of these questions in my previous work (Ruti 2012, 2015b), arguing, among other things, that Lacanian ethics draws its progressive force from being an ethics of the underdog: it is because Antigone's act defies a repressive power structure that it is ethical rather than merely capricious or pointlessly destructive. In the present context, I want to stress that, far from participating in the normativization of psychoanalysis, Lacan saw the patient's capacity to question the analyst's authority as a precondition of her ability to question the rest of social authority, to utter the *No!* or *Enough!* that I have been talking about. It is hardly a coincidence that Lacan sought to break the transferential dynamic by which the patient comes to regard the analyst as a *sujet-supposé-savoir*, as an expert who holds the key to her desire. Obviously, if the patient is to find her way out of the maze of the master's morality—as Lacan wanted her to do—she has to arrive at the recognition that, just as there is no Other of the Other, there is no secret reservoir of wisdom that the analyst possesses.

Perhaps above all else, Lacan was frustrated by the fact that many patients—and many subjects, generally speaking—were so out of touch with the truth of their desire that they were willing to sacrifice this desire to the point of self-betrayal. As he explains:

What I call "giving ground relative to one's desire" is always accompanied in the destiny of the subject by some betrayal—you will observe it in every case and should note its importance. Either the subject betrays his own way, betrays himself, and the result is significant for him, or, more simply, he tolerates the fact that someone with whom he has more or less vowed to do something betrays his hope and doesn't do for him what their pact entailed.

(1959–1960, 321)

Such a betrayal invariably results in the reassertion of the status quo, sending the subject back to the service of goods, what Lacan in this context calls "the common path" (321). And given that desire, for Lacan, is "the metonymy of our being" (321), betraying it in this way leads to the kind of psychic death that extinguishes the subject's sense of agency. To use Lacan's wording, "Doing things in the name of the good, and even more in the name of the good of the other, is something that is far from protecting us not only from guilt but also from all kinds of inner catastrophes" (319).

It is precisely such inner catastrophes that Lacanian clinical practice was designed to counter, though it may be Julia Kristeva—rather than Lacan himself—who has most clearly developed this interpretation of analytic work. Kristeva depicts psychoanalysis as a means of restoring the subject's psychic aliveness, as an explicit revolt against the numbing impact of what she calls "the society of the spectacle" (1997, 4). This society of the spectacle—of technology, image, and speed—shares many parallels with Adorno's "culture industry": a flattened surface of the lifeworld, a constriction of psychic space, a dearth of critical thought, a worship of efficiency over intellectual curiosity, and an incapacity to revolt. Against this backdrop, psychoanalysis—along with art, writing, and some forms of religious experience—offers, for Kristeva, a gateway to revolt, a way of resurrecting "the life of the mind" (a phrase Kristeva borrows from Hannah Arendt) through ongoing questioning, interrogation, and psychic re-creation.

"Freud founded psychoanalysis as an invitation to anamnesis in the goal of a rebirth, that is, a psychical restructuring," Kristeva writes: "Through a narrative of free association and in the regenerative revolt against the old law (familial taboos, superego, ideals, oedipal or narcissistic limits, etc.) comes the singular autonomy of each, as well as a renewed link with the other" (1997, 8). Given my overall argument in this chapter, it is worth noting that it is "the desire of the subject" that, in Kristeva's view, opens a place "for initiative, autonomy" (11). This is because Kristeva believes that the "Freudian journey into the *night of desire* was followed by attention to the *capacity to think*: never one without the other" (2005, 41). In other words, the psychoanalytic exploration of desire is akin to the critical (or at least curious) movement of thought—the very movement that Arendt also saw as vital to the life of the mind.

Kristeva therefore draws the same link between desire and autonomy (in this instance, the capacity for critical thought) as Lacan does. Furthermore, to translate Kristeva's point into Marcuse's terminology, one might say that analysis presents the possibility of sidestepping, or at the very least diminishing, the effects of surplus-repression. This, in turn, creates space for the truth of the subject's desire in the Lacanian sense. This does not mean that repression as such is defeated. Quite the contrary, as we will see momentarily, the truth of the subject's desire is inextricable from the primary (constitutive) repression that accompanies subject formation. But as I have already suggested, the lifting of surplus-repression renders the imprint of primary repression more clearly discernable, for when surplus-repression is removed, what remains are the always highly singular outlines of primary repression.

If Lacan—like Marcuse—sought to remove surplus-repression, it was because he understood that it is on the level of primary repression (fundamental fantasies) that one can find the most basic building blocks of the subject's psychic destiny. Stated slightly differently, primary repression is the layer of psychic life that expresses something fundamental about the distinctive ways in which the pleasure principle, in the subject's life, had become bound up with the repetition compulsion. This is why Lacan states, "If analysis has a meaning, desire is nothing other than that which supports an unconscious theme, the very articulation of that which roots us in a particular destiny, and that destiny demands insistently that the debt be paid, and desire keeps coming back, keeps returning, and situates us once again in a given track, the track of something that is specifically our business" (1959–1960, 319).

According to Lacan, analysis aims to enable us to understand something about the eccentric particularity (or truth) of our most fundamental desire as well as about the track of destiny that this desire carves out for us (and that is therefore "specifically our business"). If it is indeed the case, as I have conceded, that most of us tend to be alienated from our desire, Lacanian analysis strives to undo this alienation by familiarizing us with the truth of this desire. This process entails, among other things, recognizing that the destiny we owe to this desire can never be definitively overcome, that the debt of desire can never be fully redeemed (for how are we to compensate the signifier for having brought us into being as subjects of desire?). Our destiny—which might coincide quite seamlessly with our repetition compulsion—consists of recurring efforts to pay off this debt, which is why it keeps ushering us to the same track of desire, the same nexus of psychic conundrums, our unconscious hope being that if we wear out the track of our desire by incessant reiteration, one day we might be able to absolve ourselves of our debt. But since we cannot, the only thing to be done is to "own" our destiny even as we might seek to mitigate its more painful dimensions (the dimensions expressed by the repetition compulsion).

Jonathan Lear expresses something similar when he states:

To be committed to the task of accepting responsibility for our past (unconscious) is to be committed to the idea that the past (unconscious) cannot simply dictate an inexorable present and future. There is always a question of how the past (unconscious) can be taken up and creatively transformed. The past (unconscious) is redeemed in this world, not in the next, in the creative living with it in the present and towards-the-future.

(2000, xxxvii).

Lear here describes the process of "owning" our destiny as a matter of accepting responsibility for our past—including the unconscious currents that this past produces—in the sense that we ask how this past can be "taken up and creatively transformed." That is, instead of allowing our past to mechanically dictate the contours of our present and future, we take an active interest in the singular destiny that it generates.

This I take to be Lacan's message as well. Essentially, the only way to arrive at the kind of psychic rebirth that Kristeva advocates is to enter into a process of creative living in relation to our unconscious destiny. In the ethical act, our impulse is to embrace the jouissance of this destiny wholesale regardless of consequences (this is one way to understand what it means to plunge into the death-driven pulsation of the real). In analysis, the exploration of our destiny is more gradual, more self-reflexive. But in both cases, the point is not to obliterate our foundational destiny (or fundamental fantasies) but merely to elaborate it in more satisfying directions, away from the incapacitating effects of the repetition compulsion and toward the rewards of subjective autonomy. Furthermore, if we are to achieve this goal, nothing is more important than staying faithful to the truth of desire that, on the most elementary level, determines our destiny.

8

Let me unpack this more carefully. The track of desire Lacan is referring to must be understood in relation to what he, following Freud, calls *das Ding* (the Thing). As I noted earlier, according to Lacan's theory of subject formation, we sacrifice jouissance for the signifier, unmediated pleasure for the capacity to desire. This dynamic becomes crystallized around the fantasy of having lost the Thing, the original (non)object that offered unmitigated jouissance. We experience ourselves as deprived of something unfathomably precious—we, essentially, become the subjects-of-lack that Lacan is famous for having theorized—and we consequently spend our lives trying to find substitutes for what we imagine we have lost; we stuff one object of desire (*objet a*) after another into the void left by the signifier in the hope that one day we can heal our wound (undo alienation). Yet no object is ultimately able to satisfy us because the lack within our being is constitutive of our very subjectivity and, as such, utterly irredeemable.

However, in return for our suffering we gain the ability to wield the signifier, sometimes even in highly rewarding ways. And we also gain the capacity to be interested in the world around us, including the people who populate this world; we gain the ability to desire, and sometimes even love, others. So, all in all, we come off quite well in the sense that what we gain is arguably more valuable than what we lose, and this is all the more the case given that we have not actually lost anything to begin with, that our unconscious conviction that we were once completely satisfied is a misleading fantasy that in no way reflects the rather terrifying realities of (presymbolic) jouissance.

There is, then, an irredeemable gap between the Thing as the (non) object that causes our desire on the one hand and the objects (*objets a*) that our desire seeks out on the other, which is why we are never entirely satisfied. Many critics have fixated on the tragedy of this predicament. However, I have always read it as the source of everything that is worthwhile about human life, for the fact that we cannot attain ultimate satisfaction (absolute jouissance) does not mean that we cannot get any satisfaction, that there is no jouissance to be had, that the worldly objects we encounter cannot offer us any "real" pleasure.

In this context, it is helpful to recall that the Lacanian Thing replicates the dichotomous nature of the Kantian sublime object as one that elicits both awe and terror. As much as we want the Thing, coming too close to it is terrifying for the simple reason that we are constitutionally not designed to endure unmediated jouissance (except, perhaps, in fleeting orgasmic moments); actually possessing the Thing would instantly overload us with jouissance to the extent that we would cease to be (symbolic) subjects. As a consequence, it is precisely because we cannot have the Thing that pleasure—the kind of pleasure we are able to experience without destroying ourselves—is possible for us in the first place.

This is why Lacan emphasizes that we are always forced to approach the Thing obliquely, through the various objects of desire (*objets a*) that we discover in the world: we fixate on specific empirical objects in the hope that they will compensate for the absence of the Thing. As Lacan states, the Thing is "found at the most as something missed. One doesn't find it, but only its pleasurable associations" (1959–1960, 52). "If the Thing were not fundamentally veiled," he continues, "we wouldn't be in the kind of relationship to it that obliges us, as the whole of psychic life is obliged, to encircle it or bypass it in order to conceive it" (118). This process of encircling or bypassing the Thing—the distinctive track of desire we can never fully renounce—is governed by the pleasure principle, but quite often it takes the form of the tortured meanderings of the repetition compulsion, which is why Lacan maintains that our relationship to the Thing leads us to our "choice of neurosis" (54): it establishes the always somewhat pathological ways in which we relate to our objects of desire.

Undoubtedly, one of the objectives of Lacanian analysis—like perhaps of any kind of analysis—is to loosen the grip of the repetition compulsion (so that a more satisfying destiny might become possible). But what most interests me—and this is where I part ways with Edelman's celebration of self-shattering jouissance—is Lacan's suggestion that worldly objects can afford us "real" pleasure, pleasure that contains traces of the real, of jouissance, without pushing us so deeply into jouissance that we lose ourselves irrevocably. Simply put, Lacan implies that some objects satisfy us more than others because they seem to contain an echo of the Thing, a tiny sliver of the Thing's sublimity, with the result that they offer us manageable bits of jouissance. On the one hand, such special objects cause our desire to meet up with the jouissance of the drive, thereby bringing us within a striking distance of the Thing. On the other, because of the aforementioned gap between the Thing and all worldly objects, including the most satisfying ones, they keep us from falling fully into the whirlpool of jouissance. This is how they bring us "real" (genuine) satisfaction without causing an utter dissolution of subjectivity.

This, then, is my initial formulation of my dispute with Edelman: if Edelman would like to replace the subject by jouissance, I am interested in the kind of pleasure—modified jouissance—that we can experience while still remaining subjects, albeit fragmented and decentered ones. By this I do not mean that I do not recognize the importance of orgasmic moments of jouissance, of the kind of self-annihilating sexuality that Edelman has been so keen to promote. I merely want to be frank about the limits of that paradigm as a viable modality of living, including the fact that it loses track of our relationship to objects: as anyone who has ever experienced a really good orgasm knows, the subject in the throes of jouissance is entirely solipsistic, cut off from the world of objects, including other people (even the lover). To a degree, this is fine. I do not share Butler's insistence on the primacy of the other. Among other things, I do not believe that ethics is invariably a question of relationality. Nevertheless, it seems worth recognizing that self-shattering jouissance is not the only kind of satisfaction human beings are capable of, that Lacan gives us a way to talk about the kind of satisfaction that we derive from our relationships to objects, be they other people or inanimate entities (such as books, poems, oceans, or skyscrapers).

This kind of pleasure—pleasure that we are able to experience for longer than a few seconds—is what Lacan has in mind when he talks about the Thing's power to usher us into a singular track of desire. This singularity arises from the fact that even though the loss of the Thing is a universal precondition of subjectivity, each of us relates to this loss in a manner that is wholly peculiar to us. More specifically, every *objet a*, every object that we place into the void left by the Thing is, as Lacan puts it, "refound" (1959–1960, 118) in the sense that it always reflects something about our unique experience of the Thing as a site of melancholy yearning. This is why there tends to be a degree of consistency to our desire: we regularly find ourselves drawn to particular kinds of objects because these objects seem to resurrect some of the Thing's aura for us.

Such consistency, taken to an extreme, is what the repetition compulsion is all about. But it is also—and here we have reached the gist of my argument—at the core of the truth of desire that Lacan deems so necessary for the ethics of psychoanalysis, for the distinguishing feature of such truth is, precisely, its (obstinately consistent) singularity. The ethics of psychoanalysis "works" to the degree that it is able to conjure up this singularity, that it is able to revive forms of desire that owe their existence to primary repression (the loss of the Thing) rather than to surplus-repression (social domination), for only such forms of desire, *insofar as they meet up with jouissance* in the manner that I have described, have the power to resist the hegemonic desire of the Other. To state the matter more directly, if surplus-repression generates generic desires (such as the performance principle or the service of goods), primary repression generates inimitable desires (our specific track of desire), which is why the latter represent an ethical force that we can only betray by betraying something essential about our very being.

I am well aware that this line of argumentation only works if one is willing to accept the basic distinction between primary repression and surplus-repression that I have borrowed from Marcuse. This distinction is easy to challenge in the sense that, as I have admitted, the social codes that bring the subject into existence as a culturally intelligible entity can never be entirely divorced from hegemonic power. Yet there are still more or less oppressive ways of being interpellated into the cultural order, which is precisely why Marcuse holds open the possibility of a nonrepressive civilization.

As someone who has experienced firsthand the difference between Scandinavian and North American norms of gender and sexuality—particularly as these pertain to femininity and female sexuality—I am willing to entertain the notion that although subject formation always entails repression, this repression is existentially and epistemologically different from the kind of surplus-repression that supports "the morality of the master." As a matter of fact, if we completely close up the gap between (primary) repression and surplus-repression, we automatically conjure away any possibility of agency or individual resistance. Though this has been the direction that much of posthumanist theorizing, including that of Butler, has taken, I do not think that it represents an accurate reading of Lacan, who, as I have attempted to show, was strongly invested in the idea that analysis was a means of driving a wedge between the desire of the Other and the truth of the subject's desire. And if the Thing is where he went looking for the latter, it is because the Thing's echo connects us to an elemental realm of desire that, like a hidden subterranean stream, runs underneath the kinds of desires cultivated by the master's morality.

This is why the echo of the Thing that we discover in the objects of our desire introduces a code of ethics that is drastically different from the moral code that dictates the outlines of socially conformist modes of desire. As Lacan clarifies, "There is another register of morality that takes its direction from that which is to be found on the level of *das Ding*; it is the register that makes the subject hesitate when he is on the point of bearing false witness against *das Ding*, that is to say, the place of desire" (1959–1960, 109–110). This is an ethics that is not dictated by the instrumentalist imperatives of the service of goods but rather that assesses the value of objects—as well as of the ethical actions related to those objects—on the basis of their proximity (or loyalty) to the Thing. The object that comes the closest (or remains the most loyal) to the Thing is, ethically speaking, more important than one that is merely useful. This does not mean that we have the right to expect our objects to capture the Thing's aura with complete precision. But it does imply that objects that most powerfully emit this aura are also the ones that most readily engage our passion.

Concretely, whenever the Thing's echo resounds strongly enough in the object we have selected, it overshadows the social voices telling us that we have made a bad choice. For example, those around us may attempt to convince us that we have fallen in love with a person of the "wrong" age, race, gender, ethnicity, religion, social class, or educational level. Consider homophobia: at the present moment, powerful factions of the American cultural order are trying to convince us that love between two men or two women is an assault not only on traditional values but on God himself. This is a formidable obstacle to overcome. The miraculous thing about the Thing's echo is that it gives us the courage to fight the fight, so to speak; it is robust enough to trump the warnings and cajolings of the social order, making it possible for us to desire in counterhegemonic ways.

Think of it this way: the vast machinery of our commercial culture works overtime to eclipse the Thing's aura. We are bombarded from all sides by objects—enticing lures—that are deliberately manufactured to shine brightly enough to distract us; in the society of the spectacle, nothing is easier than losing sight of the truth of our desire. Against this backdrop, insisting on this truth becomes an ethical stance, making it possible for us to appreciate the preciousness of what we may be culturally encouraged to shun, ignore, or trivialize. As Kaja Silverman (2000) proposes, the constellation of desire that surrounds the Thing allows us to bring into visibility objects that the social order strives to render invisible; it introduces the possibility of idealizing something other than what the service of goods programs us to idealize.

When we, to borrow Lacan's well-known phrase, raise a mundane object to "the dignity of the Thing" (1959–1960, 112), we infuse it with the Thing's nobility, brilliance, and incomparable worth, thereby signaling that, as far as our desire is concerned, only *this* object will do; we, in short, deem the object in question irreplaceable. To the extent that we are able to do this, that we are able to insist on the truth of our desire, we might be said to have inherited some of Antigone's insubordination. And to the extent that we are able to hold our ground in the face of the culture industry—to the extent that we are able to resist being seduced by sparkly decoys—we are kept from becoming a mere cog in the commercial machine.

This in turn offers some protection against the impression that the world is a lackluster place where nothing can rouse our passions or move us in any meaningful manner; to the degree that the Thing's echo makes mundane objects reverberate with an exceptional dignity, it fends off the kind of complacency that strips the world of all ideals, all higher aspirations. But this only works if we are able to recognize the highly specific timbre of this echo in the first place, which is why Lacan is so adamant that psychoanalysis should help us revere the truth of our desire even when it would be easier to capitulate to the desire of the Other; it is why he asserts that there is nothing that is, ethically speaking, more important than not ceding on our desire.

9

One could say that the truth of desire, as Lacan conceptualizes it, arrests the incessant movement of desire that capitalism relies on: the subject who decides that "only this object will do" forsakes all alternative objects, thereby refusing to participate in the mentality that tells us that every object is disposable, that in fact encourages us to discard our objects almost as soon as we have acquired them. Such a subject of desire stubbornly fixates on a specific object in ways that thwart capitalism's demand that we glide from one object to the next in a frenzy of consumption; it puts a stop to the uncontrollable gluttony of the capitalist subject. Furthermore, like Marcuse, Lacan is interested in the idea that psychoanalysis, potentially at least, provides a space for a fruitful examination of the connection between so-called deviant desires—desires that respect the Thing's echo even at the cost of social marginalization—and the subject's capacity for defiance.

This is not to say that psychoanalysis is the only way to understand this connection. For example, social movements such as anticolonialism, antiracism, feminism, and queer struggles often also galvanize "deviant" desires in the service of defiant acts of rebellion. The populations that took up arms to liberate themselves from colonial rule, the proponents of the civil rights movement, the imprisoned suffragettes who were force-fed through tubes crammed down their throats, the antiwar protesters willing to endure police brutality during the Vietnam era, and defiant queer subjects (including queers engaging in socially disparaged sexual practices) all had/have one thing in common: they were/are no longer willing to give ground on their desire in order to please the Other. Similar acts of insurgence are currently erupting around the world, particularly in opposition to global capitalism and Western imperialism. To argue that psychoanalysis is responsible for such acts would be ludicrous. Yet Lacan's ethics of psychoanalysis as an ethics of fidelity to one's desire provides one way to grasp something about the psychic processes through which individuals come to possess the inclination for rebellion. This inclination, in turn, is an essential component of political action: the subject's ability to take a degree of distance from hegemonic power—or to sever the social ties that bind it to this power—may not, by itself, be enough to generate political action, but it is a necessary precondition of such action. In more Marcusian terms, it keeps the subject from "performing" in the obedient manner that it may have been conditioned to do.

A kernel of antihegemonic negativity (a trace of the death drive, of identity-dissolving jouissance) can therefore probably be found in more or less any act of defiance. At the same time, I hope to have demonstrated why there is no need to follow Edelman to a place of social suicide to appreciate the revolutionary spirit of Lacanian ethics. As I have stressed, the self-destructive act is merely the most extreme version of the Lacanian ideal of staying faithful to the singularity of one's desire; according to the interpretation that I have advanced, any subject who resists normative forms of desire by choosing to pursue the thread of its distinctive desire qualifies as a defiant subject in the Lacanian sense.

Moreover, I hope to have clarified why the act of saying *No!* to normative sociality—to the hegemonic Other—is not the same thing as rejecting intersubjectivity, why it is not necessarily an "antisocial" or "antirelational" stance in the queer theoretical sense. As my reading of the echo of the Thing, as well as the political examples I listed earlier, illustrates, the defiant subject often says *No!* to normative sociality in the name of its fidelity to intersubjective ties. Sometimes such ties link the subject to a specific object that is loved above all others, as is the case when the echo of the Thing reverberates in a cherished person in ways that render this person psychically irreplaceable. As I have argued, this type of fidelity to an object can make us socially courageous, able to resist those who seek to persuade us to shift our desire to more suitable objects. Other times, our intersubjective ties link us to political communities for the sake of which we are willing to act in rebellious ways.

I stressed earlier that even Antigone does not act on behalf of herself but on behalf of her brother Polyneces: her act is counterhegemonic *but it is not antirelational*; Antigone acts against the Other (Creon's system) but not against the other (Polyneces). This simple distinction falls out of post-Lacanian theories, such as those staged by Žižek and Edelman, that promote the uncompromising antirelationality of the act. Because Žižek and Edelman tend to view the intersubjective other primarily as a vehicle for the normalizing power of the Other, as Creon is in relation to Antigone, or as, for instance, parents are when they seek to discipline their children into heteronormative forms of gender presentation, they lose sight of the fact that there also exist loved intersubjective others for the sake of whom the subject can feel compelled to "act."

Undoubtedly, often the other who is loved is also hegemonic. This is why cruel optimism can be hard to avoid in intimate relationships. In addition, Lacan tended to foreground the terrifying aspects of the other: the Lacanian other—the other as a locus of monstrous jouissance, the other as "real"—is quite different from the largely benign other that underpins Butler's version of intersubjectivity (more on this at the end of chapter 5). But what is important at this juncture is that critics such as Žižek and Edelman give the impression that Lacan is entirely incompatible with relational theories of subjectivity and political action. This error has had far-reaching consequences for queer theory, for it is largely responsible for the antagonistic division between the antirelational and relational factions within the field. If Lacanians such as Edelman—and Bersani before him—had not interpreted Lacan as a purely antirelational thinker, this division might never have arisen. Unfortunately, one of its outcomes has been to cause those on the relational side to cast Lacan off as a "useless" thinker for their version of queer theory even though he arguably offers some very powerful tools for deciphering the ethical valence of relational bonds.

Among such tools is the ability to understand that the partially unconscious character of our desire does not make us any less responsible for its effects on others. That is, not ceding on our desire—refusing to discard the psychic destiny generated by our desire—is a matter not merely of remaining faithful to our most treasured objects but also of cultivating an awareness of the consequences of this desire on others; far from being a matter of hedonistic self-indulgence, not ceding on our desire asks us to try to understand how our desire touches, and sometimes even wounds, those we desire. In other words, because Lacanian theory implies that we are responsible for our desire as the unconscious foundation of our destiny, not ceding on our desire entails becoming accountable for what we do in the name of this desire. Conversely, when we give ground on our desire, we betray not merely our object but also the intersubjective responsibility that arises from our desire. In this sense, not ceding on our desire implies a continuous self-interrogation regarding the imprint of our desire on others. This is one reason Lacan's ethics of self-transformation is not incompatible with an ethical attitude toward others.

Unfortunately, Žižek and Edelman do not have any better grasp on this than Butler. If Butler's mistake is that she consistently—and somewhat naïvely—promotes relationality as an unmitigated virtue in ways that cause her to reject Lacan, the mistake of Žižek and Edelman is to exclude all traces of relationality from Lacanian theory. All three thinkers, in short, rely on a rigid dichotomy between antirelationality and relationality, even if they fall on opposite sides of the divide. As I will show in the next two chapters, Edelman's attempt to purge Lacanian theory of its relational elements leads to an overvalorization of the subject's solipsistic jouissance. Butler's uncritical (Levinasian) valorization of relationality, in turn, causes her to overlook what I just noted, namely, that there are times when the intersubjective other functions as a vehicle for the hegemonic injunctions of the Other; it causes her to neglect the fact that relationality is not necessarily any more pure, any more devoid of power struggles, than any other component of human life.

If Butler's earlier Foucauldian theories tended to overstate the injurious effects of intersubjectivity, her more recent Levinasian theories imply that any condemnation of the other, even of the other who promotes the inequalitarian values of the Other, is ethically unacceptable (see Ruti 2015b). In other words, if Butler's early account of subjectivity and psychic life, particularly the one found in *The Psychic Life of Power* (1997), somewhat fatalistically implied that it is impossible to escape social connections that wound us—that our psychic attachment to such connections is unbreakable—her more recent theories suggest that there is something intrinsically unethical about our attempts to do so, that we should do our best to respect the complex unconscious motivations of even those who hurt us. This is why I mentioned earlier that the good Butlerian subject these days seems to be one who accepts its violation at the hands of others while vigilantly curtailing its own aggressive impulses.

I would go as far as to say that Butler unwittingly participates in our culture's habitual glorification of the virtues of relationality. Because, as I have argued, she operates within a binaristic conceptual frame that deems autonomy to be bad and relationality to be good, she cannot account for instances where the other behaves in ways that those of us not seduced by Derrida's (2001) musings on forgiving the unforgivable deem to be truly unforgivable. Stated in less drastic terms, Butler's rote vilification of autonomy and celebration of relationality impede her capacity to acknowledge situations where things are not quite so clear-cut, where, say, autonomy is creative and relationality utterly devastating. Her theory, in short, ignores the fact that sometimes the other is . . . well . . . *terrible*: sadistic, violent, spiteful, arrogant, and so on. Like couples therapists who tell their patients to "talk through" their tensions rather than to walk out on their loved ones, Butler pathologizes opting out of relationality even in cases when it is the least pathological course of action.

This is the core of my Lacanian quarrel with her: if Butler believes that I would rather sustain wounded psychic attachments than risk losing my relational bonds—that the recognition granted by the Other (or an array of others who stand in for the Other) is so important to me that I am willing to harm myself to prolong it—I believe that there are circumstances where I am capable of cutting my connection to others who injure me even if this means risking the symbolically intelligible underpinnings of my life. Essentially, I believe that severing debilitating relational bonds is one way in which I can "choose" my autonomy over the suffocating entanglements of traumatizing relationality. Importantly, this does not mean that I reject relationality *as such*, that I want to join Edelman's antisocial strand of queer theory. As I have emphasized, I recognize not only that many relational bonds are enabling but also that some of them are so valuable to us that we are willing to sacrifice a great deal for their sake. As a consequence, my critique of Butler is not aimed at her relationality per se but at her insistence that even bad relationality is better than autonomy (in the Lacanian sense).

Butler might counter by asserting that the price of my Lacanian attitude is too high, that the annihilation of social ties—even toxic ones—in the act does not offer a viable alternative to the kind of more incremental social change that she herself tends to advocate. Yet, as those who have conjured up the courage to reject an enthralling but excruciating romantic relationship well know, it can be tremendously liberating to leave behind what has been traumatizing. The trauma will linger, of course, but its impact will be different from what it would be if we tried to negotiate with its source.

Likewise with other social ties, whether personal or collective. Imagine, for instance, the relief of a woman who is finally able to say *Enough!* to the patriarchal Law of the Father—and perhaps even to the actual father who, for her, represents that Law. Consider also the exhilaration—however fleeting—of the individual who walks out on a job rather than enduring one more day of harassment by her superiors (even when doing so puts her in financial jeopardy). What is so powerful about Lacan's ethics of psychoanalysis as a response to the master's service of goods is that it asks, quite simply, that we cease to care about what the big Other wants—that we reject the legitimacy of the Other's desire so as to create space for the truth of our own. Separation—a studied *Fuck You!* aimed at the Other—is the Lacanian antidote to alienation and thus an opening to intervention.

10

Lacan illustrates, in an explicit manner, the connection between deviant desires and defiance that (arguably all) queer theoretical attempts to conceptualize an ethics of opting out implicitly presume. One of my aims in this chapter has been to show that the Lacanian account of the ethical act offers a stronger model for political resistance than the Butlerian model of subversive reperformance, that politics is not always a matter of negotiating with power but rather of rejecting the worldview that this power represents. Butler might object that there is no such thing as desire that has not been shaped by collective norms. As she writes:

The norm does not simply enter into the life of sexuality, as if norm and sexuality were separable: the norm is sexualized and sexualizing, and sexuality is itself constituted, though not determined, on its basis. In this sense, the body must enter into the theorization of norm and fantasy, since it is precisely the site where the desire for the norm takes shape, and the norm cultivates desire and fantasy in the service of its own naturalization.

(Butler, Laclau, and Žižek 2000, 155)

I admit that there is no way to categorically contest Butler's insight: it is true that sexuality cannot be separated from normativity, that we often desire the norm, and that the norm—say, the capitalist norm—generates desires and fantasies "in the service of its own naturalization." It is also true that the norm sometimes feeds off our attempts to resist it, as capitalism does when it turns previously "deviant" modes of sexuality into the latest profitable fad. I have merely attempted to demonstrate that Butler's way of envisioning the relationship between desire and normativity overlooks the possibility that, beneath the level of culturally compliant desire, there might exist a strain of unruly desire that has to some extent—never entirely but to some extent—evaded social conditioning and that can therefore energize both our personal and political acts of rebellion.

I am not arguing that our desires—or our fantasies—can be fully dissociated from the desires—or fantasies—of our collective environment. Yet, like Lacan and Marcuse, I think that there is a distinction between the kinds of desires that respond to the performance principle (or the service of goods) and the kinds of desires that respond to the loss of the Thing (as an experience in the real). Likewise, I believe that there is a distinction between mass-generated fantasies and the singular cadence of what Lacan calls fundamental fantasies (again, fantasies in the real). This is why the "truth" of the subject's desire, for Lacan, is a kind of utopian opening, an inkling that we are not forever subjected to the modalities of life that we have inherited. In Marcuse's terms, questioning dominant forms of desire might turn the possibility of a less repressive reality principle into a real possibility. In Lacan's terms, it might lead to the surfacing of hitherto repressed desires, and perhaps even to new ways of living out our destiny (our specific track of desire).

In a certain sense, one could say that Lacan's attempt to empower the analysand to remain loyal to the truth of her desire is a form of consciousness raising. To be sure, the analyst does not necessarily actively (or deliberately) "raise" the analysand's consciousness by calling attention to, say, social injustice; the process is usually much more subtle than this. Yet analysis and consciousness raising share the same impulse of self-reflexivity: both rely on the idea that the subject possesses the capacity to become more discerning about the causes of its unhappiness as well as about the ways in which it might be able to stand up to what contributes to this unhappiness, including oppressive social formations. And once this discernment escapes the confines of the individual psyche, once it becomes a communal, collective matter, it can fuel political movements. Is this not one reason that queer theory has always emphasized the potentially subversive momentum of desire?

I have underscored that cruel optimism can cause us to wait indefinitely for whatever it is that we believe will give us satisfaction. Within this framework, what makes desire-as-drive, the kind of desire that carries some of the intensity of jouissance, such a rebellious force is that it refuses to wait: it wants satisfaction *now*. It causes us to lose our patience, jolting us to a new life because we are no longer willing to stay sheepishly devoted to the old one. In this sense, the reverse of a new desire is an alienation from previous forms of life. Alienation, in turn, is the precondition of our ability to reject the dominant happiness scripts of our society, for it forces us to recognize just how limiting such scripts can be; it causes us to become aware of how much we have sacrificed in order to conform to the master's morality (or the performance principle, the service of goods).

Desire and alienation cannot therefore be easily disentangled: new desires generate alienation and alienation generates new desires. This is precisely what Žižek means when he argues that separation from the Other is the flipside of alienation: suddenly the desires provided by the symbolic are not enough: we want something else. Once this happens, once familiar happiness scripts collapse, modes of life that might have formerly seemed unintelligible become intelligible: we start to see other possibilities, other modes of satisfaction.

In this sense, it is in the nature of desire to be transformative. It connects us to disclaimed dimensions of ourselves—dimensions that we have had to suppress to sustain the life that we have been living. Such disclaimed dimensions may have for the most part stayed invisible, but they are never fully annihilated. And when the right occasion arises, they start to clamor for recognition; they remind us of the alternative life that we could have lived—and that we might still be able to live. We may not always act on our new information, our new inclinations. But neither can we pretend that this information, these inclinations, are not now a clandestine element of our lives. Most likely, they will lie in wait for the next opening, the next time our desire is unexpectedly stirred. And the more we strive to repress them, the more momentum they are likely to gather.

I have sought to show that the moment we relinquish the distinction between desires generated by the performance principle (the service of goods) and desires generated by the loss of the Thing, we surrender the capacity to imagine agency, which is exactly the weakness of Butler's paradigm. In part because Butler does not want to acknowledge the Lacanian real as a valid theoretical concept, she is unable to envision a dimension of subjectivity that might elude total capture by hegemonic sociality. I understand her reluctance because there is always the danger that the notion of a less-than-fully-social bodily real might slide into the notion that biology is destiny. But this is not at all what Lacan suggests. Quite the opposite, he implies that the real—always incompletely—offers a way out of the destiny that our society tries to impose on us, and this includes our "biological" (sexed, gendered, racialized, and so on) destiny.

As I have explained in this chapter, the only destiny that the real guides us into is the wholly idiosyncratic destiny that arises from our fundamental fantasies (or repetition compulsion), and this destiny is much more likely to disregard, say, normative categories of gender and sexuality than it is to promote them. This is why I think that it would be a mistake to read Lacanian ethics as apolitical. If anything, this ethics is in some ways more radical than our conventional understanding of ethics for, as I have shown, it explicitly raises the possibility not only of individual transformation but also of social change. This does not mean that it is devoid of limitations, as has already become clear, and as will become more so in the chapters that follow. But it does offer a productive counterargument to Butler's contention that every desire is hopelessly caught up in the meshes of hegemonic power. While no one is saying that desire is wholly independent of such power, Lacan, Marcuse, and many queer theorists are saying that our desires can, and often do, open to undomesticated realms of experience.

Chapter Three

WHY THERE IS ALWAYS A FUTURE IN THE FUTURE

If the fate of the queer is to figure the fate that cuts the thread of futurity, if the jouissance, the corrosive enjoyment, intrinsic to queer (non)identity annihilates the fetishistic jouissance that works to *consolidate* identity by allowing reality to coagulate around its ritual reproduction, then the only oppositional status to which our queerness could ever lead would depend on our taking seriously the place of the death drive we're called on to figure.

—LEE EDELMAN, *NO FUTURE*

The moment in which I write this book the critical imagination is in peril. The dominant academic climate into which this book is attempting to intervene is dominated by a dismissal of political idealism. Shouting down utopia is an easy move. It is perhaps even easier than smearing psychoanalytic or deconstructive reading practices with the charge of nihilism. The antiutopian critic of today has a well-worn war chest of poststructuralist pieties at her or his disposal to shut down lines of thought that delineate the concept of critical utopianism.

—JOSÉ MUÑOZ, *CRUISING UTOPIA*

1

Muñoz's biting statement regarding "a well-worn war chest of poststructuralist pieties" at the disposal of any critic who wants to shout down utopia is aimed at Edelman's radical articulation of queer negativity—at Edelman's version of the ethics of opting out—in *No Future* (2004). This debate between Edelman and Muñoz about the parameters of queer politics is by now legendary. It started in 2006 on the pages of the *PMLA*, which reproduced a heated Modern Language Association forum in which Muñoz (with Tim Dean and Jack Halberstam) took issue with Edelman's formulation of the antisocial thesis. The debate crystallized the division between those—historically mostly white gay men—who promote this thesis and "the rest of us"—those interested in gender, racial, economic, and global inequalities in addition to issues of sexuality—who tend to support a more social, relational approach.

Obviously not all white gay male queer theorists fall on Edelman's side of the debate (as Dean's presence on the opposite side indicates). And those on the social side have various degrees of sympathy and antipathy toward it. Moreover, as I have illustrated, this division is in many ways misleading to begin with in the sense that even Lacan—upon whose work the anti-social school often draws—did not advocate an "antisocial" (or "antirela-tional") approach but merely tried to conceptualize what it might mean to opt out of *hegemonic* forms of sociality. This is why Lacanian theory is not incompatible with accounts of opting out—such as Halberstam's queer art of failure—developed by those who have tended to position themselves on the side of "the rest of us." By the end of this chapter, I hope to have further demonstrated why the relegation of Lacan to the antisocial side of queer theory is both misleading and unnecessary. But first it is instructive to draw out the political stakes of the divide between the antisocial and social strands of queer theory by entering the debate between Edelman and Muñoz at its sorest spot—the spot where each side accuses the other of fundamental politico-ethical lapses.

For his part, Edelman, in criticizing Muñoz's commitment to utopia-nism, accuses Muñoz of the kind of liberal inclusionism that fails to rec-ognize the insistence with which the antisocial pulse of the death drive undermines all social organization (or, in Lacanian terms, the insistence with which the real disrupts the fantasmatic coherence of the symbolic). More specifically, Edelman accuses Muñoz (and Dean) of "putting the puppet of humanism through its passion play once again" by promoting "the redemptive hope of producing brave new social collectivities" (2006, 821). Essentially, Edelman believes that Muñoz and Dean fall prey to the humanist conviction that meaning, progress, and rational understand-ing are able to transcend the foundational antagonisms of social life—antagonisms that Lacan captured through his notion of the real as an internal limit to symbolic closure.

Let me put some of my cards on the table right away: I think that this critique misses its mark quite drastically in the sense that, whatever faith Muñoz and Dean might have in new social collectivities, they do not, as Edelman implies, support liberal humanism's dreams of redemption through greater inclusion; they do not believe that simply allowing previ-ously marginalized subjects to enter the existing system would miraculously conjure away the system's problems. Quite the contrary, both are deeply critical of the homonormative quest for social respectability that charac-terizes much of liberal gay and lesbian politics. In *Cruising Utopia* (2009), Muñoz in fact explicitly condemns homonormative gays and lesbians who allow themselves to be seduced by the material and symbolic rewards of neoliberal capitalism. One could of course point out that Edelman could not have known in 2006 what Muñoz was going to say in a book that was published three years later. But this does not change the fact that Edelman's accusation rings false for the simple reason that it is aimed at two progres-sive critics who are so well versed in the basics of posthumanist theory that they in many ways take the demise of the humanist self for granted.

I cannot think of a single critic within queer theory who naïvely endorses the sovereign subject of liberal humanism. If anything—as I have already noted and will discuss in greater detail in the next chapter—the field, like the rest of American progressive theory, seems to be caught up in a compulsive cycle of needing to repeatedly expunge this subject even when very little of it remains. Furthermore, the idea that utopian think-ing is by definition liberal, that there is no room for utopianism within posthumanist paradigms, is an indication of the extent to which certain strands of posthumanist theory have solidified into lifeless patterns that no longer serve a critical function; in such instances, the monotonous rep-etition of poststructuralist dogmas—in Edelman's case, "hopefulness bad, negativity good" (which, notably, has the same starkly binaristic structure as Butler's "autonomy bad, relationality good")—serves to bar alternative perspectives that might revitalize contemporary theory by allowing us to think beyond bad-good archetypes. In this sense, Muñoz's statement regarding Edelman's "well-worn war chest of poststructuralist pieties" (2009, 10) is right on target, as is his rebuke of the "various romances of negativity" that have, within queer theory, become so predictable as to be "resoundingly anticritical" (12).

If Edelman's accusations against Muñoz are relatively easy to dismiss, the reverse is not the case, for Muñoz's indicts Edelman for perpetuating a clandestine—and therefore all the more insidious—form of white gay male identity politics: a politics that flees from the (supposedly) contami-nating impact that a consideration of gender, racial, economic, and global inequalities might have on queer theory and that refuses to recognize that the white gay male subject is just as "identitarian" as any other subject. Muñoz asserts that the only reason Edelman is able to dodge the specter of identity politics is that, in Edelman's work, white masculinity falsely configures—as it has always done—the "universal," "neutral" subject position that (seemingly) resides beyond identitarian concern. More generally speaking, Muñoz believes that antisocial queer theories "reproduce a crypto-universal white gay subject that is weirdly atemporal" (2009, 94).

Hiram Perez makes an analogous point when he criticizes not only the ways in which whiteness, in the work of many white gay men, "makes itself transparent" (2005, 187) but also the ways in which poststructuralist rhetoric is used to level charges of essentialism against anyone who dares to call attention to this problem. Along the same lines, Halberstam rails against the "invisible identity politics of white gay men," adding that when "white men (gay or straight) pursue the interests of white men (gay or straight), there's a heap of trouble for everyone else" (2006, 231). Muñoz adds a final blow when he concludes that "imagining a queer subject who is abstracted from the sensuous intersectionalities that mark our experience . . . is a ticket whose price most cannot afford" (2009, 96).

The battle lines are thus clearly drawn between those—(some) white gay men—for whom sexuality is the sole axis of theoretical investigation and those for whom sexuality is just one among many such axes. Muñoz does not pull his punches, notoriously calling—in the course of the *PMLA* exchange—the antisocial thesis "the gay white man's last stand" (2006, 825). In *Cruising Utopia*, he in turn argues that Edelman "anticipates and bristles against his future critics with a precognitive paranoia" by predicting that some identitarian critics might contest his polemic by arguing that it is "determined by his middle-class white male positionality" (2009, 95). Muñoz's candid assessment of Edelman's efforts to inoculate himself against this critique is that it "does not do the job" (95).

The stakes of Muñoz's accusation are high, revolving around the question of who can afford to relinquish all hope of a better future in the way that Edelman's rendering of queer negativity—with includes the derisive critique of the child as a sentimental emblem of reproductive futurity that I mentioned in chapter 1—calls for. Muñoz suggests that only those who "have" a future in the first place have the luxury of flirting with the idea of rejecting it; conversely, those whose futures are concretely (empirically) threatened are unlikely to advocate the annihilation of these futures. More specifically, Muñoz contends that it would be disastrous to "hand over futurity to normative white reproductive futurity," arguing that the fact that this version of futurity is currently winning "is all the more reason to call on a utopian political imagination that will enable us to glimpse another time and place: a 'not-yet' where queer youths of color actually get to grow up" (2009, 95–96). In this manner, Muñoz alerts us to the fact that while Edelman elevates the child to an icon of reproductive futurity, "the future" has never been the province of all children; that is, though Muñoz agrees with the broad outlines of Edelman's critique of reproductive futurity, he reminds us that this critique does not apply to the vast majority of the world's children, that "racialized kids, queer kids, are not the sovereign princes of futurity" (95).

Like Edelman, Muñoz admits that the world as it stands is "not enough" (2009, 96), not able to offer adequate resources for subjective flourishing. But in his view, the way to deal with the world's insufficiency and messiness is not to reject the future wholesale but rather to reconfigure its parameters. This, Muñoz asserts, can only be done by resurrecting "various principles of hope that are, by their very nature, relational" (94). As he elaborates, relationality may not always be "pretty," "but the option of simply opting out of it, or describing it as something that has never been available to us, is imaginable only if one can frame queerness as a singular abstraction that can be subtracted and isolated from a larger social matrix" (94).

In chapter 5, I discuss some of the details of Muñoz's queer utopianism. In this chapter, I want to position myself in relation to the debate between him and Edelman diagonally, in ways that cut across both perspectives without fully settling on one side or the other. I wholeheartedly agree with Muñoz's political critiques, having in fact mounted comparable ones against Žižek and Alain Badiou (see Ruti 2012, 2015b). In addition, I agree with Muñoz that Edelman's mode of abstraction leads him to ignore important nuances of subjective experience, including the fact that constitutive alienation—the subject's lack-in-being in the Lacanian sense—is far from being the only form of alienation in the world (more on this later and in chapter 4). Yet, for reasons that have to do with some of my arguments in the previous chapter, I also have a greater degree of appreciation for Edelman's theoretical perspective than Muñoz does: I believe that insofar as Edelman attempts to activate the radical kernel of Antigone's act of uncompromising defiance, there is an undeniable ethical force to his argument.

Still, Edelman leaves out significant parts of the Lacanian story, not just about the relational nature of Antigone's act that I have already emphasized but also about the complex contours of Lacan's conceptualization of nega-tivity (the linchpin of Edelman's queer ethics of opting out). As a result, my objective in this chapter is threefold. First, I wish to highlight aspects of Edelman's argument whose insightfulness risks getting lost in the fray of ideological disagreements. Second, I wish to argue that many of these disagreements arise from Edelman's one-sided of reading of Lacan. And third, I wish to offer an alternative reading of Lacan's understanding of negativity—a reading focused less on negativity's destructiveness than on the creative potential that might arise from it—in order to illustrate that Lacanian theory, overall, is not incompatible with the critical aims of rela-tional queer theorists such as Muñoz.

My goal is thus both to "rescue" Lacan from Edelman and to soften the division between the antirelational and relational orientations of queer the-ory. This division—which sometimes gets cast as one between Lacanian-poststructuralists and affect theorists—is a difficult one for me because I am a Lacanian who finds herself politically aligned with "the rest of us," including those interested in affect theory. It is also difficult for me because the "Lacan" that gets thrown around in this debate like a slippery beach ball that, to everyone's fury, only Edelman seems to be able to catch with any degree of grace is one that I scarcely recognize; problematically, queer theory's "Lacan" has congealed into a narrative about the death drive and jouissance that gets circulated without much critical distance.

Because those on the side of "the rest of us" for understandable reasons—who really wants to read Lacan beyond the few required essays?—are not always terribly familiar with the details of Lacan's vast output, they take Edelman's word on Lacan as the "truth" about Lacan. If the Lacan of the 1990s was Butler's Lacan (the Lacan of social subjection), the Lacan of the twenty-first century has been filtered through Edelman to the extent that Lacanian theory gets reduced to a provocation for defiant self-annihilation. The fundamental incompatibilities between these readings—that Butler believes that the Lacanian subject is primarily a subjected one whereas Edelman believes that this subject is primarily a rebellious one—should alert readers to the fact that, in both cases, important parts of the theory are being excluded.

This problem arises particularly strongly in queer theory graduate semi-nars where my response to my students' account of Lacan tends to be an incredulous, *Where are you getting this from? Where does Lacan say X?*

The students, unsurprisingly, do not have a good answer because most of them have not actually read Lacan beyond "The Mirror Stage"; they have merely read Edelman. At some point, I realized that this is not Edelman's fault, that if students and scholars of queer theory are citing his version of Lacan, it is because his interpretation is impressive even if it is also a bit infuriating. That "my" Lacan is largely unknown in the field is my fault in the sense that I have not presented it to those interested in queer theory (even if I have tried to present it to critical theorists, broadly understood). This book, as should be obvious by now, is in part an attempt to remedy this oversight.

2

In the next chapter, I will return to the problem of abstraction in Edelman's work by considering the disagreements between him and Lauren Berlant in *Sex, or the Unbearable* (2014). And in the second half of this chapter, I will present the alternative Lacan I alluded to above. But let me begin by discussing aspects of Edelman's argument that I believe are smarter than his critics, including Muñoz, tend to admit.

Recall the basics of Edelman's account: he connects queerness to the Freudian–Lacanian death drive as a means of opposing the future-oriented optimism of reproductive heteronormativity, an optimism symbolized by the figure of the innocent child. The antisocial thesis of his book is that instead of seeking to dismantle the homophobic representation of queers as death driven and socially disruptive, queers should embrace these negative stereotypes in order to undermine the very ideal of sociality, including its promises of political progress and a better future; essentially, Edelman asks queers to embody the destructiveness—the jouissance of the real as an impediment to symbolically viable subjectivity—that they, whether or not they so wish, always already signify for mainstream society. As Edelman states early in his analysis, "Impossibly, against all reason, my project stakes its claim to the very space that 'politics' makes unthinkable: the space outside the framework within which politics as we know it appears and so outside the conflict of visions that share as their presupposition that the body politic must survive" (2004, 3).

Within the terms I have established in this book, Edelman is advocating the Lacanian ethical act that—as I have explained—demolishes the subject's symbolic supports, thereby destroying its social viability. He is uttering a *No!* to the dominant happiness scripts of our society, asserting that the promises of political progress and a better future are intrinsically hollow, liable to generate the kind of cruel optimism Berlant analyzes. According to this viewpoint, hegemonic happiness scripts that induce us to keep trying to perfect the social order can only ultimately disappoint us. In Ahmed's terms, they are a "straightening device" (2010, 91), which, among other things, tells us that the "right" way to be queer is to approximate heteronormative kinship systems (monogamous marriage and reproduction).

I have touched on the various reasons for which wounded subjects might find cruel optimism and dominant happiness scripts difficult to discard. For example, I have explained that Berlant presents cruel optimism as a complex affective tangle in which the very modes of life, collective ideals, and intimate relationships that harm the subject simultaneously seem to guarantee its ability to go on living, with the result that they become hard to abandon; cruel optimism, we have learned, is a matter of staying faithful to injurious attachments because the idea of giving them up seems more unbearable than the injury they bring. One can see how, for many, a politics that invests in the ideal of a better future may feel like such a conflicted yet necessary site of cathexis. It is in part Edelman's lack of appreciation for such "necessary" compromise formations—the fact that he has less sympathy than Berlant and Ahmed for the painful predicament of wounded subjects—that leads him to advocate "the impossible project of queer oppositionality that would oppose itself to the structural determinants of politics as such" (2004, 4).

Perhaps the word "impossible" in Edelman's sentence conveys, in a condensed form, his recognition that many subjects find it challenging to shatter their cruel optimism. Still, Edelman's loyalty to the Lacanian notion of the ethical act as a matter accomplishing this (impossible) feat—of, as Badiou puts it, opening a space for "the possibility of the impossible" (2001, 39)—causes him to agitate for the downfall of politics as we know it; it causes him to advocate the rupturing of toxic social bonds. In the last chapter, I made a similar argument in the context of criticizing Butler's overvalorization of relationality, noting that, from a Lacanian perspective, cutting damaging relational bonds can be a courageous act. As I proposed, Lacan shows that it is, under certain conditions, possible to break our psychic investment in wounded attachments. This is why I find myself sympathetic to Edelman's impatience with cruel optimism, frustrated not only with Butler's suggestion that in rejecting such optimism I betray my ethical obligation to the other but also with the idea—more explicit in Butler than in Berlant but present in the latter as well—that I am more or less incapable of such an act of rejection. This has not been my experience in the sense that my psychic survival has always been predicated on my ability to walk away from what is debilitatingly painful.

It is true that sometimes—for practical reasons—there is no choice but to remain invested: when a Canadian immigration officer deemed me unfit for permanent residency, I did not just pack my bags and leave; I fought back even though this resulted in a year of sleepless nights. But other times, the sleepless nights are simply not worth it. Why should I waste my life attached to relational bonds, including intimate ones, that injure me? Why does Butler believe that there is something intrinsically "ethical" about doing so? These questions align me with Edelman's Lacanianism of the destructive act—which, as we have seen, can be an act of striking at what I hold most dear—even as I am somewhat startled by his attempt to equate this attitude with queer subjectivity *as such*, by the notion that, insofar as the social establishment aligns queer subjects with negativity, seeing them as a menace to its consistency, integrity, and robustness, their best strategy, *generally speaking*, is to ride the full force of this negativity. In Edelman's vision, the queer, like the antisocial pulsation of the death drive, erupts into the collective field as a site of anti-identitarian and meaningless jouissance. In Edelman's words, "the death drive names what the queer, in the order of the social, is called forth to figure: the negativity opposed to every form of social viability" (2004, 9).

3

The vocabulary Edelman uses to construct his argument about queer negativity resonates with Žižek's elaboration of "subjective destitution" as a way of stepping into—of accepting—the psychic "destiny" that arises from what Lacan calls the "sinthome." This vocabulary is slightly different from the one I have used this far, but the core ideas are the same. Recall, for example, that I have posited that Lacan asks us to remain faithful to the psychic destiny generated by our most fundamental desires, by the kinds of "true" desires that meet up with the jouissance of the drive. I have suggested that such desires function in two related ways: on the one hand, they provide an opening to Lacan's ethics of psychoanalysis, including the ethical act; on the other, they can become congealed in tenacious symptoms such as the repetition compulsion. I now want to add—as a means of entering Edelman's argument regarding what he calls "the sinthomosexual"—that the sinthome is, quite simply, Lacan's term for such a tenacious symptom, a symptom that carries the unsymbolizable energies (drives) of the real. Because such a symptom is composed of drives (jouissance) that always to some extent elude the grasp of the signifier, it does not yield to analytic interpretation or working through. This is why the only feasible response to it is to embrace it as our psychic destiny (in the sense that I described at the end of the previous chapter).

Edelman builds on these insights to argue that because the sinthome is inaccessible to symbolization, it is intrinsically resistant to hegemonic sociality; he correctly asserts that the sinthome does not communicate meaning but merely mindless enjoyment (jouissance). "Subjective destitution," in turn, is the conceptual shorthand Lacanians use for the act of identifying with one's sinthome at the cost of one's symbolic identity (as Antigone could be said to have done); in a way, subjective destitution is merely another name for the ethical act. As I have illustrated, for Lacan, this act, this identification with the sinthome—with the real as a cradle of jouissance—functions as an assertion of autonomy and resistance in suspending the sociosymbolic rules that under normal circumstances lend coherence to the subject's existence. Such an act annuls the subject as a moral agent with a binding connection to a world of shared ideals and codes of conduct. In Žižek's words, subjective destitution is "an act of annihilation, of wiping out—we not only don't know what will come out of it, its final outcome is ultimately even insignificant, strictly secondary in relation to the NO! of the pure act" (2001, 44).

This is the theoretical backdrop for Edelman's self-annihilating sinthomosexual as a figure of defiance—a figure that, despite its extremity, is not entirely unrelated to Ahmed's figures of the feminist killjoy, the unhappy queer, the melancholy migrant, and the radical revolutionary. Edelman's strategy is both dazzling in its simplicity and somewhat banal in its predictability: he associates queerness—now recoded as sinthomosexuality—with the antisocial energies of the real, asserting that queerness only attains its "ethical value" to the degree that it accepts "its figural status as resistance to the viability of the social" (2004, 3). The sinthomosexual, in other words, becomes equated with the monstrous real, with what the heteronormative symbolic deems inassimilable and what therefore resides beyond the reach of normative ethics.

In this manner, the sinthomosexual comes to metaphorize an alternative ethics—an ethics of the act, of opting out—so that antinormativity, as is common in queer theory, becomes the new ideal (or norm). This is why queerness, for Edelman, can never be an identity but "can only ever disturb one" (2004, 17). If heteronormative futurism endeavors to foreclose the disruptive force of the real—which Edelman, like Žižek, reads as an internal limit to both subjective and sociosymbolic coherence—queerness incarnates this force, thereby impeding the fantasmatic suturing of both identity and the collective political field.

To fully grasp the political poignancy of Edelman's argument, it is important to stress that the future, for him, functions as an imaginary— and therefore inherently misleading—fantasy of plenitude and wholeness. In a clever twist on the Lacanian argument that the subject's foundational lack-in-being propels it to look for substitutes for what it imagines having lost (the Thing), Edelman maintains that it is the promise of a better future specifically that serves as the ultimate substitute: the subject who pursues this promise is always, on some level, seeking to resurrect the reassuring plenitude and wholeness it (unconsciously) believes it has been forced to relinquish. In Lacanian terms, such a subject is trying to close the ontological gap (the lack-in-being) opened up by the signifier; it is striving to create a fantasmatic future in order to replicate a fantasmatic (imaginary) past without any division, antagonism, or deprivation.

This is why Edelman maintains that the fantasy of a better future promises "the coherence of the Imaginary totalizations through which [our] identities appear to us in recognizable form" (2004, 7). By screening out the lack (or emptiness, inadequacy, or castration) introduced by the signifier, the fantasy of a better future offers the dream of seamless self-actualization, of a time and place where desire is definitively quenched, where the signifier finally finds its proper signified, where "being and meaning are joined as One" (10). Unfortunately, this fantasy, while being endlessly seductive, is also endlessly deferred, thereby perpetuating the structure of cruel optimism that Edelman would like to escape; it keeps the subject from living in the present, which is why Edelman argues that it is what the queer as a figure of negativity counters (or should counter), undoing "the identities through which we experience ourselves as subjects, insisting on the Real of a jouissance that social reality and the futurism on which it relies have already foreclosed" (24–25).

Edelman, moreover, capitalizes on the Lacanian distinction between the drive and desire. In the same way that I have distinguished between repression and surplus-repression, suggesting that although repression is unavoidable, lifting surplus-repression might capture something about the "truth" of the subject's desire on the level of jouissance, Edelman implies that there is a "truthfulness" to the drive that (the more socially disciplined) desire lacks. Once again, our arguments are quite similar even though I do not wish to privilege the drive over desire in the manner that Edelman does. This is because I do not think that it is a coincidence that Lacan uses desire rather than the drive to define his ethics of psychoanalysis, of not ceding on one's desire.

Relevant in this context is the distinction I have posited between conventional desires and the kind of singular, nonnegotiable desire that relates directly to the Thing. I have specified that it is the latter that Lacanian ethics asks us not to give ground on. And I have also specified that this type of primordial desire can approach the drive as an expression of jouissance. Though I agree with Edelman that desire, due to having been subjected to more vigorous social conditioning than the drive, is forced to circle the Thing (as a site of loss) at a greater distance than the drive, it seems to me that primordial desire—that kind of desire that is able to evade surplus-repression—operates within a striking distance from the drive. Indeed, whenever such desire reaches jouissance, it could be said to more or less coincide with the drive.

My point here is that even though Edelman and I use slightly different terminologies—Edelman focusing on the drive whereas I tend to talk about desire—we are describing the same phenomenon of staying faithful to the "truth" of jouissance. Edelman locates this truth in the (death) drive whereas I locate it in the kind of desire that manages to capture something about the echo of the Thing, that discovers the aura of the Thing in mundane objects (*objets a*). Both Edelman and I connect the truth in question to the fundamental fantasies that shape the subject's psychic destiny. And both of us believe that these fantasies—often condensed in the sinthome— articulate something about the subject's singularity "in the real" (beyond symbolic and imaginary structures of personality). Both of us, in short, chart a line of reasoning that aligns the sinthome and jouissance with the subject's singularity of being, using Lacan's notion of fundamental fantasies as the hinge that connects these complex concepts.

This conglomerate of ideas is, in part at least, what Edelman is getting at when he argues that the sinthome, for Lacan, "relates to the primary inscription of subjectivity and thus to the constitutive fixation of the subject's access to jouissance" (2004, 35). "The constitutive fixation of the subject's access to jouissance" is, on some level, merely another way to describe the repetition compulsion (as a compulsion to circle the core of jouissance, the Thing). This is why Edelman goes on to propose that the sinthome operates "as the knot that holds the subject together, that ties or binds the subject to its constitutive libidinal career, and assures that no subject, try as it may, can ever 'get over' itself—'get over,' that is, the fixation of the drive that determines its jouissance" (35–36). The sinthome as the template of the subject's always idiosyncratic approach to jouissance functions as the knot that—symptomatically—holds the subject together by binding it to its repetition compulsion ("its constitutive libidinal career"), thereby ensuring that no subject will ever "get over" the fixations that determine the shape of its jouissance. The sinthome, as Edelman specifies, is " 'a pure sign,' a site of singularity and hence of nonexchangeability that fixes [the subject] as definitively, and as meaninglessly, as a fingerprint" (36).

In this manner, the sinthome bestows upon the subject's being a wholly meaningless singularity—or, if you prefer, a wholly arbitrary consistency—that makes it impossible to mistake (or exchange) one subject for another. The incessant pulsation of the drive, which the sinthome weaves into a tight knot, lends expression to this singularity/consistency without thereby facilitating self-closure in the symbolic sense. As opposed to desire—which always seeks to fill the lack of the subject's being by finding substitute objects for the primordial one it imagines having lost (the Thing)—the drive merely circles the absent center of jouissance without settling on specific objects. In this sense, the satisfaction of the drive arises from the doggedness of its movement, from the mindless repetition of its trajectory. This is what Todd McGowan, in *Enjoying What We Don't Have* (2013), dexterously captures by the idea that the satisfaction of the drive, in the final analysis, consists of enjoying what it does not have; the drive, so to speak, enjoys by enjoying "nothing" (the lack of an object). In Edelman's

words, the drive is "a pulsion that attains through insistence alone the satisfaction no end ever holds" (2004, 22).

This is how Edelman arrives at the idea that the drive offers the sinthomosexual constant access to jouissance, that the sinthomosexual "figures
the unrestricted availability of jouissance, the continuous satisfaction that
the drive attains by its pulsions and not by its end" (2004, 86). Edelman
juxtaposes this sinthomosexual to the subject of desire, the subject "who
clings to the *non*satisfaction that *perpetuates* desire and finds its defense
against jouissance in the narrative dilation that endlessly begets the future
by always deferring it" (86). That is, unlike the subject of desire—whose
satisfaction is constantly deferred to the future (whose very dissatisfaction
in the present "begets the future" as a promising but perpetually postponed
place of satisfaction)—the sinthomosexual attains satisfaction in the here
and now by replacing the fantasy of the future by the death drive, the drive
that enjoys "nothing," that enjoys no object but merely its own movement.

In this formulation, the very solipsism of the drive—the fact that it
needs no object but merely its own movement—guarantees its satisfaction;
unlike desire, the drive cannot be disappointed by the external world. In
this manner, for all his talk of antiutopianism, Edelman advances a highly
utopian vision of queer subjectivity as a site of unmediated (undiluted) jouissance. Although I concur with his assessment that jouissance functions
as the suppressed underside of the social order, I think that the idea that
any subject, however queer, could accede to an "unrestricted," "continuous
satisfaction" of jouissance sounds outrageously utopian. The fact that jouissance, in Edelman's account, serves the death drive does not change the fact
that he ends up positing a space of redemption—a kind of antiredemptive
redemption—for those who are able to utter the pure *No!* of subjective destitution (the *No!* of *No Future*).

4

Let me comment further on the fact that I am less inclined to dissociate
the drive from desire than Edelman is, for this is the main reason that,
for all their parallels, our interpretations of Lacan in the end diverge in
fundamental ways. For starters, I would argue that, despite desire's tendency to fixate on objects, it also, in its own way, enjoys what it does not
have. Edelman suggests that the drive gains satisfaction from its ceaseless

movement rather than from objects. But how different is this, conceptually, from his own definition of desire as what is endlessly perpetuated, and therefore endlessly deferred, by its nonsatisfaction? It seems to me that in both instances, it is the lack of an object—the failure to attain the object—that sustains satisfaction. In the case of desire, this lack/failure may only be partial, yet it is still a lack/failure.

As I argued in the last chapter, none of the objects that the subject lights on as substitutes for the lost Thing can ever fully satisfy it. Even the object that most faithfully resonates on the frequency of the subject's desire—that contains the strongest echo of the Thing—cannot do so consistently; the object always remains to some degree independent from the subject's desire for the simple reason that it contains characteristics that do not accord with this desire. This is why desire always, on some level, misses its object. Edelman reads this to mean that desire is politically impotent because it continuously pursues the futile promise of future fulfillment. But I am not sure how far removed this pursuit is from the drive's similarly unremitting movement.

Perhaps what bothers Edelman is that desire is a utopian force in the sense that it always seems to want "something more." Edelman interprets this as a sign that desire is a regressive attempt to regain a lost plenitude and wholeness. But one could just as easily say that desire takes a *critical* attitude toward the world precisely by wanting "something more," by refusing to be satisfied with the status quo of the here and now; desire looks toward the future because it assesses the present to be insufficient—"not enough" in Muñoz's terms. Essentially, desire is driven to ask, Could things be different? This is the critical utopian spirit that Muñoz values but Edelman devalues because he assumes that desire cannot be separated from hegemonic fantasies.

Yet, as I have demonstrated, some of our desires are counterhegemonic. One merely has to consider the countless social restrictions that have historically been placed on desire—particularly on queer, female, and interracial desire—to understand how very difficult it is to discipline; if it were easily colonized, there would be no need for the ruthless regulatory measures—such as imprisoning Oscar Wilde, cutting off women's clitorises, or hanging black men for sleeping with white women—that heteropatriarchy has over the centuries imposed on it. In other words, there is always a limit to the degree of social control that desire is willing to tolerate, which is exactly why it routinely reaches for "something more." And when it does so, it is no longer serving the hegemonic social order, as Edelman presumes, but rather turns the subject into a dissenter, a defiant subject in the sense that I outlined in the last chapter.

The arguments of the last chapter also allow me to restate my disagreement with Edelman as follows: though I concur that desire is endlessly deferred, perpetuated by its nonsatisfaction, unlike Edelman, I stress the autonomy—and therefore the politico-ethical potential—that arises from the fact that desire *does* fixate on specific objects. Indeed, these two characteristics of desire are not in the least bit contradictory: the fact that no object ever offers definitive satisfaction does not mean that no object can compel us. Quite the contrary, as I have shown, we are capable of resisting the hegemonic messages of our social environment, including the attempts of authority figures to convince us of the mistakenness of our desire, precisely because we find certain objects incomparably mesmerizing. In this sense, the ethical promise of desire derives from its stubborn loyalty to its objects, including ones that we are told are socially inappropriate. Whether or not we are able to actually attain such objects—let alone whether such objects ever offer complete satisfaction (they do not)—seems besides the point.

My reading of desire resonates with David Eng's (2010) analysis of the ethics of melancholia as a matter of remaining faithful to objects that we cannot possess, that we may even be actively asked to relinquish (more on this in chapter 5). In other words, if Edelman focuses on the ethical potential of the drive's propensity to shun objects, I focus on the ethical potential of the idiosyncratic trajectory of desire, of the track of desire that is "specifically our business," that causes the world—or pieces of the world— to "click" into place for us in meaningful ways, that allows us, however tenuously, to find value, worth, and even beauty. As I have stressed, I am less fascinated by death-driven jouissance than by the kind of (jouissance-filled) pleasure that we derive from objects (and again, bear in mind that we can derive a great deal of pleasure from objects that are not available or that only offer us partial satisfaction; there is pleasure to be had even from what cannot entirely gratify). This is why I am interested in the elaboration of desire, especially in the ways in which desire refuses to betray its most cherished objects even when holding on to these objects is socially inconvenient. That is, if Edelman reads desire's obstinacy—its tendency to solidify around particular objects—as a sign of desire's ethical failure, I read it as a sign of desire's ethical promise.

5

For Edelman, desire is automatically a regressive force and the drive is automatically a politically disruptive one. In contrast, I think that the relationship between desire and the drive is messier than this dichotomy, not the least because—as I have tried to suggest all along—our most stubborn desires converge with the jouissance of the drive. I hope to have made it clear that this does not mean that I do not recognize that desire can be hijacked by normative sociality, including the consumer fantasies of neoliberal capitalism. Yet how desire functions—regressively or disruptively— even in the capitalist context of consumption is not clear-cut.

Edelman's paradigm implies that desire, insofar as it relies on the fantasy of future satisfaction, perpetuates a capitalist logic of consumption— a logic that induces us to move from one object to the next as quickly as possible—whereas the drive, in gaining its satisfaction from the lack of objects, undermines this logic. Simply put, if the drive has no need for objects, then clearly it has no need for capitalism. By this reasoning, if we do what McGowan encourages us to do—namely, start enjoying what we do not have—we automatically thwart the foundations of capitalism. On some level, I appreciate this perspective, for I have always led a minimalist life that is not centered on possessions, so much so that I can easily live out of a medium-sized suitcase for months at end. But on another level, it makes it difficult to account for our allegiance to objects that might actually deserve our devotion. What is more, it overlooks the possibility that the fixations of desire can also disrupt the current of consumption.

As I have observed, a subject whose desire is obstinately preoccupied by a specific object is incapable of desiring other objects, thereby resisting capitalism's attempts to mobilize desire. In the last chapter, I made this point in the context of talking about how our faithfulness to a deeply loved person can keep us from participating in the capitalist mentality that tells us that every object is easily replaceable. But to some extent the same logic applies to inanimate objects as well.

For instance, I was so cathected to my ancient laptop that I used it for two years even after the components between the keyboard and the screen were so damaged that I could no longer close it: although I constantly worried that one day the screen would suddenly go blank on me, causing me to lose work—which had happened with my previous laptop—I held on to it even though it was entirely unpractical (unsuited for travel and so on). Similarly, I held on to an old cell phone that my students told me looked like a military phone from the 1980s for years after I had lost the cover to the battery. My favorite jeans are so full of holes that they are somewhat indecent to wear in public but I do it anyway. These may be banal examples, but they illustrate the manner in which our fidelity to our objects throws a monkey wrench into capitalism's attempts to encourage us to consume. When Apple releases its newest model of an iPhone, I could not care less. I trust that the phone I have—a device that looks like it was made circa 2002—will last me another decade at least.

The emphasis in my interpretation of desire falls on the object, on how the object—sometimes a culturally denigrated one—slips into such prominence for the desiring subject that the subject's bond to this object becomes nonnegotiable. In other words, even though I have stressed the importance of being able to sever ties to damaging objects, I simultaneously recognize the ethical force of insisting on the value of objects that the social order—or those who represent this order in our lives—tells us are devoid of value. For me, the matter comes down to the affective resonance of the object: some objects, however socially "appropriate," are not worth my investment; others, however socially "inappropriate," merit my unwavering fidelity. Edelman, in contrast, approaches the issue from the perspective of the subject who seeks self-closure through its objects of desire. This is what leads Edelman to argue that desire keeps jouissance at a distance by propping up the subject's fantasy of filling the void of its being whereas the drive—and by extension, the sinthomosexual who embraces the drive—"brings into visibility the force of enjoyment that desire desires to put off" (2004, 86).

I have admitted that desire strives to fill the void within the subject's being. But given that it never succeeds in this endeavor, I do not see the need to align it with self-closure; the very inability of desire to fully attain the satisfaction it seeks guarantees the subject's continued status as a being of lack (and therefore of openness). In this sense, Edelman has gotten things entirely backward: it is the subject of the drive—of jouissance—that closes upon itself whereas the subject of desire remains open to the world, including other people.

As I have remarked, the subject of jouissance is a solipsistic subject, cut off from any connection to others, even those who might facilitate its jouissance. Badiou (2012) inadvertently illustrates this dynamic when he proposes that Lacan's oft-quoted claim that "there is no sexual relation" ("il n'y a pas de rapport sexual") does not mean—as it has frequently been taken to mean—that there is an unbridgeable gap between men and women in heterosexual relationships but rather that, at the (fleeting) moment of jouissance, there is no "relation" whatsoever to another person. Orgasmic jouissance, in short, neutralizes intersubjective capacity: the drive is an antirelational force because—as I put it earlier—it shuns all objects.

On this view, the problem with ethical theories centered on jouissance is that they involuntarily resurrect the "subject" in all of its solipsistic glory at the very moment of its annihilation. I am not saying that they give us the sovereign subject of humanist metaphysics—far from it. But they do give us a self-contained subject who has severed its ties not only to the hegemonic Other but also to all intersubjective others. In this sense, Edelman's notion of the sinthomosexual as an entity with continuous access to jouissance revels in a backhanded individualism: the Edelmanian subject disappears into a vortex of jouissance that admits no trace of the other. In contrast, the subject of desire—far from being the closure-seeking arch-conservative Edelman interprets it to be—is forced to care about the contours of the surrounding world; it is forced to be curious about the world and the objects, including other people, that make up that world.

Let me press the argument a step further by proposing that desire, far from resulting in self-closure, *decenters the subject precisely insofar as it centers on an object*: the more important the object becomes, the more the subject is drained of its ego-bound cohesiveness. Freud (1914) already made this point when he argued that when we fall in love, we trade our ego cathexis for an object cathexis: we direct our libido away from the self toward the other (the object). What is more, as Roland Barthes (1977) hauntingly conveys through his "lover's discourse," the disappointments of desire can ravage us to the point of self-dissolution, with the result that even if safety is what we seek through our desire, this is frequently the last thing it delivers; the fantasies that desire generates may aim at the stabilization of life but the lived realities of desire tend to push us in the opposite direction of existential turbulence. I would even argue that the disappointments of desire derail us more effectively—and certainly for longer stretches of time—than Edelmanian torrents of jouissance, that a subject whose desire has been mortified is an inherently nonsovereign subject, a subject who has lost the coordinates of its being, a subject who has truly undergone a symbolic death (a symbolic destitution or castration).

This is why I am not persuaded by Edelman's equation of desire's future-oriented momentum with the rigidity of imaginary fantasies of plenitude and wholeness, of "eventual totalization" (2004, 101). I agree with him that fixating on the future can keep us from living in the present, can—to borrow Eric Santner's apt formulation—keep us from fully entering "the midst of life" (2001, 22); as Edelman suggests, the dream of futurity can keep "the place of life empty" (2004, 48) by robbing the present of vitality. At the same time, to cast the future as merely an attempt to recapture an imaginary past, as Edelman does, is to portray it in unnecessarily unimaginative terms. Does the future not remain inherently open ended? If so, the subject who turns toward the future by necessity remains alive to the utter unpredictability of existence. This is not a matter of denying death—or even the death drive—but merely of holding on to the possibility that between the present moment and the moment of death we are capable of meeting the world in ways that are worthy of our passion.

6

Edelman's attempt to uphold an unqualified binary between (bad) desire and the (good) drive seems to be primarily motivated by his wish to posit an equally unqualified binary between the (bad) child and the (good) sinthomosexual. I call attention to the value-laden texture (bad, good) of Edelman's binaries in order, once again, to illustrate the ways in which his antimorality remains markedly "moral." Despite its rhetorical rambunctiousness, Edelman's antinormativity does not reach "beyond good and evil" in the Nietzschean sense but merely reverses the usual valuation of the terms it deploys.

The problem with this strategy is the same as with Butler's efforts to keep (good) relationality from being contaminated by (bad) autonomy, namely, that the binary is too cleanly (and violently) delineated. There is no remainder of messiness, nothing that blurs the lines: on the side of the (bad) child we find (bad) heteronormative reproduction, the future, and the orderliness of fantasy-ridden desire; on the side of the (good) sinthomosexual we find (good) death-driven negativity, the *No!* to the future, and the disorderliness of the fantasy-shattering drive. This is a classic battle between Good and Evil, except that now what is normatively coded as Good (the child) is recoded as Evil and what is normatively coded as Evil (the sinthomosexual) is recoded as Good. Furthermore, Halberstam is surely justified in suggesting that the manner in which Edelman sets up his dichotomy unwittingly positions women—often associated with the sentimental culture of the child—on the side of future's illusory promises "while the gay man in particular leads the way to 'something better' while 'promising absolutely nothing'" (2011, 118).

That said, I would not go as far as Halberstam does when he claims that "Edelman's negativity has a profoundly apolitical tone to it" (2011, 118). I agree that Edelman fails to recognize the ways in which his version of queer negativity privileges the white gay man as a prince of destructiveness at the same time as it excludes everyone else from this noble designation; the white gay man obviously emerges as the heroic antihero of Edelman's story. Nevertheless, I wish to acknowledge that the overall ethos of Edelman's vision is political in the same sense that the ethos of the Lacanian act is political. I can certainly understand why many queer critics have been irked by Edelman's alignment of the queer with the death drive. But it should be stressed that this alignment is meant to be laudatory insofar as it depicts the queer as a discerning subject capable of seeing through the imaginary lures of heteronormative futurism.

Edelman makes his indebtedness to the Lacanian notion of the act explicit when he posits that the death-driven queer "forsakes *all* causes, *all* social action, *all* responsibility for a better tomorrow or for the perfection of social forms. Against the promise of such an activism, he performs, instead, an act: the act of repudiating the social"; the queer as a figure of defiance, in short, "stands for the wholly impossible ethical act" (2004, 101). It is clear that Edelman here flatly rejects political activism as a misguided quest for incremental change, ridiculing the efforts of such activism to improve society so as to attain a better future. But it is equally clear that this denouncement of political activism is undertaken in the name of a different kind of politics—that of the Lacanian ethical act.

That Edelman is offering us politics by another name becomes obvious when he positions himself—as I did in the last chapter—against Butlerian performativity, reiteration, and repetition, arguing that Butler's "'radical sexual politics' seems all too familiarly liberal and her engagement with psychoanalysis all too 'American,' as Lacan might say, in its promise to provide the excluded with access to a livable social form" (2004, 103–104). If Butler believes in the political potential of offering the marginalized entry into "a livable social form," and if she consequently stresses the urgency of rendering unintelligible (illegible) subjects intelligible (legible), Edelman regards the promises of intelligibility as a ruse of the hegemonic Other, asking, with reference to Butler's (2000) reading of Antigone, "What if Antigone, along with all those doomed to ontological suspension on account of their unrecognizable and, in consequence, 'unlivable' lives, *declined* intelligibility, declined to bring herself, catachrestically, into the ambit of future meaning—or declined, more exactly, to cast off the meaning that clings to those social identities that intelligibility abjects?" (Edelman 2004, 106). Edelman thus suggests that Butler's reading of Antigone romanticizes Antigone's act by drawing it back to the realm of intelligibility. Against this interpretation, Edelman insists that Antigone's act remains unintelligible, that it cannot be made legible, translated into meaning, or transformed into a recognizable identity; Antigone does not act in order to produce "livable" lives—not only does she pay for her act with her own life but this act does not resurrect Polyneces—but rather to mark, with a degree of emphasis, the space of the unlivable.

Through this interpretation, Edelman pits his radical politics of opting out against Butler's incremental politics of social change, thereby challenging, as I have done, the idea of needing to negotiate with hegemonic power. Edelman correctly recognizes that Lacan admires Antigone as an ethical heroine precisely because she refuses to enter into such a process of negotiation. This is why she functions as a precursor to Edelman's defiant queer who insists "on the unintelligible's unintelligibility, on the internal limit to signification and the impossibility of turning Real loss to meaningful profit in the Symbolic" (2004, 106).

The problem, as I have noted, is that Edelman fails to specify that Antigone does not commit her act "for nothing," that she sacrifices herself for the sake of a principle, and—most importantly for our purposes—for the sake of someone she loves. As we have seen, Antigone's act is antisocial but it is not antirelational; it opposes hegemonic forms of sociality—Creon's big Other—out of respect for a cherished relational tie. Moreover, I have demonstrated that my interpretation of Lacanian ethics diverges from that of Edelman in recognizing that Lacanian defiance does not need to reach suicidal proportions, that as much as Lacan celebrates Antigone's sacrifice, he also presents less drastic avenues for insubordination, such as the analysand's ability to utter her exasperated *Enough!* at the Law of the Father. Still, I do not want to lose track of the ways in which Edelman's critics—myself included (see Ruti 2008)—have misunderstood his argument.

Not only do I think that Halberstam is mistaken in characterizing Edelman's negativity "apolitical"; I also want to qualify my own 2008 allegation that Edelman paints the queer subject into a psychotic corner where there is no space for social viability. Given what I have just said about Edelman's rejection of social intelligibility, this reading is not unreasonable. Indeed, I suspect that even when it is not explicitly articulated, it underlies much of queer theory's resistance to Edelman's argument, for as counterhegemonic as this theory strives to be, it tends to draw a line at equating the queer with the psychotic. Yet a careful reading of Edelman's disagreement with Butler reveals what I have already alluded to in passing (but failed to adequately address in my earlier critique of Edelman), namely that in aligning the queer with the jouissance of the real, Edelman is not talking about queer subjects per se but rather proposing that "the queer" as a (culturally generated) figure *configures* the internal obstacle that the real poses to all symbolic attempts to attain closure.

This is why Edelman asserts that if Butler claims Antigone for intelligibility, for meaning, the queer "consents to the logic that makes it a *figure* for what meaning can never grasp. Demeaned, it embraces de-meaning as the endless insistence of the Real that the Symbolic can never master for meaning now or in 'the future'" (2004, 107). The queer, here, is not a psychotic subject external to the symbolic order but rather an internal irritant that, like the real that makes the symbolic cough, "de-means" the symbolic's efforts to create meaning. Like Halperin's abject gay antihero, Edelman's queer embraces its demeaned (debased) status so as to de-mean (wreak havoc with) normative meaning. That is, as a (demeaned and de-meaning) *figure* of unintelligibility, the queer takes upon itself the sacrificial task of metaphorizing "the traumatic violence of signification whose meaning-effacing energies, released by the cut that articulates meaning, the Symbolic order constantly must exert itself to bind" (106).

The acknowledgment that the queer, for Edelman, functions as a figure of unintelligibility that should not be equated with queer subjects, or even with queer subjectivity as a theoretical concept, also blunts the edge of Muñoz's accusations regarding the limited reach of Edelman's critique of the innocent child, for it forces us to admit that the child similarly functions, for Edelman, as a figure that is not necessarily meant to refer to actual children in any straightforward manner. This does not entirely neutralize Muñoz's critique, for the leap from the figure of the child to the actual child, like the leap from the figure of the queer to the queer subject, seems virtually inevitable. Indeed, one could argue that in constructing the figure of the innocent child, Edelman merely reinforces the cultural logic that excludes some (racialized, genderdeviant, and so on) children from the protection afforded children who manage to personify this figure. The same could be said about the figure of the death-driven queer: Does Edelman not, in constructing this figure, merely reproduce the very trope that mainstream society uses to oppress queer subjects? The problem is akin to the one that Irigaray (1974) and Cixous (1975) faced—and never fully resolved—when they, in deploying the stereotype of "irrational" femininity for progressive purposes, replicated the very caricature of the feminine that has historically been used to oppress flesh-and-blood female (or feminine) subjects. Nonetheless, underscoring the metaphorical dimensions of Edelman's argument complicates critiques leveled against him in the same way that underscoring the metaphorical dimensions of the arguments of Cixous and Irigaray has always complicated critiques of these thinkers, often in fact—accurately in my view—more or less absolving them of the charges of antifeminism that a more literal reading might provoke.

Perhaps most importantly, Edelman recognizes that when the "the queer" refuses the burden of (demeaning and de-meaning) unintelligibility, this burden will get displaced onto other abjected bodies. In this sense, Edelman anticipates Puar's argument—outlined in chapter 1—regarding the way in which the homonormative queer subject transfers the stigma of denigration to other "undesirable" populations, such as Muslim immigrants. Edelman points out that by denying its association with negativity, the queer subject may "enter the properly political sphere, but only by shifting the figural burden of queerness to someone else. The *structural position* of queerness, after all, and the need to fill it remain" (2004, 27). A generous reading of Edelman would here admit that he may not be as oblivious to the manner in which abjection traverses from one marginalized body (or population) to the next as Muñoz and many others have accused him of being.

However, this does not change the fact that Edelman seems to perceive any reference to concrete identities as an undoing of theoretical rigor, as a lapse into naïve identity politics. This is precisely what gives his theorizing the crypto-universal air that Muñoz detects, for Edelman appears to assume that any attempt to think through the complexities of how different bodies (or populations) are positioned in the world—and to pay attention to the variable levels of suffering that such variable positionings generate—automatically constitutes an identitarian lens (as opposed to the "universal" lens produced by unmarked—meaning, white and male—bodies). Yet there is no conceptual reason for his standpoint. There is absolutely no reason we cannot acknowledge constitutive human alienation, wounding, disorientation, and out-of-jointness—the subject's lack-in-being in the Lacanian sense—at the same time as we acknowledge that there are other, more context-specific forms of alienation, wounding, disorientation, and out-of-jointness that impact people—and cause people to suffer—in different degrees depending on their positioning within the fabric of an intrinsically unequal symbolic order.

7

This dispute will gain prominence in the next chapter. But first I want to illustrate that though the reading of death-dealing negativity that Edelman extracts from Lacan is available in Lacan's work, so is a very different reading of negativity. More specifically, though it is true that Lacan connects the death drive to the suicidal act, presenting Antigone as a heroine who is unwilling to cede on her desire even when she knows that this desire will lead to her demise, he also explicitly links the death drive to a "will to make a fresh start," "a will to create from zero, a will to begin again" (1959–1960, 212). He in fact suggests that insofar as the death drive "challenges everything that exists" (212), it can make visible what is invisible from the point of view of the social order, thereby inviting a fundamental reconfiguration (rather than simply a destruction) of that order. The same logic can arguably be applied to the subject, so that the death drive's "will to make a fresh start" might productively be taken to gesture toward the kind of psychic rebirth that clinical practice, in Kristeva's opinion, can bring about (see chapter 2). In other words, although Lacan certainly does not imply that acts of subjective destitution invariably result in collective or personal revitalization, the possibility of such revitalization—a possibility that Edelman studiously ignores—is nevertheless present in his account.

This possibility of revitalization is what Badiou has explored through his notion of the truth event as a sudden revelation that erases the individual's status quo—her "business as usual"—and brings into being the so-called subject of truth, a subject who, through its fidelity to the unanticipated insight offered by the event, engenders a new (collective or personal) order of things. Žižek, whose reading of Lacan is closer to that of Edelman, routinely takes issue with Badiou's interpretation, accusing Badiou of not fully grasping the destructive power of the death drive. Yet Žižek himself at times also views subjective destitution as a spur for a new order of things, as when, for instance, he observes that "the act differs from an active intervention (action) in that it radically transforms its bearer (agent). . . . in it, the subject is annihilated and subsequently reborn (or not)" (2001, 44). Unlike Edelman, Žižek here seems to recognize that even though the act may not consciously aim at rebirth, and even though it may not inevitably lead to such rebirth, it *can* under certain circumstances have this effect.

I suspect that the ambivalence regarding the matter arises precisely from the fact that both readings are available in Lacan, so that where one ends up—at destruction or rebirth—depends on what one chooses to highlight. Even Lacan's statement about the death drive functioning as "a will to begin again" is wrought with ambiguity. One can argue—as Philip Sayers (2014) skillfully does—that the "will to begin again," the "will to make a fresh start," refers to the will to return to the beginning of the repetition compulsion, to start "afresh" the process of pursuing the thread of this compulsion, the thread of one's fundamental psychic destiny. Read in this way, the will to begin again suggests that the subject defends against rebirth—understood as a reconfiguration of life—by opting for the familiar trajectory of the repetition compulsion.

Sayers's reading is also compatible with McGowan's analysis of the drive as what enjoys by enjoying "nothing," by never attaining its goal. Translated into my vocabulary, it implies that the death drive causes the subject to repeatedly recommence its circling around the traumatic kernel of the lost Thing. Yet even within this interpretation, there is room for a degree of "rebirth" in the sense that each new cycle of the repetition compulsion repeats slightly differently—draws new elements, new debris of life, into the groove of the compulsion—so that even when the repetition is largely predictable, it is always also somewhat unpredictable; to the extent that something new is added to the repetition compulsion with every new enactment, one can still speak of a "fresh start" of sorts.

This interpretation agrees with the conclusion regarding the repetition compulsion that I arrived at in the last chapter, namely, that the compulsion is usually impossible to break in any definitive sense, that the best the subject can do is to develop a more active—and ideally more satisfying— relationship to it. This is one reason that one cannot, in the Lacanian context, speak about an analytic "cure," about an ultimate solution (what Lacan mockingly calls "the Sovereign Good") that would, once and for all, release the subject from its suffering; the best clinical practice can accomplish is to facilitate the subject's capacity to enter into the cycle of the repetition compulsion in less injurious ways. This may, for instance, entail developing a greater degree of critical distance from the compulsion so that moments of intervention—moments when the subject decides against its "usual" manner of going about the process of living—become possible. Starting "afresh" in this sense is merely a matter of starting from a slightly different perspective.

Although I find this interpretation persuasive, I am also inclined to read Lacan's statement about the "will to create from zero, a will to begin again" alongside his famous musings about a potter who creates a vase around a void, "creates it, just like the mythical creator, ex nihilo, starting with a hole" (1959–1960, 120). In both cases, Lacan suggests that absence (zero, a hole) is a source of creativity. The zero of the death drive and the hole of the vase are far from being inert spaces of lack. Rather, they give rise to the desire to play with lack; they—to return to my wording in chapter 1— generate the impulse to work with negativity.

Essentially, Lacan stresses that emptiness and creativity—the zero of the death drive and the will to begin again; the void of the vase and the fashioning of the vase that comes to enclose it—arise simultaneously. This is Lacan's figurative means of conveying one of his most fundamental insights about human subjectivity, namely, that our sense of lack and our capacity to signify come into being in tandem: the signifier causes our lack but our lack, in turn, causes the urge to signify. Or to state the matter conversely, it is because we lack that we are prompted to signify (create) yet it is our significatory (creative) activity that allows us to (sort of) handle our lack. This is arguably what we do when we write books (yes?). In this sense, there is a direct connection between our alienation on the one hand and our capacity to envision imaginative ways of coping with this alienation on the other.

In addition, because our alienation can never be definitively redeemed, because we have no way of turning our negativity into a definitive form of positivity, our significatory endeavors are transient at best, giving us access to no permanent meaning, no solid identity, no unitary narrative of self-actualization. Any fleeting state of positivity that we may be able to attain must always in the end dissolve back into negativity; any attempt to erase lack produces new instances of lack. This means that the process of working with negativity must be continually renewed, which is why we start writing a new book the minute the old one is finished. Or at least I do. The hope is that if I work through the same ideas one more time, maybe I will finally be able to put them to rest. But they do not rest. Some of them insist on remaining wide awake, asking for yet another articulation: thus the endless recycling of thoughts, the endless "will to begin again."

In the same way that no object of desire can ever fully gratify, our every attempt to fill our lack unavoidably falls short of its goal: there will, quite simply, never be a perfect book, the book of books that extinguishes the desire for a better book. However, as I have observed, the lack of complete satisfaction does not mean that there is no satisfaction to be had. If anything, the intrinsic impossibility of complete satisfaction is what sustains us as creatures of becoming and what allows us, over and again, to take up the inexhaustible process of producing meaning, including the process of signifying beauty. As Kaja Silverman states, "Our capacity to signify beauty has no limits. It is born of a loss which can never be adequately named, and whose consequence is, quite simply, the human imperative to engage in a ceaseless signification. It is finally this never-ending symbolization that the world wants from us" (2000, 146).

8

I have demonstrated that we have two strategies for containing the void within our being: we can either find an object that snugly fits into its cavity or we can invent such an object. It may be prudent to add that, as much as I have underscored the extraordinary appeal of the object that appears to transmit an echo of the Thing, our ability to create our object—rather than randomly discover it in the world—is arguably the more reliable of these two strategies. This is why so many of us engage in various sublimatory efforts. By this I do not mean to deny that there are specific signifiers that can harm us (in the same way that there are hegemonic forms of desire that can harm us). My point is merely that the signifier is not invariably what oppresses us but also what gives us access to the kind of creative capacity that allows us to repeatedly refashion the world.

Stated slightly differently, even though the signifier (language) partakes in constraining collective regimes, it is never fully oppressive but remains open to various types of inventive reconfiguration. In his *Ècrits*, Lacan already talks about the "poetic function" of language (1966, 264), the fact that language by definition perpetuates the radical polyvalence of meaning, in ways that anticipate Derrida's commentary on the slippery nature of the signifier. But more importantly for our purposes, in his 1975–1976 seminar on the sinthome—that is, on the very concept that Edelman relies on in building his theory of the sinthomosexual—Lacan sought to rethink the relationship between the symbolic and the real through a close reading of James Joyce, coming to the conclusion that the real possesses the power to revitalize the symbolic (the signifier) from within.

Starting from the premise that the real functions as an internal limit to the symbolic's quest for closure, Lacan explores the ways in which the signifier's vulnerability in the face of the real—its tendency to be derailed by the real—holds the key to its regeneration; essentially, Lacan maintains that to the degree that the signifier is exposed to the unruly energies of the real, it can be revitalized—rather than merely defeated ("murdered," as Žižek likes to say)—by these energies. From this it follows that only those forms of signification that successfully capture something of the energies of the real—that, as it were, manage to activate morsels of the real—remain creative; without such dynamic interaction between the symbolic and the real, Lacan proposes, the signifier would rapidly grow stale and static.

Lacan renders the matter concrete when, speaking of Joyce's epiphanic writing style, he argues that Joyce is able to invent revolutionary forms of language—forms of language that alter the normal rules of signification— precisely to the extent that he manages to touch the real. More specifically, Lacan proposes that Joyce achieves inspired modes of writing—modes of writing that reveal the jouissance of the writer—because he identifies with his sinthome (note the resonances of this formulation with my earlier statements about identifying with the sinthome as one's psychic destiny). Lacan goes as far as to argue that writing, for Joyce, is *equivalent* to the sinthome: it is only insofar as Joyce is overtaken by his sinthome that he is a true artist. As Lacan posits: "But it is clear that Joyce's art is something so particular that the term sinthome is what suits it best" (1975–1976, 94). On Joyce's jouissance, Lacan in turn states: "Read the pages of *Finnegans Wake*, without trying to understand. It reads. If it reads . . . it is because one feels present the jouissance of the one who wrote it" (1975–1976, 165).

All of this implies that even though Lacan certainly draws a connection between the sinthome and the death drive, identification with the sinthome is not, for him, exclusively a matter of subjective destitution (as Edelman insists). Rather, it is a means of linking the symbolic and the real so as to replenish the signifier. Lacan goes on to interpret *Finnegans Wake* as Joyce's solution to the fact that the death drive is inherently unthinkable, stating, "The death drive, it is the real insofar as it cannot be thought except as impossible. That is to say, every time that it shows the tip of its nose, it is unthinkable. . . . What is unbelievable is that Joyce . . . could find no other solution but to write *Finnegans Wake*" (1975–1976, 25). Where Edelman advocates the vehement *No!* of subjective destitution as a response to what is "impossible" about the death drive, Lacan suggests that Joyce weaves this impossibility into the folds of his art, thereby fending off death (at least for the time being).

Without question, the insurrection of the real within the symbolic carries the destructive force of the death drive. Joyce—like Edelman's sinthomosexual—dissolves meaning. He undoes—devastates and dismembers—language. However, unlike the self-annihilating sinthomosexual, Joyce is driven by a certain élan or improvised ardor. As Lacan speculates, "Joyce felt himself overwhelmingly called" (1975–1976, 89). Joyce did not strive to choke the signifier but rather to awaken it, harnessing the destructiveness of the death drive in the service of new life (the "fresh start" I analyzed earlier). As Roberto Harari, in his reading of Lacan's seminar, aptly notes, Joyce's epiphanies allow him "to bite into bits of the real" (2002, 141). Joyce's signifiers, in other words, are unique to the extent that they breathe to the rhythm of the real. In a way, what Joyce reveals is that even though the real as such cannot be written, one can write in such a way as to brush against it; one's signifiers can transmit a sliver of the real.

There is no doubt that language is a trespasser, an intruder, in the domain of the real. However, it may be exactly because the real makes language struggle—forces it to fight for its territory, as it were—that the encounter with the real can make language fiercely inventive. If Western metaphysics has denigrated the body and its drives as the irrational (and therefore threatening) underside of meaning, and if Edelman strives to destroy meaning by unleashing the full force of the irrational upon it, Lacan wants to understand the part that the irrational plays in the creative production of meaning. He explores the potentially productive interpenetration of reason and unreason, meaning and nonmeaning, that characterizes the psychic life of all of us, and certainly of those of us who spend our time writing. I find it hard to imagine that Edelman wrote *No Future* in a state of "continuous jouissance." But that there was jouissance in the process of writing is evident in the text.

Clearly, at this late stage in his thinking, Lacan no longer sees language and jouissance as mutually exclusive, instead suggesting that the signifier transmits jouissance to the extent that it carries traces of the real. In the same way that a mundane object that contains an echo of the Thing is more galvanizing than other objects, a signifier that contains bits of the real is more galvanizing than other signifiers. This is why some signifiers speak to us on a more visceral level than others, why some signifiers seem much more alive than others. From this point of view, moments when the real infiltrates the symbolic are not necessarily indicative of the failure of signification but rather of its irrepressible vitality; they are productive irregularities that disband and displace frozen structures of meaning. In this manner, the negativity of the real becomes generative by fueling the world-shaping capacities of the signifier.

This is why I cannot fully agree with Edelman's version of Lacan. And it is also why I have never been able to agree with Butler's interpretation of the signifier as an insidious tool of subjection that divests us of agency. Nor have I been able to agree with Butler's reduction of agency to the process of negotiating with preexisting norms in the hope that something "slightly different" might come into being. Following Lacan, I believe that the signifier is capable of generating more than mere variations on—or subversions of—the norm. In other words, if for Butler there is nothing beyond power, no real that eludes the symbolic, I read the real as a source of nonsymbolic energy that to some extent evades the grip of power and that is therefore capable of enlivening the symbolic (the signifier). If the real is a gap in symbolic subjectivity—another name for the constitutive lack of our being—it is also the opening through which the drive is capable of attaching itself to the signifier, thereby animating this signifier in the manner that Lacan describes.

Another way of stating the matter is to say that creativity presupposes an encounter with negativity: with lack, castration, alienation, the death drive (the names are many). This encounter is what Butler forecloses by insisting that there is nothing beyond the symbolic (no negativity, no real, beyond disciplinary power). This is precisely why the reiteration of the norm is the only form of creativity that is compatible with the Butlerian paradigm.

Edelman in turn reads Lacanian negativity (the real) as a flat rejection of the symbolic, with the result that insofar as the queer embodies this negativity, she has no access to the signifier. The Edelmanian queer is pure drive, incapable of creativity of any kind: entirely de-meaned. Sadly, in Edelman's model, the only mode of creativity available in the world is reproductive heteronormativity. Yet surely it is not the case that only those who produce children "create" things. If anything, one could say that the queer has, empirically speaking, frequently exceeded the average level of creativity. Might this be because the queer has repeatedly had to survive the encounter with negativity?

For Edelman there is no room for nonhegemonic forms of signification: the signifier and the dominant symbolic coincide seamlessly in a manner that ensures that the signifier is intrinsically tyrannical. This explains why Edelman's "solution" to hegemonic power is to *replace* the symbolic by the real, the signifier by the sinthome (jouissance). As my objections in this chapter indicate, I find this approach largely unsatisfactory not only because of its utter lack of real-life viability but also because of its reductive binarism: the symbolic vs. the real; the child vs. the sinthomosexual; the future vs. the suicidal act. Merely reversing the customary appraisal of the poles of these binaries represents too simplistic a solution.

My more global point is that the signifier is not a monolithic monster that unilaterally imposes its hegemonic law on our psychic lives. Quite the contrary, once we have access to the signifier, we have the capacity to use it in imaginative ways, even in ways that challenge the very law that brought us into being as symbolically viable creatures. In this sense, the internalization of norms is merely one side of the process of socialization. The other side opens to creativity, meaning, and relationality (assuming that it is because of the signifier that there is lack, that it is because of lack that there is desire, and that it is because of desire that there is relationality). On this view, although the symbolic can be—and frequently is—harnessed for regulatory ends, it is not synonymous with regulation.

Finally, let us note that without the signifier, none of us would have a psyche to begin with, so that the signifier is not merely what violates the body and its jouissance but also what grants us the gift of inner life. As a result, when Butler and Edelman—and they do have this in common—demonize the signifier as a vehicle of social hegemony, my question is: Given that the signifier brings the psyche into being, what is being defended here? The sanctity of an innate human essence that predates the subject's encounter with the signifier? I doubt that such an essence is what either Butler or Edelman would promote; surely they would grant that the signifier is what brings the subject into existence. But if this is the case, I fail to see how we can treat the signifier primarily as an enemy of subjectivity. Although it is obvious that the process of symbolic interpellation includes hegemonic elements, that the subject cannot be produced without a degree of social control, it seems futile to vilify this process to the degree that Butler and Edelman do given that, without it, *there would be no subject to begin with*.

I have already noted that the poststructuralist hatred of "the subject" is another theme that Butler and Edelman have in common. Consequently, they might respond by saying that they want to get rid of the subject altogether. But it is hard to grasp what this might mean, practically speaking—a theme I will return to in the context of Huffer's analysis of Foucauldian desubjectivation in the next chapter. I know that it continues to be fashionable to speak about the demise of the subject but I have never quite understood what critics are talking about when they are talking about this demise: What exactly is supposed to take the place of the subject? Where is the critic speaking from if not from the position of being a subject of some sort? And how can Butler reconcile her admonition of the subject with her simultaneous concern for the precarity of this subject? I know that "autonomy" is the answer: it is the *autonomous* subject that needs to be destroyed. But is there really—has there really ever been—such a thing as a fully autonomous subject? Are we to take Hitler and his kin as a model for what subjectivity, as such, consists of? If not, then what the hell are we wasting ink on?

9

I will treat this question more fully in the next chapter (fun times). But, first, let me acknowledge that the interpretation of the world-shaping capacities of the signifier—and of Joyce's subversive writing practice—that I have presented is far from original in the sense that it represents a familiar line of argumentation in twentieth-century literary criticism. Kristeva's 1974 *Revolution in Poetic Language* (and it is worth noting the closeness of the publication date to Lacan's 1975–1976 seminar on the sinthome) already articulates many of the same themes. My goal, then, is not to say that Lacan presents a groundbreaking interpretation of Joyce but rather that readers of Lacan—Edelman in this case—who choose to ignore this component of Lacanian theory end up producing overly dispirited theories of subjectivity and (the impossibility) of social change.

Along related lines, they end up producing a weirdly lopsided understanding of eros (jouissance) as purely destructive. I concur that the (temporary) annihilation of sociality is the aim of eros in the sense that erotic experience ushers us beyond our symbolically mediated identities. As Bataille once put it, the purpose of eros is to defy "the self-contained character of the participators as they are in their normal lives"; because eros strikes at "the inmost core of the living being," it can bring about a momentary dissolution of the individual as he or she exists in the realm of everyday reality (1986, 17). Edelman is thus correct in suggesting that jouissance communicates the death drive. But surely this is not the entire story or even the most interesting part of the story, for eros also possesses the power to confer upon us the ardent and much-coveted sense of feeling fully alive; it can give rise to a piercing sensation of self-awakening. Precisely because eros allows us to overstep our symbolic boundaries, it activates frequencies of our being that ordinarily remain inactive. In this sense, eros is transformative as much as it is shattering, capable of reconfiguring the contours of our being; it enables us to momentarily "lose" ourselves so as to be able to resurface altered, with the parameters of our identity renegotiated.

In the same way that Joycean epiphanies lead to the reconfiguration of language, jouissance as one face of eros can lead to the reconstitution of subjectivity. Antisocial experiences can obviously be valuable in themselves. But if they entice us, it is often in part because they revive our social being; they bring the real into our symbolic existence in ways that energize our lives. In this sense, the real is not merely a harbinger of destruction but also what lends agility to our symbolic identities, including our ability to build meaningful connections to others; even if, as I have argued, jouissance itself is intrinsically antisocial, effectively cutting us off from the world of others, we can emerge from it with the desire to renew our social bonds (as lovers frequently do after jouissance has expired). This is where the intrinsically fleeting character of jouissance comes in handy, for it allows for a momentary dissolution of sociality without thereby irrevocably demolishing our capacity to relate to others.

That we routinely reap the benefits of the interplay between the symbolic and the real, the social and the antisocial, is one reason I think that conceptualizing the relationship between these concepts as a binary structure where the subject either inhabits the symbolic as a fully conformist being or casts it all off through a subversive act of subjective destitution is largely counterproductive. I agree that the real can destabilize the ideologically complacent structures of the symbolic. At the same time, taking up permanent residency in the real is hardly a viable option. Peering into the abyss, remaining aware of lack, tarrying with the negative, and momentary self-annihilation as a means to self-transformation (or subjective revitalization) all make sense to me. But the idea of the real as an *alternative* to symbolic existence does not. What would such existence mean in concrete terms? Why the impulse to delimit resistance to one experiential register— the real—instead of interrogating the vibrant interaction between the symbolic and the real (and the imaginary, for that matter)? And why the urge to cast the real wholly outside of life? If the goal is to escape the constraints of the dominant social order, why build an equally constraining escape?

Allow me to approach the matter from yet another angle. It is true that the Lacanian real can signal the dissolution of social subjectivity. Yet moments of such dissolution are not solely self-negating; they can also make us feel . . . well . . . immediately real. They may in fact be the closest we ever get to feeling fully present to ourselves. Poststructuralist theory has insisted that the subject, insofar as it is a split, alienated subject, can never be fully present to itself. But I would argue that the Lacanian real gives us a posthumanist manner of understanding what it might mean to attain a momentary glimpse of self-presence.

The fact that touching the real annihilates structures of language and sociality—that it arrests the customary workings of consciousness—allows for a relatively unmediated encounter with our bodily being; jouissance defies social intelligibility, but it enables us to feel immediately intelligible to ourselves. Such moments of hitting the real—moments when we find ourselves at the outer edges of coherent subjectivity—offer us the kind of intensity of experience that normally eludes us; in Harari's words, they usher us to "the hiding place of being" (2002, 74). This is exactly why Lacan (1972–1973) links jouissance to mystical experiences that transport us beyond everyday life, that, as it were, slice the world open in order to create space for the sublime. Christopher Bollas in turn describes such ephemeral states of altered perception in more mundane terms, as "simple self" experiences—moments of simplified or suspended consciousness— that allow us to fall to a place of depth "beyond thinking" (1993, 17). We emerge from that place amplified.

In this context, it is useful to recall Santner's distinction between two forms of interpellation. The first is what we usually understand by the term, namely our induction into the normative symbolic structures of the world (interpellation in the Althusserian sense). The second is a function of being summoned to an inspired manner of encountering the world. Santner talks about divine revelation as such an alternative form of interpellation— a calling that cannot be resisted—but he also implies that we can envision it in broader, less theological terms as a matter of being called upon to meet whatever it is that, at any given moment, takes on a force of necessity for us.

The encounter with the real conjures up the latter kind of interpellation. What is at stake here is the difference between a socially mediated identity on the one hand and a certain kind of subjective singularity on the other— a difference, that is, between an identity that relies on collective forms of authorization and one that in some ways eludes or exceeds these forms. The latter ushers us into the path of our drive destiny—our destiny "in the real"—rather than into the path of the destiny that the Other has designated for us; it is what causes us to make the kinds of life choices that seem insane from the perspective of the symbolic but that make sense to us on some alternative ("real") level. This far, I have talked about such choices in the context of our faithfulness to "inappropriate" objects of desire. But one can also imagine them in other realms of life, as when we, for instance, give up a prestigious job in order to pursue a less prestigious but more rewarding one.

Precisely because the real does not enter into the domain of social negotiation—because it only reveals itself in the fissures of the symbolic— it marks what is unique about each individual: it represents an uncontrollable eruption of singularity beyond the social. As Santner remarks, the singular self—the self that can "most truly say 'I' " (2001, 86)—possesses an actuality beyond all social generality or classification. This singular self conveys the fact that after the subject has been divested of its symbolic commitments there is still something that remains: the indigestible real of being. Although Santner reasons along the same lines as Edelman in the sense that he links subjective singularity to the death drive—to the utter alterity, asociality, and existential loneliness of death—his analysis remains more sinuous in that he never loses track of the vitalizing potentialities of the real: the fact that it can give us access to what he calls the "sparks" of more life (142).

Subjective singularity in the Lacanian sense always borders on the death drive. But, as I have tried to demonstrate, it is also a matter of creative living, of the always idiosyncratic ways in which we manage to bring the energies of the real into the symbolic realm. Lacan in fact explicitly stresses that Joyce is singular to the extent that his art draws on the real. More specifically, Lacan maintains that it is because Joyce embraces his sinthome (as the depository of the real) "that one can say that Joyce, as it is written somewhere, identifies himself as an individual" (1975–1976, 168). On this view, it is not only how we die—or face the prospect of our mortality— but also how we inhabit the intersection of the signifier and the real that singularizes us, that gives our identities a distinctive resonance. Although being compelled to participate in a common symbolic system deprives us of individuality, the fact that we always bring the real of our bodies into this system in idiosyncratic ways singularizes us.

Harari points out that "when the symbol and the sinthome are separated, this is an effect of the discourse of the master" (2002, 88). In other words, when our discourse fails to carry bits of the real, it obeys the master's dominant law. In contrast, discourse that touches the real crafts what I have elsewhere called a character (see Ruti 2013). In this sense, the act of identifying with one's sinthome is less a matter of self-annihilation than of actualizing one's singularity. From a slightly different viewpoint, one might say that if the process of fashioning a singular place within the world results in a distinctive subjective "style," this style always expresses something about the manner in which the symbolic and real, however tenuously, come together and amalgamate.

This is why one of the most arduous facets of human life is the necessity of maintaining a balance of sorts between the symbolic and the real, between the signifier and the bodily remainder that resists signification. As Lewis Kirshner posits, "To summarize the Lacanian position, self-maintenance (a sense of embodied existence) entails preservation of a certain equilibrium with the real" (2004, 76). On the one hand, if the subject is to feel alive, it must, as Kirshner puts it, "preserve contact with the traces of the 'thing' (the unsymbolized part of the real), without being overwhelmed by it"; on the other, an excessive weakness of social links exposes the subject "to destabilization by a real that cannot be contained" (76). This is to say that whenever the symbolic gains too much power at the expense of the real, life loses its passion and forward-moving cadence. But when the symbolic fails to adequately mediate the chaotic energies of the real, the subject feels terrorized by the overproximity and overwhelming intensity of its own jouissance; it fails to gain a steady foothold in cultural narratives and other collective landmarks that anchor it in the social world and lend a degree of cohesion to its identity.

This is why Lacan (1955–1956) posits that, if we are to lead manageable lives, we need a number of key signifiers—what he calls "quilting points"—that connect us to a universe of familiar meanings. This is an aspect of Lacanian theory that Edelman chooses to overlook, with the result that he loses sight of the interplay between the symbolic and the real. This in turn means that he fails to recognize that the real is not necessarily what destroys the future but rather what, from time to time, puts it on hold by allowing us to experience the full impact of the here and now. It is true that during our fleeting encounters with the real we are without past or future, our entire being unified in a single instant of the present. But this does not mean that our future is permanently foreclosed.

10

I have countered Edelman's reading of Lacan with an alternative interpretation in order to illustrate that Lacanian negativity opens to processes of becoming as much as—and perhaps even more than—processes of self-annihilation. When Muñoz and Dean defend queer utopianism against Edelman's nihilism on the pages of the *PMLA*, they seem to be getting at something similar. Muñoz, for his part, opposes Edelman's contention that there is "no future" for the queer by asserting that "queerness is primarily about futurity" (2006, 826). Hope, he asserts, is not a conservative form of complacency but rather a way of sustaining a spirit of imaginative inquisitiveness that allows us to envision alternatives to the life-arresting logic of the heteronormative present.

Dean in turn argues—along lines that have obvious parallels with what I have just said about eros—that the shattering of normativity that queer eros enacts "betokens not the end of sociality but rather its inception" (2006, 827). That is, the antisociality of eros is not merely, or even primarily, destructive but instead gives rise to fresh forms of erotic connectivity—forms that are not governed by the demands of reproduction but that open to a more promiscuous array of intersubjective possibility. The problem with Edelman's argument, Dean correctly suggests, is less its antisociality than the fact that it cannot admit that anything constructive could ensue from this antisociality.

It seems to me that this distinction between antisociality (negativity) that is wholly destructive and antisociality (negativity) that, potentially at least, yields to something more affirmative is a good way to capture the gist of the disagreement between Edelman and his more utopian critics. Among other things, it offers a way to parse Muñoz's conviction that the antisocial thesis represents "the gay white man's last stand" (2006, 825). As I have already suggested, to some extent this conviction arises from the recognition that the kind of radical self-dissolution that Edelman celebrates can only be undertaken from a position of relative security, that deprivileged subjects—many women, racialized subjects, and those who lead economically precarious lives (that is, subjects whose claim to symbolic identity is shaky to begin with)—simply cannot afford to abandon themselves to the jouissance of the death drive in the way that more secure subjects might be tempted (or even compelled) to do. Many queer subjects of course also lead precarious lives, so that my formulation is not meant to create unnecessary divisions between, say, queer theory and feminism, or queer theory and critical race theory, but merely to call attention to the conditions under which the act of subjective destitution becomes a feasible option. It seems understandable that those who feel that they cannot afford such an act—as I certainly have felt for much of my life—will be on the lookout for ways to conceptualize negativity as the underside of possibility rather than as a pure site of loss; those who have experienced an excess of loss are unlikely to be looking for an additional helping of it.

Conversely, one could hypothesize that the romance of self-annihilation that Edelman promotes speaks to those who experience their subject positions as *too secure,* who feel suffocated and oppressed by the strength (and rigidity) of their symbolic identities, and who consequently yearn for the release offered by jouissance. In other words, while those whose symbolic identities are already slipping might need the support of affirmative, even utopian theories, those whose symbolic investments protect them from the more shattering frequencies of life might be drawn to theories of self-dissolution. In this context, it may be useful to recall that poststructuralist theory—with its vehement rejection of agency, coherence, rationality, and mastery—*was* largely an invention of white men (though white women and racialized subjects quickly followed suit).

I am not saying that there were no good theoretico-political reasons for this invention, for there were, such as the recognition that humanist discourses of self-mastery all too easily spawn colonialist and imperialist fantasies of mastering the world. But it may also be that there is a connection between the rise of poststructuralism and the unacknowledged guilt of those who, in the post–World War II (and postcolonial) context, felt themselves to have *too much agency* (and who therefore wanted to theorize it away). A prime example is Althusser, who both strangled his wife and developed a theory of social interpellation that more or less completely erased the concept of personal agency, thereby rendering responsibility for one's actions an intrinsically elusive goal (see Kirshner 2004). This is why a cynical view of poststructuralism would see it as a symptom of white men fleeing from the burden of their egos, from the terror of their (excessive) sovereignty. Though I do not invariably hold such a cynical view, though I am as enamored of Derrida as the next theorist trained within the 1990s American academy, I do not think that it is a coincidence that, within queer theory, "hardcore" poststructuralism continues to be aligned with white gay men whereas the softened version associated with affect theory has become aligned with female critics and critics of color.

Fortunately, as I have noted, this division is increasingly breaking down as a result of the sweeping popularity of the trope of opting out within queer theory. At first glance, this may imply that the pendulum is swinging toward Edelman's antisocial thesis. But as I will show in the chapters that follow, the counterforce of sociality and relationality is not being run over by antisociality. Rather, it is being rearticulated in more sophisticated ways. More specifically, it offers a convincing alternative to Edelmanian antisociality by sidestepping some of the latter's theoretical weaknesses. As I have attempted to illustrate in this chapter, foremost among these is the idea that sociality *as such* is the enemy of queer subjectivity, for this conception fails to adequately differentiate between hegemonic and enabling forms of sociality; it fails to take into account the fact that even though we are inevitably interpellated into dominant sociosymbolic structures, we remain capable of generous kinds of sociality (and intersubjectivity).

Along related lines, as I have argued, Edelman's insistence on equating jouissance with the death drive overlooks inflections of jouissance that reach toward the inspired. It is true, of course, that the Lacanian notion of jouissance connotes a pleasure that is so acute as to border on the painful, and that it is consequently impossible to divorce it from the death drive. But to fully subsume it to this drive is to deny the possibility that jouissance can potentially rejuvenate—rather than merely obliterate—the subject. In this sense, Edelman faithfully repeats the sterile tenets of the kind of poststructuralist theory that insists on the emptiness of subjectivity, that sees no value in regeneration, and that cannot admit notions of psychic reparation into its steely vocabulary. In contrast, more relational critics strive to retheorize these concepts without thereby losing sight of the centrality of negativity in human life.

It seems to me that the humanist subject can die in a variety of different ways. Edelman's account of queer antisociality drains the subject of creativity, meaning, relationality, and agency, allowing it to be overtaken by the mindless pulsation of the death drive. But there are those of us who would like to reconfigure the posthumanist subject in less dejected terms, who, instead of dismissing notions like creativity, meaning, relationality, agency, and inner restoration, would like to figure out what these concepts might mean in the posthumanist context. This is not a matter of returning to a time before poststructuralism but rather of working toward a place beyond it; it is not a matter of discarding the critical tools that we have gained from poststructuralism but rather of putting these tools to less doctrinaire use; and it is not a matter of holding on to an outdated vision of the masterful and self-transparent subject but rather of building a better understanding of what it means to live in the world as an embodied creature who can never fully master or understand the parameters of its own being.

It is not insignificant that those of us advancing this softer version of posthumanist theory tend to possess a strong commitment to matters of social survival, justice, and responsibility. Among other things, this commitment explains why we are not averse to the possibility that hopefulness may at times be more radical than the cynicism of neo-Lacanian austerity. I would propose that it is in these more limber genres of posthumanist theory that the innovative (rather than merely defensive) spirit of poststructuralism lives on in a reinvigorated form. I would also argue—and this point should not be taken as a criticism of Edelman, whose stylistic acrobatics I count among the merits of *No Future*—that insofar as these new forms of posthumanist theory reject faithfulness to torpid forms of overworked rhetoric, they exemplify what is most revolutionary about queer theory, namely, its resistance to obsolete kinship structures of all kinds. For me at least, there is nothing as strange as queer theory that remains intractably devoted to the most sacrosanct pieties of poststructuralism.

Let us assume from the outset that the subject is alienated, fragmented, and non-self-identical, that its every attempt at self-mastery is undermined by unconscious currents of desire, and that its sociality is always to some extent disrupted by the antisocial energies of the real. Let us also assume that nonreproductive pleasure is valuable, that eros in its unshackled form is rebellious, and that we want to defeat heteronormative, patriarchal, and racist structures of social organization. What we are then left with is the dicey question of how the queer subject—or any subject for that matter—is to proceed with its life. After all, the fact that the subject is socially constituted rather than essential, that it only manages to attain a culturally intelligible identity at the price of lack, and that it is internally torn by antagonistic forces that pull it in contradictory directions does not mean that it is released from the task of fashioning a livable life for itself; if anything, it means that this task is all the more demanding, sometimes even perhaps calling for the type of negotiation with hegemonic power that Butler advocates.

The main fissure I see in contemporary queer theory resides between those who recognize the necessity of such existential negotiation—affect theorists such as Berlant being the most obvious example—and those who persist in the notion that any concession to the idea that there are lives to be lived in the "real" world leads to soft-hearted and naïve forms of theorizing. Even though I believe that Butler negotiates too willingly, I find Edelman's extreme version of queer antisociality even more problematic, which is why I have sought to offer an alternative reading of Lacanian negativity. I have sought to show that, far from foreclosing the future in the manner that Edelman proposes, Lacanian negativity holds open the future as a space of ever-renewed possibility. This insight in turn allows me to conceptualize the contours of (queer) subjectivity along less nihilistic lines. After all, barring some life-erasing catastrophe, there will always be a future in the future, even (hopefully for some time) for Professor Edelman. The question that remains—the only question worth asking—is what this future should (or could) entail.

Chapter Four

_____

BEYOND THE ANTISOCIAL-SOCIAL DIVIDE

The vocabulary for articulating any reader's reparative motive toward a text or a culture has long been so sappy, aestheticizing, defensive, anti-intellectual, or reactionary that it's no wonder few critics are willing to describe their acquaintance with such motives. The prohibitive problem, however, has been in the limitations of present theoretical vocabularies rather than in the reparative motive itself. No less acute than a paranoid position, no less realistic, no less attached to a project of survival, and neither less nor more delusional or fantasmatic, the reparative position undertakes a different range of affects, ambitions, and risks. What we can best learn from such practices are, perhaps, the many ways selves and communities succeed in extracting sustenance from the objects of a culture—even of a culture whose avowed desire has often been not to sustain them.

—EVE SEDGWICK, *TOUCHING FEELING*

Eve hopes for something other than drama that feels dramatic and threatening to the possibility of staying attached to life.

—LAUREN BERLANT, *SEX, OR THE UNBEARABLE*

1

I place Sedgwick's well-known statement about paranoid and reparative reading at the head of this chapter because it hovers in the background of the taut exchange between Berlant and Edelman in *Sex, or the Unbearable* (2014)—the text I will use to continue the reconsideration of queer negativity I began in the previous chapter. This reconsideration leads to larger questions about subjectivity, autonomy, and ethics that I will pursue, in the second half of this chapter, through Lynne Huffer's arguments in *Mad for Foucault* (2010) and *Are the Lips a Grave?* (2013). But first, let me restate the obvious, namely, that negativity has been an important trope for thinkers on both sides of the antisocial–social divide, that even those who seek to replace Edelmanian paranoia by Sedgwickian reparation have tended to align queerness with negativity.

One might say that the theoretical skirmishes between antisocial and social queer theorists have been less about negativity per se than about the level at which this negativity should be understood to operate: if antisocial theorists, such as Edelman, tend to emphasize—along Lacanian lines—the constitutive role of negativity in human life, those on the social side of the debate tend to focus on more circumstantial and context-specific forms of negativity, wounding, decentering, and suffering; those on the relational side challenge the idea that the subject's foundational lack-in-being is the only, or even the most important, form of alienation in human life, calling attention to the myriad ways in which the subject can be injured (even "negated") by structural inequalities such as racism, sexism, homophobia, and global economic injustices. This fundamental disagreement then generates further disagreements about the appropriate contours of politico-ethical intervention: if Edelman regards the disruptive force of the death drive—the most radical expression of constitutive negativity—as intrinsically counterhegemonic, more relational critics acknowledge the need for reparation in response to circumstantial forms of injury. That is, relational critics recognize what I argued at the end of the previous chapter, namely that the call for subjective destitution in the context of lives that are already destitute merely adds insult to injury, that those whose claim on subjectivity is precarious to begin with may not find the idea of plunging into the suicidal jouissance of the real a particularly appealing prospect.

This explains why critics such as Muñoz, Eng, and Love—and to some extent Berlant—emphasize the need for reparation. As we will discover toward the end of this chapter, Huffer straddles the divide between the antisocial and social, paranoid and reparative, attitudes. Her stance interests me not only because Sedgwick already noted that sometimes it is the most paranoid critics who are most capable of reparation but also because, as should be clear by now, I view the division between the antisocial and social factions as largely unnecessary in the sense that the recognition of the subject's constitutive lack-in-being should not, in principle, keep critics from acknowledging the importance of more circumstantial forms of wounding (and vice versa).

One could even posit that these two levels of lack—constitutive and circumstantial—are intimately related in the sense that it is often through circumstantial experiences of wounding that we are brought face to face with our constitutive wounding. If it is the case—as Edelman himself, following Lacan, suggests—that we spend much of our time building fantasy formations that allow us to avoid confronting our constitutive lack, then moments when something goes wrong in the concrete texture of our lifeworlds are ones when our carefully constructed fantasies collapse and we have no choice but to stare right into the abyss (in the Nietzschean sense); moments when a painful event scrambles the coordinates of everyday life force us to grapple with the fundamental uncertainties of human life. An excellent example of this dynamic is the failure of love: when we are abandoned by a loved person—a person who seemed to contain a tiny sliver of the lost Thing—we experience two levels of deprivation: we mourn not only the person we have lost but also the promise of wholeness and plenitude that this person represented; our circumstantial deprivation leads us to a direct confrontation with our constitutive deprivation (the lack of the Thing). This is precisely the lot of the melancholic who mourns not only the lost object but also the loss of the fantasy of overcoming alienation; in melancholia, the subject's circumstantial loss cuts into the wound of its constitutive alienation, causing this wound to bleed anew by deepening it.

From this perspective, queer theory's acrimonious fights over constitutive versus circumstantial forms of negativity—fights that have in recent years consumed huge amounts of energy—have been much ado about nothing. Moreover, it saddens me as a Lacanian that much of the blame for the rancor must be placed on Edelman's side: simply put, it is because Edelman keeps denying the importance of context-specific modalities of wounding that the debate remains at a deadlock. Yet what is so difficult about admitting that human beings can be wounded in a variety of ways? What could possibly be lost by such an admission? On the most basic theoretical, let alone political, level, I just don't "get" Edelman's resistance to this admission: I do not understand why the decade that separates the 2004 *No Future* from the 2014 *Sex, or the Unbearable* seems to have merely fortified his resistance to the—in my view, entirely uncontroversial—idea of multiple levels of deprivation.

In marked contrast, Huffer manages to revise her stance on the matter in the relatively short span of three years. In the 2010 *Mad for Foucault*, Huffer's antisociality is perhaps even more pronounced than that of Edelman—as we will see below, Huffer criticizes Edelman for not going far enough!—with the result that I find myself disagreeing with her on a number of key issues, including her uncompromising antifoundational-ism. But the tone of Huffer's 2013 *Are the Lips a Grave?* is entirely differ-ent in the sense that Huffer's antisociality is tempered (but not necessarily compromised) both by her attention to circumstantial forms of wounding, such as racism, and by her recognition that intersubjectivity—the always unpredictable, and sometimes injurious, impact of the other on the self—is one of the principal ways in which the subject's quest for secure ontological foundations is challenged. That is, the division between antisociality and sociality dissolves in *Are the Lips a Grave?* in ways that offer one possible route out of the impasse that has haunted queer theory for what to me seems like an absurdly long time.

It may be that I am intrigued by Huffer's attempt to bridge the antisocial-social divide because of my own predicament of being a Lacanian drawn to Sedgwickian reparation. I hope to have gone some way in illustrating why this theoretical intersection is not quite as bizarre as it may at first seem. As I have proposed, as much as Lacan criticizes the hegemonic aspects of the symbolic order, he also emphasizes—in ways that Edelman leaves out of the story entirely—that it is through the signifier (through symbolic structures of signification) that we access many of the more reparative frequencies of life, such as creativity, meaning, relationality, and psychic renewal. In the same way that Foucault sees power as both constraining and productive, Lacan views the symbolic as both oppressive and enabling, as a complex nexus of signification that both limits our options and—ideally at least—grants us the ability to transcend these limitations. In Sedgwickian terms, one might say that Lacan gives us excellent reasons for feeling paranoid about the symbolic at the same time as he points to the reparative resources made available to us by the signifier.

Moreover, as I turn to the next stage of my argument, I want to acknowl-edge that there is a great deal of clandestine Melanie Klein—one of the main sources of Sedgwick's reparative thinking—in Lacan's work, starting with the key concept of the Thing. Julia Kristeva (2000) goes as far as to accuse Lacan of having plagiarized Klein. The details of this accusation, like the details of Kleinian theory, are beyond the scope of this book, but it may help to bear in mind—as we enter the exchange between Edelman and Berlant—that, in Kleinian terms, the impulse to repair, in its infantile form, arises from the child's depressive assumption that its paranoid fantasies of being persecuted by the external world have caused it to harm the (m)other: reparation is aimed at mending a relationship that has been damaged by the child's (fantasized) aggression.

In adult life, a similar anxiety about one's capacity for violence can generate a wish to neutralize the impact of this violence by repairing one's bonds to the surrounding world. The attitude of the Kleinian subject vis-à-vis the world is therefore deeply ambivalent: the tendency toward paranoia (which causes violence) and the tendency toward reparation (which seeks to undo the effects of violence) commingle in the subject's psychic life. As a consequence, the paranoid and reparative attitudes, for Klein, are not stable character traits but rather psychic "positions" that the subject (more or less) fluidly circles in and out of.

From Sedgwick's perspective, the main problem with paranoid queer theory—and recall that in making her argument she draws on the early work of Butler, D. A. Miller, and herself—is that, unlike the Kleinian subject, this theory is not able to move, even temporarily, to the reparative position. Sedgwick admits that there are good reasons for this resistance to the reparative position, among other things stressing—as her statement earlier attests—that this position remains unpalatable to many progressive critics because it has historically been aligned with the impoverished theoretical vocabularies of conservative, anticritical traditions; affirmative reading practices have taken an unnecessarily saccharine tone, thereby converging with mainstream platitudes about the good life, such as the phony celebration of positivity, cheerfulness, and self-actualization that I criticized in chapter 1. Sedgwick correctly points out that this is not the only way to understand reparative interpretive practices, which can be just as complex, as capable of critical acumen, as paranoid ones.

It is also worth noting that, at the end of the passage I have quoted, Sedgwick expresses the gist of what Berlant develops through her notion of cruel optimism (see chapter 1), namely, that people (and communities) are often driven to "extract" sustenance from attachments to modes of life, ideals, and objects that have historically denied them this very sustenance. This detail is important because it expresses the basic insight of relational queer theorists that I flagged earlier, namely, that negativity is variable and unevenly distributed, which is precisely why it cannot be valorized in the unqualified manner that Edelman does. Berlant recognizes this, which is why she is pulled to the relational side even as she retains a strong allegiance to the antirelational stance. The core disagreement between Edelman and Berlant, in short, is that if Edelman views negativity's power to destroy the subject's aspirations toward sovereignty as an intrinsically ethical force, Berlant is concerned with the subject's capacity to survive forms of negativity—or negation—that are forced upon it by wounding personal, cultural, and socioeconomic conditions.

2

In *Sex, or the Unbearable*, both Edelman and Berlant position themselves against "projects of queer optimism that try to repair the subject's negativity into a grounding experiential positivity" (2014, 5); both critics, in short, endorse notions of queer negativity, subjective undoing, and nonsovereignty. But while Edelman clings to the hardnosed line of death-driven queer destructiveness that he developed in *No Future*, Berlant is interested in the subject's ability to navigate—and persist through—scenes of negativity, undoing, and nonsovereignty. Within the terms that I have established, while Edelman adheres to a strictly Lacanian notion of constitutive alienation (or lack-in-being), Berlant is interested in the material and affective effects of more concrete forms of alienation; though Berlant certainly recognizes the importance of constitutive alienation, she is more invested in mapping out the messy, multiple, and often compounded ways in which specific subjects are negated by specific circumstances.

As was already the case with her analysis of cruel optimism, Berlant sheds light on the ambivalent attachments that subjects form to modalities of life that seem necessary for survival—that appear to provide the conditions of life's possibility—even as they bring injury. Conversely, Berlant recognizes that optimism—and perhaps even utopian hopefulness—may be a precondition of the subject's capacity to sever its bonds to wounding existential scenarios; that is, even though Berlant, like Butler, emphasizes that people are often not able to extricate themselves from damaging attachments, she simultaneously stresses that if they are to have any chance of doing so, they need to retain a degree of hopefulness about the possibility of an alternative future. In this sense, though Berlant shares some of the Butlerian willingness to negotiate with power that I have criticized, her relationship to power seems less deterministic than that of Butler: Berlant's subjects may be as tightly caught up in the meshes of power as Butler's subjects are, but they are not as helpless against it, let alone invested in their own subjection.

In the present context, what is important is the manner in which Berlant draws the distinction between herself and Edelman:

While [Edelman] focuses on "story" as *always* enacting negativity's drama and expectation and refusal, I am more concerned with that muddled middle where survival and threats to it engender social forms that transform the habitation of negativity's multiplicity, without necessarily achieving "story" in his terms. For, you know, I am a utopian, and Lee is not. I do not see optimism primarily as a glossing over, as "fantasy" in the negative sense of resistance to the Real. I am interested in optimism as a mode of attachment to life. I am committed to the political project of imagining how to detach from lives that don't work and from worlds that negate the subjects that produce them; and I aim, along with many antinormative activists, to expand the field of affective potentialities, latent and explicit fantasies, and infrastructures for how to live beyond survival, toward flourishing not later but in the ongoing now.

(Berlant and Edelman 2014, 5)

Berlant's allusion to "story" here refers to Edelman's conviction that any future-oriented story of life—any attempt to fasten a life to a hopefulness about a better future—represents an imaginary fantasy that seeks to foreclose the self-shattering negativity of the real. As I have explained, Edelman views the ideal of a better future as a fantasy formation aimed at denying the trauma of constitutive alienation, with the result that the subject who banks on the future is, in Edelman's assessment, deluded in ways that keep it from living in the present. In addition, for Edelman, any attempt to find a feasible foothold in the world represents an illegitimate quest for mastery: "Such transformative self-perception achieved amid affective discontinuity implicitly presumes a mastery of, and a capacity to include in our calculations, our unknowable primary attachments. In this it risks a regression from engaging the nonsovereignty of the subject" (Berlant and Edelman 2014, 65).

What Berlant reads as an effort to survive, Edelman—true to his allergy to subjective viability and comfort—reads as a defensive pursuit of mastery. This is why his disagreements with Butler do not keep him from agreeing with her on the matter of "the subject": like Butler, Edelman judges every attempt at recentering the self to be intrinsically unethical. If there is no place for even a momentary stabilization of subjectivity in Edelman's vision, it is because he equates all efforts to find a respite, however temporary, from the experience of nonsovereignty with a conservative—and therefore unethical—adherence to fantasies of coherent subjectivity. This is why Edelman claims, in response to Berlant's point about the ambivalent manner in which many subjects are struggling to detach from lives that "don't work," that his notion of negativity "speaks to the fact that life, in some sense, *doesn't* 'work,' is structurally inimical to happiness, stability, or regulated functioning" (Berlant and Edelman 2014, 11).

In this statement, there is a willful blindness to Berlant's basic point, namely, that there is a difference between life "not working" in the ontological-existential (constitutive) sense and life "not working" in the circumstantial (context-specific) sense. *Of course* life is never going to "work," existentially speaking; of course none of us will ever be perfectly happy, stable, or fully functioning. This is an ontological given. But surely this predicament is quite different from the realities of lives that "don't work" because there are systemic roadblocks—such as racism—to their flourishing. It seems entirely obvious that we need to be able to think these two levels of life "not working" simultaneously, which is why I remain perturbed by Edelman's inflexibility on the issue. Berlant is hardly trying to replace Lacanian lack by the neoliberal dream of autonomy, so why the fuss? Unfortunately, it is Edelman's refusal to give an inch on the matter that leads to his rather chilling conclusion that anyone interested in survival—in repairing and rebuilding lives that have been torn apart—by definition violates ethics as an expression of nonsovereignty.

Edelman is unwilling to concede what Berlant readily recognizes, which is that many subjects experience nonsovereignty as an ordinary, even banal component of everyday life rather than as an exceptional state brought about by radical acts of subjective destitution. As Berlant remarks:

I think that subjects are not usually shocked to discover their incoherence or the incoherence of the world; they often find it comic, feel a little ashamed of it, or are interested in it, excited by it, and exhausted by it too, by the constant pressure to adjust that is at the heart of being nonsovereign, subjected to the inconstancy and contingency that they discover in and around themselves.

(Berlant and Edelman 2014, 6)

Berlant stresses that because nonsovereignty—incoherence—is a commonplace part of the lives of many subjects, these subjects are unlikely to be shocked by it; they may experience a variety of mundane feelings—amusement, shame, interest, excitement, or exhaustion—in response to it but they may not find it all that remarkable. In contrast, Edelman insists on the extraordinary status of nonsovereignty, writing: "So for me, the structuring incoherencies that queer the self as the center of consciousness, and so of a pseudo-sovereignty, remain unavailable to the subject except in rare moments of traumatic encounter, moments when the potential for shock gets activated by the nearness of the unbearable, which is to say, of our own enjoyment: the enjoyment 'we' never own" (Berlant and Edelman 2014, 9).

Edelman here admits what he did not in *No Future*, namely, that no subject, however queer, can have continuous access to jouissance—that it is, instead, a momentary state of (non)being. However, what I want to focus on is his assertion that the decentering jouissance of the real, the kind of jouissance that erupts in orgasmic spasms of "enjoyment," represents a "traumatic encounter," a "shock" that renders life "unbearable." Unbearable? Seriously?

My skepticism regarding this argument may be due to my Scandinavian matter-of-factness about sex, for I have never found my "enjoyment" (jouissance) particularly unbearable. What exactly is it about sex that is supposedly so deeply traumatizing? I am not here referring to the injurious stigmas attached to queer sexuality by the heteronormative social order but to the idea—promoted not just by Edelman but also by critics such as Bersani and Halperin—that there is something about the sheer experience of sex that is *intrinsically* traumatizing. It seems to me that (consensual) sex does not necessarily do much damage to our sense of self. It may decenter us momentarily but it does not inevitably leave any lasting imprint of trauma: often we simply just tidy up our hair, give our clothes a good shake, and get going with the rest of our (more or less coherent) lives.

As I mentioned in the context of discussing online pornography as a break from the workday in chapter 2, far from dissolving the subject in some definitive manner, sex can facilitate its symbolic endeavors (its ability to keep up with our society's performance principle). I proposed that it is, rather, desire—particularly the disillusionments of desire generated by the failures of love—that tends to devastate the subject. The same could be said about a number of physical and affective experiences that cause pain, whether this pain is temporary or prolonged: from bodily injury to emotional suffering, people undergo traumatizing experiences that reconfigure the basic parameters of their lives. From this viewpoint, if you want to talk about experiences that are genuinely "decentering" (or "unbearable"), the places to look are oppressive social circumstances. In contrast, jouissance as a release of sexual tension is merely a fleeting—though repeatable—swerve in the coherence of being. Consequently, when white gay men sing the praises of the nonsovereignty (or "abjection") arising from sex, I cannot help but think that if the disorienting effects of (consensual) sex are the only form of nonsovereignty you ever experience, then you really do not have much to grumble about.

Sex may be "inconvenient," to use Berlant's expression. It may be embarrassing, tiresome, annoying, or wonderful. Furthermore, as I myself proposed at the end of the previous chapter, eros can be profoundly transformative (see also Ruti 2011b, 2013). Toward the end of this chapter we will see that Huffer, following Foucault, agrees. But it seems to me that it is an exaggeration to argue, as Edelman does, that sex, in its consensual form, causes nonsovereignty in some enduring (ontological) sense. Frankly, what I hear behind white gay male tributes to jouissance are all-too-familiar Anglo-American anxieties about sexual surrender (which Anglo-American culture, including queer culture, routinely confuses with masochistic submission and problematically codes as "feminine").

Edelman posits that "the closer we come to enjoyment, the greater our need to defend against it—to defend our putative sovereignty against the negativity that empties it out" (Berlant and Edelman 2014, 8); on this view, sexual experience is "unbearable" because it is filled with intensities we can never fully manage, intensities that "signal our too-near approach to what we are driven to enjoy" (8). I understand Edelman's Lacanian point regarding the impulse to protect our social viability against the turbulence of excessive jouissance. But from my skeptical perspective, this also sounds like puritanical defensiveness about getting too close to enjoyment, about losing control, and about—gasp!—being feminized.

Along closely related lines, it also sounds like the kind of "crisis" that is likely to strike a hypercoherent, hypermasculinist (which is not necessarily the same thing as "male") subject more forcefully than other kinds of subjects for the simple reason that this subject finds the prospect of losing its self-mastery terrifying. As Lacan (1972–1973) observes, masculinist subjects can be burdened by their phallic identities, can find it difficult, even impossible, to access jouissance because they are protecting their symbolic cohesiveness too tightly. As a result, I am not sure that all subjects experience their jouissance as quite as "unbearable" as Edelman would like us to believe; subjects who are used to living in a state of nonmastery—subjects for whom nonsovereignty is a normal part of the muddy river of life—may not regard their temporary disintegration in sexual jouissance as particularly challenging (or even very interesting).

3

Although Berlant has more respect for the "unbearability" of sex than I do, her overall theoretical impulse is the same as mine, namely to steer clear of the hysterics that frequently characterizes posthumanist theorizing about the general human condition, including the fact that we (most of us) are sexual creatures. As she remarks, "I tend to dedramatize the experience of being a sexual subject in the ordinary, while Lee sees the subject's reeling experience of his subjective negativity as a drama that becomes dramatized" (Berlant and Edelman 2014, 6). This statement echoes the one Berlant makes about Sedgwick that I placed at the beginning of this chapter: "Eve hopes for something other than drama that feels dramatic and threatening to the possibility of staying attached to life" (46).

This notion of dedramatization—the possibility of "something other than drama that feels dramatic"—resonates with me because I have long been irritated by progressive theory's tendency to dramatize, and endlessly whine about, entirely unavoidable components of subjectivity, such as our constitutive opacity, alienation, incoherence, and nonsovereignty. This is one reason I have sought to highlight the rewards of our foundational lack-in-being, for it seems to me that the complaints about this lack that fill the pages of poststructuralist tomes are often hugely overstated, giving the impression that to be a subject—not the (bad) sovereign subject of humanist metaphysics but the (good) nonsovereign subject of posthumanist theory—is always and automatically the same thing as being deeply wronged, victimized, dispossessed, persecuted, and so on.

There are probably times in the lives of all of us when we feel wronged. And—as I have argued all along—there are plenty of individuals who are forced to habitually feel wronged due to structural inequalities. But the idea that we are somehow intrinsically wronged by our constitutive vulnerabilities, like the idea that jouissance is intrinsically shattering, turns entirely ordinary components of human experience into scenes of extraordinary suffering, thereby distracting attention from the kind of context-specific suffering that actually *is* unbearable. This is why I think that contemporary theory's rhetoric about the traumatizing effects of our constitutive lack-in-being needs a serious dose of dedramatization.

Edelman is self-reflexive enough to recognize that his tendency to dramatize the constitutive insecurities of human life at the expense of more context-specific varieties of insecurity renders him contemporary theory's "Darth Vader, a form of the father we love to hate: withholding, histrionic, life-negating, and full of inhuman enjoyment" (Berlant and Edelman 2014, 58). More specifically, he acknowledges that, in the context of Sedgwick's distinction between paranoid and reparative reading, he embodies "the negativity Eve distrusts in paranoia: the negativity she associates with the demystifications practiced by the Yale school, whose 'masculine' regime of epistemological power she opposes to 'vitality and value'" (57). Yet Edelman does little to dispel this self-imposed caricature, so that the Yale school's "'masculine' regime of epistemological power" seems to function, for him, as a source of deep pride rather than as a fantasy to be interrogated (one has to wonder why this is the point at which the deconstructive–Lacanian impulse to dispel the conservative force of fantasies peters out).

Most notably, Edelman does nothing to repair "the micro-abrasions that tear the relational filament" (Berlant and Edelman 2014, 69) between himself and Berlant during their exchange. For him, their dialogue gains strength from these microabrasions "much as a muscle develops through the repetition of stress" (69). Again, one can only wonder how this sudden fetishization of robust musculature fits into a theory that sees radical nonsovereignty as a politico-ethical virtue; for all his talk about destroying the masterful self, few critics in contemporary theory display a greater tendency toward mastery than Edelman.

In (aggravatingly gendered) contrast, Berlant, true to her allegiance to Sedgwickian reparation, does her best to repair the damage. Though she, toward the end of their dialogue, comes close to accusing Edelman of "bullying pedagogy" (Berlant and Edelman 2014, 124), she simultaneously takes the sting off this accusation by resorting to a placating image of camaraderie, collaboration, and laughter. For instance, she states, "What does surprise us . . . is how close we come to each other in certain crucial formulations" (119).

At this point in the text one could start to get annoyed at Berlant's attempts to accommodate Edelman in the absence of any reciprocation on his part; one could get annoyed at her willingness to let Edelman mow over her more nuanced understanding of negativity with his obstinate repetition of the idea that any impulse toward reparation betrays the negative force of the Lacanian real. At the very least, she could mock (even just a little) his assertion that, in the dialogue between them, he is committed to "thinking in the absence of predetermined outcomes" (Berlant and Edelman 2014, 4). I would say that—for those of us used to reading poststructuralist–Lacanian theory—there is absolutely nothing unpredictable, nothing surprising about Edelman's thinking. We know ahead of time how things are going to go: subjective coherence and viability bad, incoherence and negativity good.

Like much of antisocial queer theory, Edelman's discourse is characterized by a mechanical celebration of incoherence—nonsovereignty, dissolution, fragmentation, instability, and so on—that forecloses all other registers of being, that valorizes life's most exhausting frequencies. The thing is, some of us, even some of the Lacanians among us, are tired of dwelling in these frequencies. And we are tired of the ruthless attempt to deny the reality of context-specific forms of traumatization in the name of the gaping wound of Lacanian lack-in-being. Indeed, in refusing to think beyond this lack-in-being, Edelman plays right into Muñoz's accusation about the antisocial thesis being "the white gay man's last stance." His poststructuralist–Lacanian hardline overlooks the existence of precarious subjects, which means that his deconstructive gesture of undoing the subject is indiscriminately aimed at the kinds of subjects—subjects who are already fraying around the edges—who should not logically be its target.

4

The same celebration of incoherence can be found in Huffer's *Mad for Foucault*, which, with some help from Deleuze, outlines Foucault's theory of desubjectivation so as, among other things, to accuse (the rest of) queer theory of a secret allegiance to the very subject that it seems to demolish. In the course of proving her point, Huffer—somewhat astonishingly—accuses the Edelman of *No Future* of falling asleep at the poststructuralist wheel, suggesting that the subject needs to be even more traumatized, even more thoroughly decentered, defeated, and destroyed, than the Edelmanian subject. More specifically, Huffer proposes that what the concept of the sinthomosexual "takes away with one hand it gives back with the other, as it continues to assume the existence of a psyche as container of the subject's death" (2010, 115). Drawing on Nietzsche's argument that the psyche represents the outcome of a violent process of internalizing hegemonic morality, Huffer posits that, for all of Edelman's talk about self-shattering, "the death drive of the queer antisocial thesis epitomizes the self-hating violence of the moral 'I'" (116), of what Nietzsche in *On the Genealogy of Morals* (1989) describes as "wild, free, prowling man turned backward against man himself" (85). "In dialectical terms, negation alone does not undo the 'I,'" Huffer reminds us, for "every assassination of morality is still a morality" (116).

As a Nietzschean observation, Huffer's insight is accurate. But I do not think that it entirely holds as a criticism of Edelman. On the one hand, I agree with Huffer that Edelman's antinormativity remains a "moral" stance. As I have argued, Edelman's antinormativity does not reach beyond good and evil in Nietzsche's sense but merely renames as good what normative society deems bad (and vice versa). Essentially, Edelman pits the sinthomosexual against the child in much the same way that Christianity pits God against Satan or *Superman* comics pit Clark Kent against Lex Luthor. To paraphrase today's teenagers, the sinthomosexual is so bad that he is totally awesome. On the other hand, Huffer is mistaken in insisting that the sinthomosexual fails to sever its attachment to the psyche, for it is impossible from a Lacanian perspective—which is Edelman's perspective— to equate the sinthome with the psyche (as Huffer seems to do).

Let me explain the matter in terms that might make sense to Huffer because of her appreciation for Deleuze. I have demonstrated that the sinthome expresses something about the fixations of the subject's jouissance, about its singular way of enjoying itself as an embodied entity, which is why Lacan aligns it with the drive. The Lacanian drive, in turn, is more or less identical to what Deleuze, with Guattari, theorizes as the rhizomatic desiring-machines that undo every Oedipal attachment, that overflow all subjective coordinates, and that cannot therefore possibly be contained within the individual psyche. As Deleuze and Guattari admit, the "drives are simply the desiring-machines themselves," adding that Lacan "was the first . . . to schizophrenize the analytic field" (1972, 35; 363).

Despite their hostility to psychoanalysis, Deleuze and Guattari concede that what was astute about Lacan in comparison to other analysts of his era was that he was "not content to turn, like the analytic squirrel, inside the wheel of the Imaginary and the Symbolic," that he refused the reterritorialization of subjectivity accomplished by Oedipalization by focusing on the deterritorializing force of the drives (1972, 308). Consequently, when Edelman, drawing on Lacan, aligns the sinthome with the homosexual (in order to arrive at the notion of the sinthomosexual), he is conceptualizing the kind of Deleuzian–Guattarian massacre of subjectivity that cannot but obliterate the psyche. This is why—and I will return to this point later—Huffer's efforts to dissociate her argument from that of Edelman are mostly unsuccessful: her Foucauldian–Deleuzian theory of desubjectivation is simply not that different from Edelman's Lacanian theory of self-shattering jouissance.

More generally speaking, I would say that even though the various post-'68 French (male) thinkers all had their distinctive vocabularies, they were for the most part preoccupied by the same ideas: the death of the humanist subject, the transvaluation of all values, the transgression of normative morality, the questioning of the limits of thought, the deconstruction of the reign of reason, and so forth. Lacan, Blanchot, Derrida, Foucault, Deleuze, Guattari: they were all after the same thing (more or less). They all wanted to question the ways in which subjectivity had, in the Enlightenment model, become tangled up in fantasies of autonomy, transparency, and self-mastery. They used different terms to describe the downfall of the humanist subject—jouissance, transgression, contestation, *différance*, desubjectivation, desiring-machines. But their overall goal was always the same: the destabilization of the subject of reason. This is why I believe that whether one follows Lacan or Foucault, one is likely to arrive at a very similar place.

Huffer, however, is less interested in such convergences of thought than in illustrating the superiority of Foucauldian–Deleuzian desubjectivation over queer theory's tendency to cling to the subject. What is perhaps most interesting about her attack is that it encompasses both the antisocial approach represented by Edelman and the performative approach represented by Butler. Regarding the former, Huffer argues that, despite its claims to the contrary, it "cannot let go of the 'psyche' or 'soul' which constitutes the rationalist modern subject," with the result that "the moral violence of the swamp remains" (2010, 116). Regarding the latter, Huffer asserts that

Butler merely "undoes gender but not the subject itself" (112). More specifically, Huffer maintains that inasmuch as Butler relies on a Hegelian logic of negation, reversal, and sublation, she fails to do away with the subject, merely enacting the kind of "negation of negation" by which a new positivity is installed; the Butlerian subject, Huffer stresses, may not be a normative subject but it is nevertheless a subject. As she sums up the matter, "With performativity, the subject is not undone but rebelliously remade: she is a joker, a trickster, a sassy artist who operates in the camp mode of ironic subversion" (119–120).

To complicate matters, Huffer appears to think that there is such a thing as "antisocial performativity" (2010, 115). Given Edelman's vehement critique of Butler's all-too-social, all-too-liberal, and all-too-American brand of theorizing, I am not sure what this might consist of, unless one reads the fall into the jouissance of the real as a "performance." But the relevant point here is that Huffer believes that queer theory—whether antisocial (Edelmanian) or performative (Butlerian)—"dialectically unravels the subject's interiority as 'sex,' but leaves intact the internalizing violence that produces the moral soul" (116). In other words, queer theory (generally speaking) may strive to negate morality but this morality sneaks back in because the subject that queer theory keeps reconceptualizing has still been constituted through the internalization of morality.

To this stealthy and illicit perseverance of morality, Huffer, following Foucault and Deleuze, juxtaposes a process of desubjectivation: a draining away of the psyche, the soul, identity as such. That is, Huffer's antidote to queer theory's (alleged) cathexis to the subject is a Foucauldian–Deleuzian pulverization of the subject so that what is left is not a psyche, let alone a soul, but an event of sorts: a fleeting saturation of energies, perhaps a style, perhaps a rhythm. According to Huffer, desubjectivation moves "the subject away from himself (or his dialectical negation) toward the place of anonymity that is the promise of the subject's undoing" (2010, 117). In more visceral terms, it—as Huffer puts it—enacts "the terrifying disintegration of the face in madness: Nietzsche's lifeless eyes, his corpselike body" (118).

This formulation gives me pause. First of all, I am not sure that queer theory's attempts to do away with the subject have been as unsuccessful as Huffer suggests, for I do not think that critics in the field—and certainly not Edelman—retain any allegiance to "the rationalist modern subject." But even more fundamentally, Huffer's argument, for me, raises some basic theoretico-political questions, the foremost of which is *why we want this degree of subjective disintegration to begin with*. Why do we want Nietzsche's lifeless eyes, his corpselike body? Did even Nietzsche want these? Personally, I would prefer Nietzsche's overactive mind (his psyche, his soul); I would prefer Nietzsche before his tragic descent into madness, the Nietzsche who sought to reinvent himself, to become the poet of his own existence.

My point is that we—posthumanist critics, including queer critics—are so used to reading the types of pronouncements that Huffer makes about the need to destroy the subject that it is easy for us to glide over them without much resistance, with a distracted "yes, yes, of course we want the subject dead." Yet stopping for just a moment reveals that things are perhaps not quite so straightforward: Why do we want a subject without a psyche? I understand the Nietzschean idea that the psyche cannot be dissociated from the hegemonic morality that is in part responsible for bringing it into being. Still, would not a subject without a psychic life—without any sense of subjective continuity—be a fairly lackluster one? Is the Christian notion of the soul the only way to conceptualize inner lives that feel meaningful, that feel affectively resonant?

These are questions that I have been asking since *Reinventing the Soul* (2006), for I believe that there are ways to think about the psyche, and even the soul, that do not fall into either the Cartesian paradigm of reason or the Christian paradigm of salvation. Psychoanalysis is full of such ways, despite what Edelman's version of it might suggest. So is affect theory, which, among other things, focuses on how currents of both tangible and intangible energy surrounding the psyche impact its functioning. This may be why I have trouble seeing the (theoretical or political) rewards of eliminating the subject altogether.

I once had a graduate student who wanted to reduce the subject to its digestive track. Her response to my query about *why* she wished to accomplish this extraordinary feat was to give me the usual litany of the crimes of the Enlightenment subject: too autonomous, too transparent, too masterful, too unitary, too agentic, too arrogant, too moralistic, and so on. By now I find this litany quite tiresome. In addition, the efforts to slay this monstrous subject have become so preposterous that I can no longer take them seriously (even as a rhetorical game). As I have repeatedly acknowledged, I appreciate the impulse to loosen the parameters of how subjectivity was conceptualized in Enlightenment philosophy. But sometimes it seems to me that progressive theory gives the Enlightenment subject far too much power in the sense that it does not seem to be able to stop framing its arguments as critiques of this subject, with the result that it routinely ends up overstating its case.

5

The autonomous, transparent, and masterful (and so on) Enlightenment subject was a philosophical abstraction—a fantasy of humanist philosophy—that French posthumanist theory, for excellent reasons, sought to take down in the second half of the twentieth century. I have never had a problem with this per se: the takedown was long overdue. However, as I stated at the beginning of this book, my sense is that over the decades the slaughter of the humanist subject has become largely ritualistic, undertaken with an automatism that, among other things, loses track of the fact that the lives of most human beings have never come anywhere close to approximating the abstraction under attack. I am not certain that even Descartes experienced himself as fully autonomous, transparent, and masterful; if he had experienced himself as such, he might have never written his *Meditations*.

To be sure, I understand the impulse to take down the Donald Trumps of the world. And I understand that neoliberal capitalism is doing its best to convince us of our agentic status so as to be able to instill in us a sense of individual responsibility, including the idea that if we fail to succeed according to the terms set by the dominant happiness scripts of our society, it is because we have not tried hard enough (or because we have not sustained a positive enough attitude). Still, where are the people who have managed to live up to the ideals of neoliberal capitalism? Where are the arrogant selves of Enlightenment philosophy? If they are nowhere to be found, or if they can only be found with considerable effort, then what is the point of raising the destruction of "the subject" to the epitome of politico-ethical virtue?

In this context, it is worth recalling Sharon Holland's critique of "subjectless" queer theory in *The Erotic Life of Racism* (2012). If the Huffer of *Mad for Foucault* believes that queer theory has not taken the destruction of the subject far enough, Holland argues that, to the extent that queer theory has conjured away the subject, it has lost the capacity to interrogate the specificity of subjective experience, such as the material, psychic, and affective effects of sexism and racism on particular subjects. Holland further claims that insofar as queer theory has equated attempts to investigate such effects with a hopelessly parochial identity politics—envisioned as the slightly embarrassing country cousin of an urbane and stylish queer theory—it has effectively destroyed second-wave feminism, including the black feminism of Audre Lorde's generation.

My commentary on Edelman's anti-identitarianism certainly points in this direction. Holland, however, throws a wider net for her critique, implicating even explicitly profeminist and antiracist critics such as Butler and Muñoz. Regarding the latter's wish, articulated in *Disidentifications*, to "supersede the limits of feminism" (1999, 22), to replace second-wave feminism by a more capacious (less identity-based) postmodern feminism, Holland writes: "By this time in the theoretical game, feminism has solidified as a project that should be superseded, which gives it the status of a relic and simultaneously excises the very contributions of women of color to the production of a very diverse feminist discourse that queer of color critique is poised to commit itself to" (2012, 78). In other words, even as queer of color critique seeks to forge an alliance with a "diverse feminist discourse," it eliminates the contributions of feminists of color, such as Lorde, who are considered to be too "essentialist," too devoted to the epistemological value of "experience." In this manner, Muñoz's well-meaning gesture of transcending the historical failures of second-wave feminism, paradoxically, participates in the vilification of the very strand of feminism that queer of color critique is arguably most indebted to.

Holland claims that the relationship of Butler to Simone de Beauvoir is similar: "Butler's early work on feminist philosophy was engaged in a concerted dismantling of Beauvoir's essentialist existentialism" (2012, 51). Ironically, I got a perfect illustration of the problematic of erasure that Holland is referring to when I taught her book in my feminist and queer theory graduate seminar. One frustrated student objected to Holland's repeated allusions to Beauvoir, asking "Why is she not talking about Foucault?" I could not help but laugh out loud, responding: "Well, perhaps she is trying to counter the fact that queer theory has mowed over key feminist thinkers, such as Beauvoir, by implying that they have nothing cool to say."

My more global point is that the "brain drain" from feminism to queer theory that Janet Halley, in *Split Decisions* (2006), reads as an indicator of feminism's hopelessly pedestrian and reductive nature did not happen spontaneously but was, in part at least, brought about by strands of queer theory that, sometimes (though not always) quite deliberately, chose to portray feminism as pedestrian and reductive. This dynamic is what leads Holland to remark that "in recent years, it has become almost impossible to speak for or about women within emerging feminist/queer theorizing because of the call to a *subjectless* feminism" (2012, 50).

Heather Love seems to be raising a related concern when she maintains that the fact that queer critics "have generally understood the concept of identity to be both politically and philosophically bankrupt . . . has short-circuited important work on the history of identity" (2007, 44). Love goes on to concede that identity is "a deeply problematic and contradictory concept" (44). Nevertheless, she believes that it remains a powerful organizing principle of life, linking us to personal histories within which we, however incompletely, recognize ourselves. I agree, which is why I find attempts to obliterate the psyche, such as Huffer's, so bizarre. Even if it is true that the psyche can never be dissociated from its normative—including moralistic—constitution, surely it cannot be reduced to this constitution, surely it also retains the capacity to critically assess the very forces that have brought it into being. If it could not, there would be no such thing as self-reflexivity or social change.

On the one hand—as I emphasized earlier—posthumanist theory tends to equate subjectivity with victimization, incessantly complaining about the hardships of constitutive alienation. On the other, poststructuralist critics such as Edelman and Huffer keep wanting to hack the subject to pieces. At some point, one has to start wondering about the contradiction at hand: What is the purpose of the hacking if we are simultaneously convinced that to be a subject is to be inherently lacking and out-of-joint (even victimized)? This contradiction is usually resolved through a by now familiar strategy: it is only the *bad* Enlightenment (or neoliberal) subject that is sovereign—and therefore in need of being annihilated—whereas the *good* posthumanist subject is nonsovereign, incoherent, decentered, fragmented, precarious, dispossessed, persecuted, and so on.

As I argued in the context of my critique of Butler in chapter 2, such dichotomizing gives the impression that the posthumanist subject has been fashioned out of everything that was left out of the humanist subject, with the result that it becomes impossible to theorize the ways in which sovereignty and nonsovereignty—autonomy and various types of vulnerability—might commingle in the lived experience of many, if not most, subjects. Moreover, it all too easily generates the tendency to see the utter mortification of the subject as a politico-ethical *ideal*, so that the only "proper" way to be a subject is to model oneself on the severely traumatized subject.

The Huffer of *Mad for Foucault* falls prey to this tendency just as much as Edelman does, which is why her text, for me, raises the same reservations about the desirability of desubjectivation as I feel about Edelmanian self-shattering. I guess I do not wish to become a Deleuzian–Guattarian schizophrenic in the throes of desiring-machines any more than I want to become an Edelmanian sinthomosexual in the throes of continuous jouissance. Indeed, trying to imagine an orgasm—jouissance—that lasts a lifetime is enough to render the dream of desubjectivation genuinely alarming.

I suppose I find Huffer's disagreements with Edelman less interesting than the relentlessness with which both critics cling to the ideal of nonsovereignty. As may be obvious by now, my hesitation regarding this ideal arises in part from my suspicion that it is purely rhetorical in the sense of being utterly unlivable. As Huffer herself admits in *Are the Lips a Grave?*, some of queer theory's most cherished dogmas—such as the notion of queer "undecidability"—"are *not* borne out in the lives of people who, whether they identify as queer or not, are continuously interpellated as subjects" (2013, 66). In other words, regardless of how rebellious an attitude we adopt to the world, being a "subject" of *some* kind is a nonnegotiable precondition of living, unless we are willing to descend into psychosis (which even Deleuze and Guattari did not seem to want to do). This is why my level-headed response to queer theory's idealization of nonsovereignty is: If you can't put your theory into practice, if you aren't willing to destroy the very foundations of your existence, then why is the death of the subject such a goal for you? Essentially, my question is: If you're not gonna do it, why are you even talking about it?

Though I in many ways agree with Wendy Brown's assertion, in *Edgework* (2005), that theory should not necessarily be expected to reflect the concerns of real life because its main task is to envision alternatives to this life, there are limits to my willingness to go along with this perspective. Brown states:

As a meaning-making enterprise, theory depicts a world that does not quite exist, that is not quite the world we inhabit. But this is theory's incomparable value, not its failure. Theory does not simply decipher the meanings of the world but recodes and rearranges them in order to reveal something about the meanings and incoherencies that we live with. To do this revelatory and speculative work, theory must work to one side of direct referents.

(80)

Fair enough. But I am not sure I would go as far as to argue, as Brown does, that "theory is never 'accurate' or 'wrong'" (80). When evolutionary psychological theory—which I discuss in detail in another book (see Ruti 2015a)—claims that every aspect of human sexual behavior can be traced back to the drive to produce children, it is simply just wrong (even stupid).

6

Although I concur that the task of theory is to reinvent the world rather than to merely describe its existing—impoverished—forms, there is, for me, a difference between theorizing that provides alternatives to lives as they are currently lived and theorizing that sounds like futile talk about visions that are entirely untenable as real-life options. Extreme accounts of the politico-ethical benefits of nonsovereignty veer toward the latter. Bear in mind, for instance, that a subject without a psyche, a fully desubjectivized nonsubject, would be a creature without memory, a wholly ahistorical creature (and in this sense, ironically, antithetical to Foucault's historically grounded method). On the one hand, Nietzsche is surely right that a subject who is too full of memories is weighed down by these memories, perhaps even paralyzed by them, and consequently unable to embrace new forms of life; according to Nietzsche, such a subject is like a dyspeptic who "cannot 'have done' with anything" (1989, 58). On the other, the opposite extreme— a subject wholly devoid of memory—hardly seems more desirable.

Memories add weightiness to our being, among other things allowing us to learn from past experiences. This is nifty in the context of everyday tasks such as starting the dishwasher. Imagine what it would be like if you had to read the manual every time you wanted to use it (plus would you find the manual in the first place, or even the kitchen, you creature without memory?). It is arguably also useful that most of us do not immediately forget the lessons of toilet training. But I imagine you would prefer me to prove my point by talking about "meaningful" things such as how we relate to others. Wish granted: because we remember what it feels like to be wounded, and because we also remember times when we ourselves might have acted in hurtful ways, we may be able to stop ourselves from injuring others in the present; though we are often haunted by our memories, particularly by their traumatic frequencies, these memories can also make us more ethical in our relationships with others.

Moreover, we need memory to feel the bittersweet sentiments that queer theory has recently made so much of: sadness, melancholia, nostalgia, regret, and so on. A subject without memory would be a flattened subject, a subject without the capacity to connect one point of its life to other points. This type of subjective continuity is not at all the same thing as a stable core of personality. Quite the contrary, memory with its gaps, flaws, lapses, and complex entanglements with affect—with its tendency to scramble the relationship of the past, present, and future—is among the many factors that keep human beings from being fully coherent. This is why I do not see any reason to equate our capacity to link events from the past to events in the present with humanist progress narratives: surely having a sense of subjective singularity—having a sense of the historical reasons that make it impossible to exchange my life for another—is quite different from feeling that I am on a teleological trajectory to perfection.

My discomfort with the valorization of desubjectivation does not end here, for this valorization tends to engender another problem I have identified, namely, the idea that antinormativity alone—defiance without any particular "content"—represents a sufficient ethical platform. I have stressed at key points in my analysis that queer theory has turned antinormativity to a new norm. The flipside of this is that it has flatly rejected normative ethics, which presupposes a socially viable subject, a subject capable of a degree of accountability for its actions. Though I understand queer theory's antipathy to norms—particularly sexual norms—this antipathy can, like the rhetoric of desubjectivation, be taken to such an extreme that it becomes spurious. How many of us can honestly say that we want a society with no limits on behavior? How many of us would be willing to give up basic rights, such as formal equality under the law?

For many queer theorists, rights-based models of justice—models that rely on a set of normative ideals—are merely an insidious form of biopolitical control, a means of further constraining us even as they profess to protect us. Undoubtedly this is sometimes true. And it is also true that rights-based models of justice cannot solve structural problems such as sexism, racism, homophobia, or poverty and that their practical application consequently often falls short of the ideals they profess. But this does not mean that I am prepared to simply just throw out the ideals in question, for I do not believe that the system's inability to live up to its ideals automatically means that the ideals themselves are intrinsically corrupt. The ideal of formal equality under the law may frequently be violated in practice. But the demise of this ideal would arguably have even more drastically oppressive consequences.

Nor is it the case that normative ethics is inextricably tied to the Enlightenment subject of abstract reason. As feminist philosophers such as Amy Allen (2008), Seyla Benhabib (2006, 2011), and Nancy Fraser (2010, 2013) have illustrated, it is entirely possible to envision a set of a priori norms that are historically constituted—rather than metaphysically grounded—and that therefore remain open to continuous modification. Indeed, many of the norms that we, collectively speaking, live by have been conjured into existence through relatively recent processes of negotiation. Though there is no doubt that such negotiations always exclude certain individuals and populations—and though there is consequently no doubt that we need to stay vigilantly attentive to the constitutive exclusions of our normative systems—the alternative of discarding all attempts to improve these systems by, say, rendering them more inclusive or more consistent in their application would hardly be a productive course of action.

In this particular instance, Butlerian negotiation with power seems like a better option than Lacanian–Edelmanian and Foucauldian–Hufferian antinormativity. I would in fact go so far as to say that queer antinormativity can only survive to the degree that it operates against the backdrop of basic rights. As deficient as these rights are, as insincere as the foundations of contemporary liberal democracy may be, their absence would obliterate the political space within which queer antinormativity can operate. In this sense, antinormativity presupposes the persistence of "liberal" values even when it engages in a vehement critique of (neo)liberalism; ironically, as I already mentioned in chapter 1, the antinormative critic can only flourish to the extent that she can implicitly "count on" the practical (boringly prudent) liberal to keep defending the very rights that she shuns.

In this context, it seems fitting to raise the possibility that queer antinormativity, like queer performativity, might in some ways play right into the hands of neoliberal capitalism. Is it not the case that capitalism, like antinormativity, despises limits? Does it not thrive in the absence of constraints? After all, the self-absorbed neoliberal individual who is used to an endless array of existential possibilities and who does not like limitations on her freedom—including her freedom to choose her hair color, breakfast cereal, video game, and mode of exercise—may be perfectly happy with the idea that she should not be beholden to norms that might restrict her in some way. From this perspective, a priori norms could be argued to war against the neoliberal capitalist ethos of unmitigated choice, perhaps even decentering the neoliberal subject (and its projects of self-actualization) by introducing within its being "alien" elements (norms) that it experiences as constraining. As a result, queer theory's categorical rejection of a priori norms can come across as a bit too convenient, as a symptom of the very neoliberal system that this theory condemns.

In addition, though collective norms that trump the wishes of the individual can be tyrannical, so can a radical antinormativity that veers into anything-goes relativism and that consequently fails to distinguish between just and unjust actions. Though there is no doubt that there are norms that are simply just oppressive—such as heteropatriarchal norms of gender and sexuality—there are others that may be the most effective way to counter the abuses of power. Yet other norms can cut both ways. For example, Benhabib (2011) points out in the contexts of global human rights discourses that even though such discourses can be—and have frequently been—used to advance Western economic and political interests across the world, they can also be—and have sometimes been—used to protect non-Western populations from precisely these interests (for instance, by placing restrictions on the exploitation of labor in free-trade zones).

That so many individuals and political groups around the globe are demanding basic human rights may on some level signify the triumph of Western imperialism; but on another level, it is an indication that there is something appealing about the prospect of such rights (my assumption being that people outside the Western world are not mere passive dupes of Western values, that they are perfectly capable of deciding which political goals they want to support). Likewise, even though rights discourses within Western societies can promote the socioeconomic agendas of the powerful, they can under certain circumstances be used to shield the less powerful against such agendas. The fact that rights-based justice fails as often as it succeeds does not mean that it never succeeds, that it accomplishes nothing.

While I am at it, let me put some pressure on the wholesale rejection of reason that tends to characterize posthumanist theory, including some versions of queer theory. I am of course aware of the historical violences of Enlightenment reason, including its connection to Western imperialism's "civilizing" mission. Furthermore, as a feminist, I am familiar with arguments regarding reason's masculinist biases. And as a psychoanalytic thinker, I recognize the brutality of models of life that overvalue our rational agency at the expense of the body, the passions, the unconscious, and so on. I therefore agree that rationality is not the defining ingredient of human beings. Yet a blanket condemnation of reason seems both reductive and hypocritical—reductive because it discounts the considerable role that rationality plays in human life and hypocritical because it denies that, as academics, we rely on our rational capacities to stage our arguments.

Is it not the case that my ability to speak to you on these pages—and your capacity to process my arguments, critique them, and (hopefully) use them in your own thinking—is predicated on a degree of reason? Indeed, do we not spend much of our careers trying to reason with, and sometimes even outreason, each other? Furthermore, are we not usually trying (at least partially) to "master" something, such as the movement of thought, the organization of ideas, or the craft of writing? This may be idiosyncratic, but I spend a lot of time telling the graduate students whose dissertations I supervise that the organization of their ideas could use some work and that the syntax of their sentences (sometimes) sucks. And I spend even more time rereading my manuscripts in an attempt to make sure that my syntax does not (always) entirely suck. Perhaps this is why I find the unqualified rejection of both reason and mastery that has become habitual in contemporary progressive theory so absurd. True, none of us is fully rational. Nor can we ever fully master anything. Yes, my syntax still sometimes slips. But fortunately it is considerably better than it was when I was nineteen and barely spoke English. Have I tried to master the damn language? Hell yes.

It is in part for such banal reasons that I appreciate Amy Allen's observation that there is an enormous difference between categorically rejecting reason on the one hand and trying to reenvision it along less tyrannical lines on the other. Referring to Huffer's interpretation of Foucault in particular, Allen maintains that it is erroneous to assume—as Huffer does—that

Foucault's celebration of madness amounts to an attempt to do away with reason. According to Allen, Foucault undertook "neither a rejection of reason nor a romanticized idealization of unreason" (2013, 22). In other words, Foucault was not interested in destroying reason but rather in historicizing it by examining how it had been constructed at various points in time, how it had been shaped by disciplinary power, and how it had been deployed to meet specific socioeconomic and political goals.

There is no question that this project entailed a critique of the failings of Enlightenment reason. There is also no doubt that reason, for Foucault, was always impure (biased) in being socially contingent. This is why it must be diligently questioned, why we are right to ask how our dominant models of rationality have been implicated in various relations of power. But this does not mean that reason is altogether useless. For example, Allen observes that even though feminists have been at the forefront of criticizing the abuses of reason, they have frequently also found it enabling because it has allowed them to mount their intricate critiques of social hegemonies, including, somewhat ironically, reason's patriarchal underpinnings. Furthermore, it is precisely the impurity of reason that opens up the possibility of alternative—less repressive, less objectionable—forms of reason. As Foucault explains, "If critical thought itself has a function . . . it is precisely to accept this sort of spiral, this sort of revolving door of rationality that refers us to its necessity, to its indispensability, and, at the same time, to its intrinsic dangers" (2000, 358). Reason, for Foucault, was always contaminated by its context but this, far from negating its value, was what made the reconceptualization of reason feasible in the first place.

7

Queer theory has been right to criticize both normative justice and the oppressive reign of reason. Yet the idea that we can (or should try to) replace these components of social life by an antisocial plunge into the jouissance of the real—or by an equally antisocial process of desubjectivation—can only weaken our understanding of the complexities of human life, which consists of both sociality and antisociality, relationality and antirelationality, rationality and irrationality, and which, to complicate matters even more, is characterized by a degree of self-reflexivity even as it is driven by unconscious motivations that elude comprehension. To her credit, Huffer recognizes this complexity in *Are the Lips a Grave?*, with the result that she, among other things, arrives at the same insight about the potentially normative force of queer theory's antinormativity that I have articulated throughout this book:

If we define ethics, in its broadest sense, as reflection that responds to the Socratic question how are we to live? queer theory must engage the ethical in ways that are more nuanced and varied than its now stock array of antinormativities allows. Indeed, the fact that queer theory's antinormativities have acquired a normative moral force of their own dramatizes a crucial Nietzschean point: simply negating moral norms will not prevent the rebounding force of new moralities precisely at the site where morality has been contested.

(2013, 30)

On the one hand, Huffer reiterates the Nietzschean point about the covert morality of queer antimorality that she made in *Mad for Foucault* in the context of criticizing Edelman and Butler for their continued investment in the psyche. On the other, Huffer's tone in this statement is quite different from the one she used in her earlier text, for ethics here is no longer a matter of rejecting the social coordinates of human life but rather of reflecting on these coordinates, of engaging with the Socratic question about the best way to live. At first glance, this may seem like a conservative descent back into humanistic concerns about the parameters of the good life, but I prefer to interpret it as a welcome shift from the Foucault of desubjectivation to the Foucault of the care of the self.

I do not mean to imply that Huffer entirely abandons the rhetoric of desubjectivation. But in part because her aim in *Are the Lips a Grave?* is to build a bridge between queer theory and feminism—to dilute the bitter aftertaste of queer antifeminist discourses, such as Halley's—Huffer is now interested in combining the best of antisocial theory with the best of more relational approaches. Indeed, if destroying the subject is no longer enough for Huffer, it is because she now recognizes that, logically, this would lead not merely to the erasure of the self but also to the erasure of the other, including the other who has already been erased by various collective inequalities; the other, after all, is also a self. That is, instead of liberating both self and other, the ideal of desubjectivation all too easily depletes the already depleted, thereby making it impossible to attend to the ills of social injustice. As Huffer maintains, "To simply shatter [the] subject—and along with it, morality—is to ignore the first burden of a nonviolent practice: the acknowledgement of harms, including, most importantly, the constitutive exclusion or forgetting of the other" (2013, 44).

As violent as morality can be, we also need it—or at the very least we need some conception of relational ethics—in order to be able to acknowledge intersubjective harms, including the harm caused by the constitutive exclusion or forgetting of the other. Though Huffer still on some level adheres to the ideal of desubjectivation, she now emphasizes that this ideal does not necessarily work for marginalized subjects who already experience their lives as being devoid of agency and subjective integrity. Drawing on the work of Muñoz and Roderick Ferguson, she admits that "the standpoint epistemology undergirding a specifically queer of color claim gives epistemic and moral authority to the experiential truths of a coherent subject in ways that are in tension with Foucauldian desubjectivation" (2013, 16).

Huffer goes on to argue that because queer of color critique focuses on the desubjectivizing force of various historically specific (empirical) forms of marginalization, it tends to advocate "critical resubjectivation" rather than further desubjectivation: even though queer of color critique—like other forms of progressive critique—certainly interrogates the ideal of an integrated identity, it "tends to reclaim subjectivity" rather than to agitate for its demise (2013, 16). In this manner, Huffer recognizes the validity of queer of color critiques of "subjectless" queer theory. Partly for this reason, she proceeds to call for a new model of ethics that "puts the autonomous status of the sovereign humanist subject into question without shattering subjectivity altogether"; she wishes to rethink "the antifoundationalist claims of postmodernism together with the ethical dimensions of intersubjectivity" (60). In this way, Huffer arrives at a conceptual crossroads that is very similar to the one I have tried to advance in this book (as well as in much of my earlier work). Among other things, she acknowledges that the subject who seeks empowerment is not necessarily following a path of breadcrumbs back to the fully agentic Enlightenment subject.

If I in the final analysis find myself agreeing more than disagreeing with Huffer, it is because her goal in *Are the Lips a Grave?* is the same as mine has always been, namely, to figure out how to address the realities of circumstantial forms of dispossession without thereby revalorizing the "self-possessed" subject of humanist metaphysics. This is not an easy task, which may explain why Huffer ends up with some startling theoretical choices, such as the attempt to turn Foucault into a relational critic and Butler into an antirelational one, so that Butler—whose theory of performativity Huffer still in many ways juxtaposes to Foucauldian desubjectivation—is now *also* lumped together with antisocial Lacanians such as Bersani and Edelman whereas Foucault slides into the relational side. While I agree with Huffer's global vision, I do not find these conversions entirely convincing, not the least because, as I hope to have shown in this book, it is difficult to reconcile Butler with Lacanian theory, particularly the antisocial version of this theory advanced by Edelman.

It seems to me that Huffer's attempt to turn Butler into an antisocial thinker arises primarily from her wish to keep agreeing with Foucault and disagreeing with Butler even through her efforts to reconcile antifoundationalism with relationality arguably bring her closer to Butler than to Foucault. In other words, Huffer strives to rescue Foucault from the taint of antisociality—which is now a problem for her in ways that it did not appear to be before—by transferring this taint to Butler. This can only be done by replacing the early Foucault of desubjectivation by the later Foucault of the care of the self (which is fine) and by ignoring Butler's (2004, 2005, 2009, 2012, 2013; Butler and Athanasiou 2013) recent work on dispossession, biopolitics, and the ethics of precarity, that is, work that is premised on a deeply intersubjective model of human life (which is less fine). The result is uneven but there is still something to be learned from it. How does Butler, who has developed one of the most relationally grounded ethical theories of the twenty-first century—who, as I have argued, tends to fetishize relationality to the point of suggesting that any glimmer of autonomy amounts to ethical violence—get cast as an antisocial critic? And how does Foucault, the advocate of self-pulverization, become a relational one?

8

Let us tackle Butler first. On the one hand, Huffer persists in contrasting the furtive foundationalism of Butler's approach with Foucault's antifoundationalism, which "not only troubles identity but undoes subjectivity itself" (2013, 16). On the other, she accuses Butlerian performativity, along with Sedgwick's early theories of performativity, of the kind of self-absorption and self-referentiality that effectively excludes the other. In a sense, Huffer suggests that antisociality was not invented by Lacanians such as Bersani and Edelman but rather by theorists of performativity (Butler and Sedgwick) who, even as they sought to dismantle the sovereign subject, remained obsessed with the self and its subversive resignification at the expense of any sustained analysis of this self's relationship to others.

The implication of Huffer's argument is that early theories of performativity functioned as precursors to antisocial queer theory. As Huffer claims, queer theory's performative subject "emerged as fractured, unstable, and permanently dislodged not only from its humanist foundations in the 'grand narratives' of History, Truth, and Man but also, and more significantly, from any sense of the interdependency and connectedness with others that lie at the root of the social realm" (2013, 62). As a consequence, the performative subject paved the way for queer theory's subsequent (general) disavowal of "any sustained investment in intersubjectivity and community" (62).

Huffer acknowledges that queer of color critique is an exception to this trend. But, in her view, the rest of queer theory—*whether performative or antisocial*—has detached itself not merely from humanism but also from sociality. As I just noted, this assertion does not sit well with Butler's more recent ethical theories, which are predicated on a Levinasian-psychoanalytic understanding of the primacy of the other. And I wonder about its accuracy even in relation to Butler's performative theories, for these already incorporate a deeply psychoanalytic understanding of the ways in which the other takes up residence within the self, so that the very distinction between self and other is blurred (Butler's elaboration of melancholia as a process of incorporating aspects of otherness is a good example of this). Nor does Huffer's critique capture the social valences of Sedgwick's later work on relationality and reparation. But if we, for a moment, follow Huffer's line of reasoning, the implication is that, despite their significant divergences, theories of queer performativity and theories of queer antisociality both mark "a philosophical move away from the other as constitutive of the queer subject"; both occlude "the problem of otherness, and therefore ethics" (2013, 62).

By focusing on this unexpected point of continuity between performativity and antisociality, Huffer puts her finger on their shared narcissism, namely, that insofar as both exclude the other, they secretly prop up the subject even as they seem to trouble or demolish it. This in turn leads to what Huffer reads as queer theory's hypocritical tendency to celebrate the undoing of the subject at the same time as it persists in defining "the queer subject." As Huffer explains, "queer theory's performative first person—the radically unstable queer 'I' or 'we'—simultaneously assumes and denies its own claim to discursive authority" (2013, 63).

Paradoxically, then, queer theory's disavowal of sovereign subjectivity establishes the unstable (nonsovereign) queer subject's legitimacy as uniquely antinormative, subversive, and deviant. According to Huffer, such a stance—which I have earlier in this book defined as one of the pillars of queer exceptionalism—valorizes undecidability "to the point where being 'queer' and being 'undecidable' have become virtually synonymous" (2013, 66). In this manner, queer theory creates a counterintuitive dynamic by which the queer subject appears more heroic than other subjects by virtue of its intense instability; in a way, the less of a subject the queer subject is, the more powerful it becomes. Challenging this "universalist logic at work in the development of the seemingly anti-universalist category of 'queer'" (64), Huffer calls for a greater degree of accountability for those who cannot or do not wish to approximate queer theory's ideal of instability. Furthermore, she posits that queer theorists frequently appear "disingenuous in their embrace of the queer subject's radical instability" (62) in the sense that even they are not able to live up to this ideal.

Huffer is here close to the objection I have raised against Edelman's antisociality, namely, that there is something meaningless about a theoretical ideal that no one—not even the author of the theory—can ever approximate. As I have suggested in this chapter, the same critique could be leveled against the Foucauldian ideal of desubjectivation that Huffer herself upholds in *Mad for Foucault*, which may be one reason that she now insists on Foucault's relationality (a relationality that would, logically, be more appropriately assigned to Butler). Huffer does this, once again, by downplaying the conceptual similarity between Foucault and Edelman's Lacanian approach, this time by emphasizing Foucault's historico-genealogical method over his ideal of desubjectivation:

Foucault would implicitly reject antisocial queer theory's plunge into the abyss of a negative ethics. Foucault's explicitly genealogical approach to the other would disallow the psychic ahistoricity of such abyssal conceptions of self-undoing: in his heterotopian histories of the present, the spatio-temporal particularities of lives in relation to others matter more than the frozen negativity of an antisocial death drive.

(2013, 46)

Earlier I demonstrated that in *Mad for Foucault* Huffer—largely unsuccessfully—attempts to distinguish between Foucauldian desubjectivation and Lacanian–Edelmanian jouissance. In this passage from *Are the Lips a Grave?*, desubjectivation drops out of the picture altogether so that it is now the Foucault of genealogy—the Foucault who (supposedly) investigates "lives in relation to others"—who is pitted against antirelational queer theory's "abyssal conceptions of self-undoing." In other words, it is only by shifting her emphasis from the Foucault of desubjectivation to the Foucault of genealogy that Huffer is able to drive a wedge between Foucault and Lacanian–Edelmanian antisociality. I certainly understand this impulse to align Foucault with historicity and relationality against the "frozen negativity" of antisociality. But the cost of doing so is high, for it keeps Huffer from recognizing the parallels between the ethical visions of Foucault and Lacan, and not only between the Foucault of desubjectivation and the Lacan of jouissance but also between the Foucault of the care of the self and the Lacan of clinical practice.

9

One of my aims in this book has been to demonstrate that the fissure within queer theory that separates the Foucauldians from the Lacanians is both conceptually and politically pointless, needlessly draining a great deal of the field's energy. I hope to have already clarified the similarities between the Foucault of desubjectivation and the Lacan of jouissance (as well as between Huffer's antifoundationalism and Edelman's antisociality). As a result, I would like to end this chapter by briefly outlining some other (to me, obvious) parallels between Foucault and Lacan, first by illustrating the convergences between Huffer's Foucauldian ethics of eros in *Mad for Foucault* and the Lacanian ethics of the act that I outlined in chapter 2, and second, by illustrating the convergences of the later Foucault's care of the self and Lacan's conception of the clinical goals of psychoanalysis.

Regarding the first of these comparisons, consider that Huffer portrays the ethics of eros that she derives from Foucault as an interrogation of the values of conventional morality, which Foucault viewed as "catastrophic" (2010, 245). Could not the same thing be said of the Lacanian ethics of the act, which, as I have explained, opposes the master's morality and the service of goods that this morality supports? Is it not the case, in short, that Foucault and Lacan both work with a basic distinction between (conventional) morality and (rebellious) ethics? In addition, both seem to align morality with (conventional) knowledge and ethics with (rebellious) "truth." As I have illustrated, in Lacan, the master's discourse (morality) is destabilized by the truth of desire (ethics). This seems strikingly compatible with Huffer's claim that the Foucauldian ethics of eros "asks about the relation between subjectivity and truth" (247).

In the *History of Madness*, Foucault describes madness as follows: "a truth of man, very archaic and very near, very silent and very threatening, a truth the underlies all truth, the truth closest to the birth of subjectivity, and the most widely spread at the very level of things; a truth that is the deep retreat of man's individuality, and the inchoate form of the cosmos" (1961, 517). I would say that Foucault is here getting at something very similar to the Lacanian notion of the real (which, recall, saturates the subject's most fundamental fantasies) as a site of the subject's most archaic, and therefore most threatening, truth—that is, precisely, "the truth closest to the birth of subjectivity." Even Foucault's reference to truth as "the deep retreat of man's individuality" resonates with Lacan's arguments regarding the real as the seat of the subject's singularity of being (see Ruti 2012). Consequently, when Huffer proposes that "eros is the name we can give to an ethical practice of embodied subjectivity in relation to truth" (2010, 269), I cannot help but think that Lacan might have said the same thing about desire (about the kind of desire that catches up with the jouissance of the real). Likewise, when Huffer glosses Foucault's conceptualization of eros as a "transformative rethinking of life," as "biopolitical life's transfiguration" (270), it seems to me that she is talking about something very similar to the Lacanian act, which also enacts "life's transfiguration" by undoing the master's morality (which, arguably, is just another designation for biopolitics).

When we shift our focus to the second of my comparisons—the convergences between Foucault's care of the self and Lacan's conception of the clinical goals of psychoanalysis—the analogies between the two thinkers are equally pronounced. In Foucault, we find the opposition between Cartesian rationality and the care of the self as a spiritual, bodily practice of self-interrogation and self-transformation. In Lacan, in turn, we find the opposition between the master's discourse—which sometimes takes the form of a university discourse fixated on knowledge in the Cartesian sense (see Lacan 1969–1970)—and the truth of desire that analysis is designed to release. In both scenarios, (sterile) knowledge is, once again, juxtaposed to (transformative) truth. Truth, in turn, is aligned with eros (Foucault) and desire (Lacan).

It is therefore not surprising that, in *The Hermeneutics of the Subject*, Foucault states: "Lacan actually reintroduced into psychoanalysis the oldest tradition, the oldest questioning, and the oldest disquiet of the *epimeleia heautou*, which was the most general form of spirituality" (1981–1982, 30). Foucault here admits that Lacan's version of clinical practice is close to his own notion of *epimeleia heautou*, the ancient spiritual practice of caring for the self which was intended to augment one's ability to treat oneself as an object of inquiry, examine the movements of one's interiority, and attain more profound levels of self-relation. As Foucault specifies, the care of the self consists of "the search, practice, and experience through which the subject carries out the necessary transformations on himself in order to have access to the truth"; "there can be no truth without a conversion or a transformation of the subject" (15).

Huffer correctly recognizes that the Foucault of the care of the self is not only interested in self-undoing—desubjectivation—but also in self-making (self-transformation). Huffer describes the process as follows: "The ethics of the self as a practice of freedom is, above all, the practice of critical reflection that will allow us to practice a different living through the art of ethical self-transformation" (2010, 264). This is a conclusion I can support. I would merely add that such an ethics of the self as a practice of critical reflection cannot be undertaken without a psyche, so that if this ethics is what Huffer wants to endorse, she cannot simultaneously advocate for the collapse of the psyche.

Nor can Foucault's ethics be undertaken without some relationship to the unconscious. Perhaps this is what Foucault is getting at when he describes eros as "a blind madness of the body," "the great intoxication of the soul where Unreason is in a position of knowledge" (1961, 88). It seems to me that what perhaps most unites Foucault and Lacan is their shared appreciation for the ambivalent intersection where self-reflection meets the passions of the body. Foucault's term for these passions was eros; Lacan called them desire (or the jouissance of the real). Foucault talked about the care of the self; Lacan talked about analysis as an elaboration of the subject's desire. Neither thinker believed in the notion of a definitive cure; but both were interested in the subject's capacity to develop an inquisitive relationship to its destiny.

The parallels between the two thinkers do not stop there, for if Foucault recognized that the subject's destiny can get caught up in the tentacles of biopolitical control, Lacan similarly recognized that it is often excruciatingly caught up in the tentacles of the master's discourse, the discourse that strives to replace the truth of the subject's desire by the Other's desire. However, both thinkers had faith that, through processes of self-examination, at least some of that destiny could be released from the grip of hegemonic power, that the subject could arrive at an—always partial, always slipping— understanding of its singular "truth." Such a truth is obviously not Truth in the metaphysical sense but rather the idiosyncratic, flickering truth of the kind of eros, the kind of desire, that has not been entirely subsumed to the dictates of disciplinary power. To express the matter in slightly different terms, it seems to me that both Foucault's care of the self and Lacanian clinical practice aim at a revitalization of being; both, in short, aim at the rewriting of destiny.

10

Huffer's antipathy to psychoanalysis—and therefore, indirectly, to Lacan— is understandable in light of Foucault's justifiable criticisms of the normalizing tendencies of analysis in the *History of Madness*. As we know, in this text Foucault rejected psychoanalysis fairly unconditionally, seeing it as the culmination of the Cartesian triumph of reason over unreason, of the self-mastering subject of "knowledge" over the madman. Moreover, Huffer reveals that Foucault had good private reasons for this rejection by quoting Foucault's explanation—given in an interview—about why he wrote the *History of Madness*: "In my personal life, from the moment of my sexual awakening, I felt excluded, not so much rejected, but belonging to society's shadow. It's all the more a problem when you discover it for yourself. All of this was very quickly transformed into a kind of psychiatric threat: if you're not like everyone else, it's because you're abnormal, if you're abnormal, it's because you're sick" (quoted in Huffer 2010, 23). One can certainly appreciate why 1950s versions of adaptive psychoanalysis—which Lacan was also hugely critical of—would have contributed to Foucault's sense of ostracization. Yet by the early 1980s, by *The Hermeneutics of the Subject*, Foucault had come to recognize that psychoanalysis, particularly its Lacanian version, could be an important intellectual ally. More specifically, he had come to see that even though psychoanalysis, like Marxism, could easily ossify into normalizing forms through processes of institutionalization, it also had the capacity to resist such ossification. Foucault in fact proposed that it is precisely when institutionalization is avoided—when one is able to preserve the critical edge of Marxism and psychoanalysis—that one discovers in these fields the same "questions, interrogations, and requirements which . . . are the very old and fundamental questions of *epimeleia heautou*, and so of spirituality as a condition of access to the truth" (1981–1982, 29). Foucault continues as follows:

In both Marxism and psychoanalysis, for completely different reasons but with relatively homologous effects, the problem of what is at stake in the subject's being (of what the subject's being must be for the subject to have access to the truth) and, in return, the question of what aspects of the subject may be transformed by virtue of his access to the truth, well, these two questions, which are once again absolutely typical of spirituality, are found again at the very heart of, or anyway, at the source and outcome of both of these knowledges.

(29)

Here Foucault once again aligns self-transformation with "access to the truth" in ways that resonate with Lacan's analysis of the truth of desire, this time explicitly admitting that both Marxism and psychoanalysis retain the capacity to deliver the subject to its truth through the practice of *epimeleia heautou*. In this context, I want to reemphasize—because this helps me further explain why Lacan tends to be congruent with Foucault's care of the self—that in Lacanian theory, there is no such thing as a decisive cure. Like Foucault, Lacan had no patience with the ideal of psychic "health" as a route to happiness. Quite the contrary, Lacan announced that for the analyst to make himself "the guarantor of the possibility that a subject will in some way be able to find happiness . . . is a form of fraud" (1959–1960, 303). That happiness is what the analysand is looking for tends to be a given. Lacan, however, saw this as a "bourgeois dream" designed to distract the subject from "the reality of the human condition": "the state in which man is in that relationship to himself which is his own death . . . and can expect help from no one" (300, 303–304).

Lacan links this "human condition" to anguish, distress, and psychic disarray, suggesting that the purpose of analysis is to reconcile the subject to the realization that there is no ultimate remedy or salvation, no "Sovereign Good" that can secure its happiness (1959–1960, 300). As he starkly states:

That's something to remember whenever the analyst finds himself in the position of responding to anyone who asks him for happiness. The question of the Sovereign Good is one that man has asked himself since time immemorial, but the analyst knows that it is a question that is closed. Not only doesn't he have that Sovereign Good that is asked of him, but he also knows that there isn't any.

(299–300)

The analyst, then, does not have the Sovereign Good; he does not have the key to the analysand's happiness. This is why the revitalization of subjectivity, the rewriting of destiny, that takes place in Lacanian analysis is not a matter of translating the bad into the good, illness into health, pathology into normalcy, but rather of learning how to live out the singular destiny that arises from the singular cadence of the truth of one's desire. Am I mistaken in seeing the correspondences between this understanding of clinical practice and Foucault's care of the self as an ongoing interrogation of subjective truth (as opposed to knowledge)?

In *Mad for Foucault*, Huffer approvingly quotes Didier Eribon, who asks, "I wonder if it is really possible—and desirable—to engage in a project to join queer theory or, in a more general way, radical thought . . . with psychoanalysis" (2010, 35). The implication is that psychoanalysis has nothing to offer to queer theory. Critics such as Halperin (2007) have made comparable arguments, dismissing psychoanalysis on the basis of Foucault's early condemnation of it. I hope to have illustrated that such dismissals not only misunderstand Foucault but also prematurely close up the conceptual space between Foucault and Lacan.

On my interpretation, Foucault and Lacan were both trying to figure out how to destabilize the humanist subject without thereby annihilating the subject entirely. This is one reason that reading them together can help heal the rift between the antisocial and social strands of queer theory. Granted, both thinkers entertained fantasies of utter subjective pulverization, Foucault through the notion of desubjectivation and Lacan through the notion of the ethical act as a plunge into the jouissance of the real. Ultimately, however, both retained an appreciation for the richness of psychic life, for subjective "truth," and for the transformative potential of self-interrogation. Both also stepped away from the solipsistic asociality of desubjectivation and jouissance by emphasizing the necessarily intersubjective setting of self-transformation, Foucault by investigating the social context of self-care and Lacan by investigating the transferential potential of the analytic dyad. This does not mean that they discarded the radical potential of desubjectivation and jouissance altogether but merely that they recognized that human life also contains other, more social, more affirmative frequencies.

This is what Edelman denies. Huffer, in turn, tries to resurrect the affirmative side of Foucault—his love of eros as what not only unbinds but also binds and, by binding, transforms—without thereby acknowledging Foucault's theoretical proximity to Lacan. At one point in *Mad for Foucault* she in fact wonders how it has come to be that both Foucault and Freud (psychoanalysis) have played such an important role in queer theory. I hope to have shed some light on the matter: when I read Huffer's engaging description of Foucault's care of the self as a form of self-reflexivity saturated by eros, I immediately think about the clinical practice of psychoanalysis as an open-ended exploration of being, as a space where the signifier and the real, word and affect, thought and eros (potentially at least) come together to generate what Kristeva calls the rebirth of the subject.

Chapter Five

THE USES AND MISUSES OF BAD FEELINGS

Queerness is a longing that propels us onward, beyond romances of the negative and toiling in the present. Queerness is that thing that lets us feel that this world is not enough, that indeed something is missing. . . . Queerness is essentially about the rejection of a here and now and an insistence on potentiality or concrete possibility for another world.

—JOSÉ MUÑOZ, *CRUISING UTOPIA*

I pay particular attention to feelings such as nostalgia, regret, shame, despair, *ressentiment*, passivity, escapism, self-hatred, withdrawal, bitterness, defeatism, and loneliness. These feelings are tied to the experience of social exclusion and to the historical "impossibility" of same-sex desire.

—HEATHER LOVE, *FEELING BACKWARD*

1

At first glance, it may seem that the forward-looking queer utopia Muñoz promotes in *Cruising Utopia* (2009) has little to do with Heather Love's backward-looking analysis of bad feelings in *Feeling Backward* (2007). If anything, even though Muñoz's wish to move beyond "romances of the negative" is first and foremost a response to Edelman's antisocial thesis, his statement—when extracted from the context of his critique of Edelman—could in principle be applied to Love as well inasmuch as she seems engaged in her own version of "romancing" the negative. Yet pitting Muñoz against Love—or against other critics such as Sara Ahmed (2004, 2006, 2010, 2014), Lauren Berlant (2008, 2011), Ann Cvetkovich (2003, 2012), or David Eng (2001, 2010) who have explored the sadder frequencies of queer life—does not make intuitive sense. In part this is because the latter critics do not share Edelman's antisociality. But it is also because they are interested in how bad feelings—negative affects—accrue and stubbornly cling to subjects who have been traumatized beyond the constitutive traumas of subject formation: as opposed to Edelman, who insists on bypassing trauma's circumstantial modalities in favor of the foundational negativity of human life (the way that life, inherently, "doesn't work"), they are invested in understanding the ways in which context-specific negativity—marginalization, dispossession, exclusion, and abjection—is unevenly distributed across the collective field (the ways that life works less for some subjects than others).

Muñoz shares this outlook, which is why his utopianism has a rather somber tone. As he notes in the statement quoted in the epigraph, queer utopianism arises from the recognition that the world as it stands—the here and now—is "not enough." In this sense, this utopianism, like bad feelings, strives to exit a cruel, corrupt, and stultifying world. In other words, if bad feelings, especially sad ones such as despair, nostalgia, and melancholia, opt out of an unsatisfactory present by withdrawing from it, Muñoz's utopianism does the same by turning toward the promises of the future. Although Muñoz's strategy, on the surface, seems more optimistic, his utopia, as we will shortly discover, can only be accessed by a detour through the past, which is why it easily meets up with backward-looking feelings such as melancholia.

Muñoz draws on the Frankfurt School scholar Ernst Bloch to construct a utopian hermeneutics of hope that—he hopes—will revive a flagging queer imagination. He does so in order to counter two very different forms of political failure. One is obviously the antisocial strand of queer theory championed by Edelman—which Muñoz acerbically calls "a poor substitute for actual critical intervention" (2009, 4). The other is the neoliberal pragmatism of the mainstream lgbtq movement that I discussed in chapter 1. Such pragmatism, Muñoz asserts, tells us not to dream of an alternative world "but instead to dwell in a broken-down, toxic present" (30). Queer utopianism, in contrast, insists on the possibility of a more welcoming world. As a matter of fact, queerness, for Muñoz, is *intrinsically* utopian in that, like Jacques Derrida's (2005) "democracy to come," it persists as an elusive ideal that we strive to approximate even if we can never quite reach it. As Muñoz explains, "We may never touch queerness, but we can feel it as the warm illumination of a horizon imbued with potentiality" (2009, 1). Somewhat paradoxically, it is because queerness is "not yet here" that it can be "distilled from the past and used to imagine a future" (1).

Some queer subjects might object to Muñoz's claim that "we have never been queer," but his emphasis lies on the idea that because queerness is inherently open ended, because it cannot be fixed into a definition, it "allows us to see and feel beyond the quagmire of the present" (2009, 1). Undoubtedly Muñoz could here be accused of aligning queerness with undecidability—and thereby of fanning the fires of queer exceptionalism—in precisely the way that Huffer criticizes (see chapter 4). But what interests me in the present context is that queerness, as Muñoz envisions it, turns out to be a great deal like Lacanian desire: propelled by lack, never fully satisfied, but potentially endlessly inventive in its quest for satisfaction. And it is also like Lacanian desire in the sense that it searches the past for a trace of what has been lost so as, however temporarily, to render the present incandescent, so as, however temporarily, to make the present a place where the utopian longing for a more beautiful future has already been met. I want to linger for a moment on the fact that Muñoz, in criticizing Edelman's Lacanianism, converges with "my" Lacan, for this further confirms that Edelman's Lacan is not the only possible Lacan.

In chapter 2, I talked about how, in Lacanian terms, desire revolves around a primordial (non)object—the Thing—that has been irrevocably lost. I talked about how every worldly object of desire—every *objet a*—is "refound" in the sense that it contains an aura of this lost object. And I talked about how desire fixates on specific objects (as opposed to others that might be equally or even more available) because it recognizes the Thing's echo in the objects in question. This, I argued, gives rise to an ethical attitude which deems objects that carry the Thing's echo to be irreplaceable, valuable beyond reckoning, and therefore worth protecting and preserving.

It seems to me that the queer utopianism that Muñoz derives from Bloch relies on a similar logic of finding the echo of the past—of what is no-longer-conscious—in the present so as to discover a potentiality for the future. As Muñoz states: "Bloch invites us to look to this no-longer-conscious, a past that is akin to what Derrida describes as the trace. These ephemeral traces, flickering illuminations from other times and places . . . extend a glance toward that which is forward-dawning, anticipatory illuminations of the not-yet-conscious" (2009, 28). The no-longer-conscious, in short, offers a glimpse of the not-yet-conscious (the not-yet-here) as a way to "combat the devastating logic of the world of the here and now, a notion of nothing existing outside the sphere of the current moment, a version of reality that naturalizes cultural logics such as capitalism and heteronormativity" (12).

Muñoz's claim, in a sense, is that what is no-longer-conscious is also not yet entirely voiced: it is a trace of a potentiality that has not yet reached full expression. This is why it is possible to mine residues of the past—including objects that retain a residue of the past—for the "anticipatory illuminations" that they reveal about a future potentiality. In the same way that Lacanian desire finds the aura of the Thing (the no-longer-conscious) in worldly objects it wishes to honor with its searching (and even loving) attention, Muñoz's queer utopianism discovers the no-longer-conscious in objects—or moments, spaces, and sites of queer life—it wishes to honor with its searching (and even loving) attention. As he observes: "A posterior glance at different moments, objects, and spaces might offer us an anticipatory illumination of queerness" (2009, 22).

2

Arguably the most engaging parts of Muñoz's text are ones where he activates such a glance, as he does when he reads Charlie Chaplin and Kevin Aviance as "masters of the historically dense queer gesture" (2009, 67). Muñoz is here referring to the kinds of fleeting gestures that, like dance moves, vanish as soon as they are completed but that, nevertheless, point to the future in constructing the kind of queer archive that allows diverse queer subjects to meet at a shared space of recognition. That is, subjects who might otherwise have little in common will understand certain gestures—certain tonalities of being—as belonging to a queer past (and therefore possibly to a queer future).

As Cvetkovich (2003), among others, has noted, much of the historical archive of queer lives relies on ephemera: passing impressions that have produced no enduring record or that have merely produced scraps of a record that cannot easily be reconstructed into a coherent whole; in part because of the relentless criminalization of queer lives, these lives have eluded the tentacles of "official" history, persisting instead in furtive modalities that defy detection even as they invite it from those "in the know." Muñoz is getting at something similar, except that his emphasis lies in the sudden illumination, the sudden revelation, that a tiny sliver of experience floating up from the past can provide. Muñoz specifies that queer energies and lives are laid bare "through small gestures, particular intonations, and other ephemeral traces" that are "utterly legible to an optic of feeling, a queer optic that permits us to take in the queerness that is embedded in gesture" (2009, 72). Indeed, not only have queer experiences been lost as a result of persecution; it may also be that queerness is "filled with the intention to be lost," "to slip through the fingers and comprehension of those who would use knowledge against us" (72, 81). Yet the ephemerality of the queer archive does not render it immaterial, for the "hermeneutics of residue" unearths "vast storehouses of queer history and futurity" (81).

Muñoz finds such lingering residues, among other objects, in Tony Just's photographs of public men's toilets in New York City. Just selected run-down toilets—ones that would have been likely to be used as venues for fleeting sexual encounters before being closed down due to the AIDS crisis—and scrubbed them sparkling clean. He then proceeded to photograph the bathrooms, focusing on their immaculate details. Influenced in part by Derrida's (2006) notion of hauntology, Muñoz explains: "The urinals, tiles, toilets, and fixtures that are the objects of these photo images take on what can only be described as a ghostly aura, an otherworldly glow" (2009, 40–41). This otherworldly glow recalling "the ghosts of public sex," in turn, deconstructs the binary of actuality and ideality: "In pan, I see the ghosted materiality of the work as having a primary relation to emotions, queer memories, and structures of feeling that haunt gay men on both sides of a generational divide that is formed by and through the catastrophe of AIDS" (41). The ghosts in Just's photographs appear material—tangible in conjuring up the AIDS crisis—without being visible.

One could say that the ghostly presences in Just's photographs animate what Eng describes as affective—as opposed to empirical—history. Eng explains that if empirical history demands a foundation in verifiable events—in what "really happened"—affective history arises from, and honors, "the realm of ghosts" (2010, 183). "The figure of the ghost," Eng continues, "introduces the what-could-have-been as that privileged category through which history becomes both haunted and an alternative historical understanding emerges into a horizon of being oriented toward a doing in futurity" (184). This alternative historical understanding cannot be conveyed by cognitive, purely empirical accounts of past events any more than it can be expressed through liberal narratives of historical progress. Rather—Eng maintains—it conjures up affect "as a tool for political disenchantment and social reform" (186). It renders suffering political, creating a social, collective response to the losses of the past.

This I take to be one of Muñoz's points as well. More specifically, Muñoz views such a political response to loss as a reparative alternative—in Sedgwick's sense—to Edelman's paranoid conviction that because the past has shunned the queer, the future must necessarily do the same, the future must necessarily exclude all possibility of queer intervention. For Muñoz, the encounter with negativity, with a historically particular (rather than constitutive) record of pain, shame, despair, and anguish, is not invariably a pure experience of loss but, potentially at least, an opening to something worthwhile, such as a collective political response. This is why, as an alternative to Edelman's negativity, Muñoz offers the "scandal" of the nonopposition of the negative and the positive, where "the negative becomes the resource for a certain mode of queer utopianism" (2009, 13).

In this manner, Muñoz counters the fetishization of negativity that characterizes the antisocial rhetoric of opting out with a critical utopian rhetoric of hope. This is not hope in the banal sense that mainstream culture markets to us through popular psychology, advice columns, sappy television shows, and the idea that thinking good thoughts will bring good things into our lives. Instead, it is hope as a tool of critical thought, as a means of envisioning alternatives to an impoverished present: in the same way that I have proposed that critical forms of desire can lead us to ask for "something more," Muñoz believes that critical forms of hope can lead us to insist on a better future. Indeed, even the fact that hope is regularly thwarted does not alter Muñoz's conviction that it is "indispensable to the act of imagining transformation" (2009, 9). Hope can obviously be disappointed but disappointment must be risked "if a disabling political pessimism is to be displaced" (9).

Muñoz is here close to Ahmed's argument that pessimism can function as a disabling defense against disappointment. In other words, as critical as Ahmed is of the overly optimistic happiness scripts of our society, she recognizes that pessimism can become a bad habit of sorts, a strategy of "preparing" oneself for disappointment well before one has had a chance to be disappointed. Pessimism, according to Ahmed, mitigates the anxiety that might arise from being (hopefully) invested in the future, thereby serving as "a way of inhabiting the world through shielding oneself from possibility" (2010, 178). That is, if being optimistic about the future can keep one from living in the present, pessimism—when it becomes excessive—can foreclose the future as a space of possibility (as it does for Edelman). Moreover, like Sedgwick's paranoid position, it can be used to fend off any and all surprises, with the result that the pessimist may even come to enjoy "other people's disappointment as a sign of their failure to be prepared" (178).

For both Ahmed and Muñoz, the antidote to this state of affairs is holding the future open as a place where unexpected things can happen. Admittedly, Ahmed is more hesitant than Muñoz, pointing out that optimism can be confused with neutrality—so that an optimistic assessment becomes conflated with how things supposedly actually are (even when they are not)—in ways that more or less guarantee disappointment. Ahmed moreover cautions us against using optimism as a means of converting bad feelings into good ones, of viewing bad feelings as a mere stepping-stone to eventual happiness. As I have observed, this is precisely what the American dream tends to do, which is why its progress narrative includes the idea that we should be able to turn hardship into some sort of personal profit. In Ahmed's terms, the problem with this is that such optimism involves a "commitment to happiness as the endpoint of human action, as what all experiences of bad feeling enable us to reach" (2010, 177).

Still, Ahmed does not reject the idea that hopefulness can function as a valuable political (or personal) affect. Though she is critical of the hegemonic imposition of hopefulness as a default stance with respect to the future, of the promise of happiness as a dominant ideal, she does not deny the political (or personal) potential of hopefulness. Muñoz in turn believes that hopefulness about the possibility of a better future is the only way to move forward in queer politics, that surrendering the future to the heteronormative establishment is more risky than the risk of getting one's hopes dashed.

3

It may be helpful to recognize that although Muñoz is primarily interested in circumstantial rather than constitutive forms of negativity, his approach—which views the negative as a resource for future potentiality—is not entirely unlike the one I took toward the Lacanian notion of constitutive lack in chapter 3, where I read this lack as a source of creative energy, of the desire to populate the world with various products of our imagination. I admit that this approach can be co-opted by the progress narratives of dominant culture, including the American dream. And I also admit that both Muñoz and I could be criticized for harboring a theoretico-politico impulse to turn the negative into a positive in an effort to make the unbearable more bearable. Edelman might argue that both Muñoz and I refuse to confront the negative head on, that we are engaged in various tactics of distraction that keep us from acknowledging the impossibility of queer lives (Muñoz) or, quite simply, the abyss of existence (me). I have often thought about this counterargument because it captures the gist of my disagreement with the reigning strands of poststructuralism and Lacanianism within the American academy—strands that come together seamlessly in Edelman's work. I suppose that the matter, for me, once again comes down to two different conceptions of what it means for the humanist subject to die.

As we have seen, for Edelman, this subject dies in a suicidal act; it is undone by jouissance. For me, in contrast, this subject dies so as to be reborn into new processes of becoming and humbled-yet-still-viable agency. As I have tried to demonstrate, the rebirth I am referring to is not akin to the Christian notion of resurrection by divine grace but rather to "revolt" in the Kristevian (1997) sense of regaining enough psychic aliveness to be able to rethink, revisit, revise, and rework what does not work. It is also related to Berlant's (2011) description of our belabored efforts to break our cruelly optimistic attachments to forms of life that "don't work." And it is conceptually connected to Cvetkovich's attempt, in *Depression: A Public Feeling* (2012), to pursue the pathways through which depression can sometimes—though not always—generate tenuous yet life-sustaining modes of creativity. As I admitted in chapter 2, I recognize that there are situations where a categorical *No!* to the status quo brings enormous relief. But, for me, such a *No!* can only mean something in the context of a life that—beyond that *No!*—still remains livable (unless, of course, it is uttered for political purposes, as when the subject sacrifices itself for the sake of a cause, as Antigone arguably does).

At this juncture, Heather Love's nuanced analysis of the role of negativity in queer politics and theory is instructive. On a basic level, Love is critical of the mainstream gay and lesbian movement's attempts to translate a shame-filled past—a pre-Stonewall past—into a triumphant future by simply just discarding what was excruciating about this past; she is critical of the attempt to translate shame into pride, as happens when, "in the darkroom of liberation, the 'negative' of the closet case or the isolated protogay child is developed into a photograph of an out, proud gay man"

(2007, 20). In such instances, the trace of the suffering that has been suppressed remains "visible right on the surface of this image" (20). What is more, such a barely suppressed trace can start to clamor for recognition, as is the case, for example, when pre-Stonewall feelings of shame find their way into the lives of present-day queer subjects: such feelings are doubly disconcerting because they are detached from their "proper" historical context and therefore seemingly irrational and irrelevant, out of place in a world that in principle is supposed to be accepting of queer lives.

According to Love, such circulation of pre-Stonewall feelings within a post-Stonewall world suggests a "complex, incorrigible, and fatal" historical continuity (2007, 20). Essentially, Love believes that political efforts to transcend the pain of the past will never be entirely successful, that no matter how much gay, lesbian, and queer subjects try to repress the traumatizing aspects of queer histories, these aspects will always infiltrate the present. For instance, she analyzes the image of the melancholy lesbian who never gets the girl in traditional Western literary depictions of same-sex love, proposing that present-day young lesbians who do not have any trouble getting the girl are still, in some ways, living in the shadow of this historical figure whose romantic endeavors were always tinged by disappointment. Though Love does not use psychoanalysis in her discussion, her basic insight is deeply psychoanalytic, namely, that the past will always be a part of the present and that our attempts to deny this reality will only make this past more powerful.

Along closely related lines, Love is suspicious of modalities of queer criticism that seek to overcome difficult histories by transforming "the base materials of social abjection into the gold of political agency" (2007, 18). Among such modalities Love counts the ever-popular Foucauldian–Butlerian "reverse discourse," which recognizes histories of injury while simultaneously seeking to rework them for current political purposes. Within such reworking, the acceptance of stigma is "conditional on its ability to be 'turned' to good use" (18). In other words, if early gay and lesbian criticism tended to ignore the painful aspects of the past in order to construct a positive history, more recent queer theory, drawing on the Foucauldian–Butlerian reverse discourse, "has focused on negative aspects of the past in order to use them for positive political purposes" (18–19).

Love's concern about this strategy is that, in its haste to refunction the legacies of abjection, queer theory may not adequately account for the lingering effects of these legacies, the fact that they may motivate the present moment in ways that cannot be translated into positive politics; in Love's view, the attempt to transform negative affects into affirmative politics may keep us from fully grappling with the persistent power of queer abjection. This is why Love's own endeavor focuses less on moving beyond a difficult past than on developing "a politics of the past" (2007, 21): a theoretico-political practice of exploring the impact that the past continues to have on the present through bad feelings such as shame, sadness, despair, bitterness, and self-hatred. Such feelings, Love notes, tend to be seen as politically "useless" in the sense that, unlike more "dignified" sentiments such as anger or outrage, they are not easy to translate into collective resistance. If anything, such feelings block action by paralyzing the subject. Yet Love finds much to honor in her queer archive of bad feelings, advocating the act of taking an unflinching look at this archive so as, precisely, to understand why action is thwarted.

At the same time—and here I return to the potential value of the approach that Muñoz and I favor, the approach that seeks to resurrect the kernel of positivity within the negative—Love recognizes that the central paradox of transformative criticism is that it cannot help but wish for a better future: "The emphasis on damage in queer studies exists in a state of tension with a related and contrary tendency—the need to resist damage and to affirm queer existence"; "despite our reservations, we just cannot stop dreaming of a better life for queer people" (2007, 3). Indeed, as much as Love stresses that she wants to dwell within the damaging aspects of the past, ultimately even she cannot entirely avoid implying that such dwelling within damage will do some good. In saying this, I do not mean to criticize Love, for it seems to me that, theoretically speaking, the only alternative would be the route taken by Edelman (which Love explicitly rejects).

Love's analysis may foreground what is ambivalent and embarrassing—and it may wish to live with injury instead of fixing it—but there is still something affirmative, even comforting, about it. After all, making (some) sense of past suffering may help us make (some) sense of present suffering: understanding the historical sources of abjection may shed light on current sources of abjection in ways that offer solace. In this sense, Love's project may be closer to that of Muñoz than her dismissal of utopian, hopeful attitudes may suggest.

I would say—once again returning to the terminology that I established at the beginning of this book—that the key distinction to be drawn here is between approaches that celebrate negativity for its own sake, as Edelman does, and those that try to do something with it (that work with it). Both Love and Muñoz do something with negativity, even if they go about this task in different ways, Love by looking backward, Muñoz by looking forward. Both refuse to disavow negativity. But neither do they valorize it as a heroic counterhegemonic stance. There is a certain working through of suffering that takes place in the theorizing of both thinkers, which suggests that both are interested in the rebirth—rather than merely just the death— of the subject, particularly the queer subject.

I see my own relationship to negativity along similar lines: I do not wish to avoid a confrontation with suffering—how could I?—yet I am also interested in the unpredictable effects of suffering. Such effects are not always positive; sometimes suffering merely produces more suffering. I would never argue that all suffering yields meaning. Much of it is "useless," as Emmanuel Levinas (1991) once put it. Indeed, it may be that none of it is "useful" in a conventional sense. But parts of it may be *usable*. Occasionally, parts of it may even be enriching in the sense that, without suffering, human beings might be somewhat boring, devoid of emotional depth and capacity for empathy. I am the first to admit that the amount of suffering in human life, particularly in the lives of those who are socioeconomically or otherwise marginalized, can be so excessive as to be unbearable. Yet I am also interested in how the unbearable can be borne (if and when it is). That is, unlike Edelman, and like Berlant, I believe that survival—living on despite everything, limping forward despite injury—is worth talking about.

This may explain why I am drawn to Muñoz's model of quotidian utopianism, of finding the luster of the transcendent, however fleetingly, in the texture of the everyday. On the one hand, as I have shown, Muñoz's utopianism arises from the recognition that the present is inadequate. On the other, Muñoz is careful to specify that his utopianism is not an attempt to reject the present. As he states:

To critique an overarching "here and now" is not to turn one's face away from the everyday. Roland Barthes wrote that the mark of the utopian is the quotidian. Such an argument would stress that the utopian is an impulse that we see in everyday life. This impulse is to be glimpsed as something that is extra to the everyday transaction of heteronormative capitalism. This quotidian example of the utopian can be glimpsed in utopian bonds, affiliations, designs, and gestures that exist within the present moment.

(2009, 22–23)

In other words, while the queer utopian impulse is motivated by the insufficiencies of the present, it simultaneously looks into the quotidian details of this present in the hope of discovering something "extra"—and "extra" here should perhaps be taken as a synonym for "anticipatory illuminations"—in these details. Stated slightly differently, queer utopianism strives to detect the gaps, breaks, and fissures in the normative narrative of what the good life is supposed to entail in order to conjure up an alternative understanding of what "reality" consists of. Moreover, Muñoz believes that such an alternative understanding of the everyday can—potentially at least—alter the way the future will be lived. In his words, it signals "a queerness to come, a way of being in the world that is glimpsed through reveries in a quotidian life that challenges the dominance of an affective world, a present, full of anxiousness and fear" (25).

4

Despite his appreciation for the transcendent valences of the quotidian, it is arguably memory—particularly glimpses of the no-longer-conscious—that, for Muñoz, holds the most powerful "world-making potentialities" (2009, 35). This is one reason that his project intersects in such productive ways with Love's more explicitly backward-looking project. And it is also why it overlaps with recent accounts of melancholia, such as Eng's (2010) analysis of racial melancholia, despite the fact that melancholia, on the surface, may seem like the very antithesis of utopian thinking in the sense that the melancholic cannot by definition get interested in the future. As Freud (1917) already maintained, the melancholic copes with his or her loss by incorporating the lost object into his or her psyche, thereby transforming a loss in the external world into an internal possession, with the result that the psyche, for the time being, becomes closed to new objects; it becomes closed, precisely, to the future. The memory of the lost object, as it were, crowds out the possibility of new affective ties, which is why, for instance, the melancholic finds it hard to cathect to a new love object when he is still mourning a lost one.

Freud explains that this predicament is partly due to the ambiguous nature of the loss in question: the melancholic knows whom he has lost—knows the identity of the person who is no longer available—but not "what" he has lost in that person. In other words, the melancholic is mourning not just the loss of a given person but also the affective promises that this person offered but that have now irrevocably vanished. The melancholic's grief, in short, arises in part from the fact that he will (now) never know what he *could have had* with the person who has been lost; it is the loss of future possibility—as well as the promise of plenitude and wholeness that the loved object tends to contain—that is so painful. A loved person's death, for example, is devastating in part because we know that we can never have another conversation, another interpersonal encounter, with that person, so that what has been lost, along with the person, is the bit of life we could have had with this person.

How, then, can utopia and melancholia be reconciled? I have already started to answer this question by emphasizing that both utopia and melancholia are modalities of opting out of an unsatisfying present, utopia by looking forward, and melancholia by looking backward. But Julia Cooper offers a more precise explanation when she writes:

The melancholic knows that what she has lost is never to return, but by restaging its return through dream, thought, and fantasy, is able to engage anew with what is perpetually absent. Likewise, she who believes in utopia knows that her ideal society will never actualize, but by insisting on its necessity and charting its tenets and principles, engages with the nothingness of utopia. . . . Utopian thinking requires a leap of faith that surely it would be easier and more comfortable *not* to take, and melancholia demands a fidelity that is without a doubt exhausting.

(2016, 72)

In Cooper's view, utopia entails a demanding leap of faith in relation to an ideal that will never materialize whereas melancholia entails a demanding, even exhausting, fidelity to what will never return. Both are ways of cathecting to a place of impossibility, of insisting on the affective necessity of what is absent: for utopia, the absence in question is the not-yet-present (an ideal future) whereas for melancholia it is the no-longer-present (the lost object or ideal).

This shared insistence on the nonnegotiable value of what is lacking is what places utopia and melancholia on the same conceptual map.

I would merely add that what makes Muñoz's utopianism particularly compatible with efforts to theorize the politico-ethical potential of melancholia, such as Eng's analysis of racial melancholia, is the complex temporal structure that I have outlined, namely, that Muñoz's utopianism nostalgically looks to the past for the raw materials from which a better future can be fashioned. In other words, Muñoz, like Eng, believes that residues of the past can alter the parameters of the future in ways that carry politico-ethical significance.

In drawing this analogy, I do not mean to suggest that Eng seeks to translate melancholia into political or ethical action in any straightforward sense. If anything, inasmuch as melancholia indexes the affective register of being stuck in sadness, it—like the bad feelings Love describes—resists such translation. Nevertheless, Eng highlights the politico-ethical valences of the melancholy subject's refusal to relinquish its most cherished objects or ideals. As he explains: "The melancholic's absolute refusal to relinquish the lost other—to forfeit alterity—at any cost delineates one psychic process of an ethical death drive in which the loved but lost racial object or ideal is so overwhelmingly important to the ego that it is willing to preserve it even at the cost of its psychic health" (2010, 157).

The "ethical death drive" that Eng presents here is very different from the one advocated by Edelman, for it bypasses the solipsistic loop of self-shattering jouissance by placing an emphasis on the subject's faithfulness to objects and ideals that are deemed so precious that the subject is willing to preserve them even at the cost of its psychic health. The parallels between this formulation and my formulation of Lacan's ethics of desire—an ethics centered on the persistent affective imprint of the lost Thing—should be immediately discernible: in the same way that the specificity of desire, in my formulation, introduces an ethical code that differentiates between objects that reverberate on the frequency of the lost Thing and others that do not (or that only pretend to do so), melancholia, in Eng's formulation, introduces an ethical code that values lost objects and ideals over the subject's own ego. Eng's reading also resonates with Lacan's interpretation of Antigone as an ethical actor who rates her own survival lower than her duty to her dead brother. In all of these instances, the subject, unlike the Edelmanian ethical subject, is motivated by a fierce loyalty to what has been lost.

Eng analyzes melancholia as a collective racial formation among Asian Americans specifically:

> To the extent that Asian Americans are perpetually consigned to foreigner status and continue to be considered eccentric to the U.S. nation-state, and to the extent that ideals and standards of whiteness remain unattainable for them, it might be said that Asian Americans are denied the capacity to invest in new people, places, and ideals. . . . Racial melancholia thus describes a psychic condition by which vexed identification and affiliations with lost objects, places, and ideals of Asianness, as well as whiteness, remain estranged and unresolved.
>
> (2010, 115–116)

Eng thus identifies two related causes of Asian American racial melancholia: on the one hand, an ambivalent identification with ideals of whiteness that remain forever out of reach, and that consequently undercut the Asian American subject's sense of cultural belonging and, on the other, a perhaps equally ambivalent identification with lost ideals of Asianness. This is how melancholia, in Eng's view, can become "a normal everyday group experience" (121). Within this framework, melancholia no longer signifies a psychic pathology but is best understood as a reasonable response to social exclusion.

The matter is further complicated by the fact that neoliberal multiculturalism seeks to deny the realities of racism by insisting that we live in a postracial society. Eng explains that the "stuttering logic" of multicultural colorblindness *"goes something like this: we are all different, but we are all the same too . . . but it doesn't really matter"* (2010, 117). This logic erases the racialized subject's capacity to address the various ways in which "it" does actually matter, thereby merely deepening this subject's malaise. In this sense, Asian American melancholia is an indicator of the extent to which social problems such as racism can be privatized, banished to the individual psyches of those who, for reasons that they cannot always identify, feel bad. This in turn absolves the collectivity of any responsibility for these bad feelings, which can be construed as individual failures. In this manner, political problems become personal ones, silently borne by subjects who may not even always be fully aware of their social origins.

Eng renders his analysis concrete by discussing melancholia in the context of Korean female adoptees, calling attention to the psychic complexity of situations where Korean birth parents and cultural ideals—many of whom/which were lost so early that they only persist as fantasmatic ghosts, as inchoate traces, in the psyches of the adoptees—are replaced by middle-class white parents and cultural ideals. In such cases, melancholia can arise not only from the often unnameable losses of cultural dislocation but also from the adoptee's inability to ever fully embody the white ideals that surround her. The Korean girl may be assimilated into her new family, she may feel part of the family, but she is also, due to racial difference, always to some degree othered.

Furthermore, the situation of transnational adoptees is doubly challenging because their grieving is, by necessity, done in isolation rather than in immigrant families. Indeed, the adoptive family may find it difficult to recognize, let alone empathize with, the adoptee's sadness for the simple reason that, from their perspective, everything is (or should be) fine. The adoptee has been "rescued" and successfully delivered to her white middle-class environment, with the result that, as Eng states, her new family "cannot easily conceive of her adoption as involving loss," "cannot easily imagine her arrival in the United States as anything but an 'unequivocal gain'" (2010, 122).

Eng further observes that one reason Asian girls are particularly popular among white American couples may be that the stereotype of the meek Asian girl promises an adoption process that is hassle-free: the girl is expected to assimilate without difficulty. Needless to say, this puts pressure on the adoptee to play her part, to show no signs of discontent, thereby depriving her of a much-needed space to grieve whatever it is that she has lost (her birth parents, country, culture, and so on). Eng is not trying to demonize white adoptive parents—many of whom are obviously well meaning—but merely to elucidate a structural problem that arises when racial inequalities meet socioeconomic global inequalities in ways that generate taxing affective economies for transnational adoptees. In such scenarios, any sign of grief on the part of the adoptee can be read as ungratefulness, for nothing signals a lack of appreciating more clearly than being depressed when one is expected to be happy; the sad adoptee is, in a way, betraying the pact of happiness that her new family is counting on. As a result, Eng notes, there can be an unstated "affective embargo" against grieving that may cause the adoptee to slip into silent melancholia (2010, 123).

5

Given Eng's poignant account of the ethical death drive that animates melancholia, I find it noteworthy that it is Edelman's version of the death drive that routinely gets equated with queer rebellion (even by those who disagree with it). As a matter of fact, my experience in teaching Eng's analysis of racial melancholia has been that students often struggle to see its relevance to queer theory. Though there are many ways in which I could defend the "queerness" of Eng's text, ranging from its critique of neoliberal heteronormativity and homonormativity to its dexterous treat-ment of the nexus of capitalism, racialization, kinship, and gender in the lives of transnational adoptees, I want to pause on the fact that queer theory has—wittingly or not—drawn its parameters in such a way that it is easier for my students to discern the queerness of Edelman's death drive than that of Eng's. Although it is possible to argue, as I have done in this book, that bad feelings such as melancholia can be just as much a matter of opting out of neoliberal capitalist heteronormativity as Edelman's self-shattering jouissance, it appears that the latter has come to be regarded as virtually synonymous with queer defiance. Ironically, this may—and here we arrive at one of the limits of theories that promote self-annihilation—be because it remains largely metaphorical, because it offers an exciting depiction of something that few people actually experience (for longer than a fleeting moment).

I have already expressed my deep skepticism regarding the matter. In the present context, it also seems relevant to interrogate the fact that while earlier thinkers, such as Leo Bersani (1995), followed Lacan (1972–1973) in aligning jouissance with femininity, Edelman masculinizes the concept, stripping it of its customary feminine intonation. Indeed, it may well be this masculinization of jouissance that most bothers me about Edelman's appropriation of Lacanian ethics. And it may also be why I resist Fou-cault's notion of desubjectivation. It seems to me that, in both instances, beneath the image of the self-shattering, self-pulverizing subject lurks the image of a subject *who is brave enough, valiant enough, and strong enough* to undertake such acts of self-shattering and self-pulverization—that is, a (conventionally) masculinist image of the subject.

The Edelmanian and Foucauldian models of self-undoing both presuppose a robust subject who is tough enough to risk utter ontological instability; they are both characterized by a backhanded heroism, not the heroism of a subject who insists on the truth of its desire—as the Lacanian subject of the act does—but rather the heroism of a subject who is able to *endure its own death* (a bit like Jesus). Perhaps it truly is the case that, for (some) white men, the only way to lose their autonomy is to beg God to take it away (which is one way to understand Lacanian jouissance). As David Halperin admits, courting self-shattering abjection may be the privilege of white gay male subjects who are seeking to take a vacation from their will (to power) (2007, 97). Be this as it may, Eng's melancholic—though also expressing something about the subject's intimate encounter with the death drive—seems to fall short of the queer allure of Edelman's muscular antihero.

I wonder about the degree to which this has to do with the feminization of Asian Americanness that Eng (2001) has treated in his earlier work. Likewise, I wonder about the degree to which it has to do with the general denigration of femininity within queer theory. In other words, if Edelman's sinthomosexual appears so gallantly queer in contrast to Eng's melancholic, it is in part precisely because it has evaded the mark of femininity. Let's face it: queer theory tends to align queerness with masculinity, including the masculinity of female-bodied people. I am not saying that it does not talk about femininity, for it does so incessantly, and usually offensively—a theme I return to shortly—but merely that it has not been very successful at envisioning what queer femininity might look (or feel) like.

To be sure, "feminine" men, and even some femmes, find their way onto the pages of queer theory, but usually only as supporting actors to its masculine superheroes (who are by no means always men). Even more disturbingly, queer theory recycles misogynistic tropes of femininity that it—seemingly without much critical distance—lifts from mainstream straight culture, which is why it repeatedly aligns femininity with masochism, passivity, submission, abjection, humiliation, mortification, and "receptivity" (whatever the hell that means). This alignment is so pervasive that one must ask why queer theory, which has made a point of deconstructing more or less every naturalized myth of our society, *persists in fetishizing more or less every naturalized myth about femininity that our*

culture has managed to produce, including the idea that there is something
intrinsically masochistic about female sexuality.

A generous reading of Edelman would argue that he masculinizes the
figure of the sinthomosexual in order to sidestep this association of femininity with masochism. But I am more inclined to believe that he masculinizes the figure in order to avoid the taint of masochism (which remains
with the excluded feminine): the sinthomosexual accesses jouissance in a
courageous rather than masochistic register. I find it equally impossible
to offer a generous reading of queer theory's general alignment of femininity with masochism, passivity, submission, and so on. Such a reading
would take queer theory at its word when it claims that this alignment is
not degrading because, within the field, masochism is glorious, passivity is
fabulous, submission is just another name for sublimity, and so on. But I
am not persuaded, not the least because queer theory's depictions of femininity always in the final analysis seem to come back to a brute biological
equation of femininity with "penetrability." That is, much of queer theory
jumps from the fact that women have vaginas to the bizarre but pervasive
notion that lesbians and gay men who allow themselves to be penetrated
are automatically "feminized" (whereas lesbians and gay men who do the
penetrating are automatically "masculine").

There are of course various attempts among gay men to flee this stain
of femininity. The barebackers Tim Dean (2009) studied, for instance,
find a way to translate the "abjecting" process of receiving dicks—the
more the merrier—into a sign of virility. But the effort that goes into this
translation—as well as the vehemence with which the translation is insisted
on—merely proves that gay culture, like much of queer theory, is still
haunted by the following (maddeningly conventional) logic: women are
penetrated, and because women are feminine, gay men who are penetrated
are also feminine (whereas lesbians who do not allow penetration are masculine), and with penetration comes masochism, passivity, submission, and
so on because . . . well, penetration is a form of violation, so that whoever
is penetrated is automatically victimized.

When it comes to "femininity," much of queer theory sounds like the
early Catherine MacKinnon. All of the field's attempts to flip things around
by recoding masochism, passivity, submission, and so on as desired sexual-
affective states have not managed to change the fact that the field clings to
a naturalized chain of reasoning that links penetrability to femininity and

femininity to victimization, that it continues to rely on a binary of masculine aggression and feminine capitulation that even many straight people these days find hopelessly outdated. In reading queer theory, one gets the impression that having/using a dick to penetrate somehow automatically renders one an aggressor and not having/using a dick to penetrate automatically renders one a victim. But really, who, besides missionary-style Christians and prominent queer theorists, thinks about sexuality in such starkly gendered terms in the twenty-first century? What does it matter who puts his/her dick where? Why is the one who is penetrated dominated, rendered "passive," "emasculated," and so on?

6

To be clear, I am not arguing that queer theory should talk about femininity in more laudatory terms (though that would be nice too); rather, I am saying that it should stop envisioning queer sexuality through gendered imagery borrowed from the straight culture of the 1950s (the butch-femme subculture of that era may have had good reasons for doing so but contemporary queer theory surely does not). At this point in the theoretical game, queer theory's depictions of "feminine" masochism, passivity, submission, and so on sound like a flimsy excuse for misogyny. And they also sound like an equally flimsy excuse for dissociating queer theory from feminism. Worse still, they can be used to redefine feminism *as* masochism, passivity, submission, and so on, as Halberstam insists on doing.

Halberstam calls his new feminism "shadow feminism," which should already raise our eyebrows, given that shadows do not have a great deal of world-altering power. Halberstam strategically relies on the powerful signifiers of "Mahmood" and "Spivak" to establish the foundations of this shadow feminism:

When feminist freedoms, as Mahmood shows, require a humanistic investment in both the female subject and the fantasy of an active, autonomous, and self-activating individualism, we have to ask who the subjects and objects of feminism might be, and we need to remember that, as Spivak puts it, to speak on behalf of someone is also to "restore the sovereign subject within the theory that seems most to question it."

(2011, 129–130)

We are here back at the all-too-predictable—to me tedious in its utter inevitability—critique of the "active, autonomous, and self-activating" humanist subject. What is more, it turns out that it is *feminists* specifically who are the most arrogant supporters of this sovereign subject, nay, perhaps the most arrogant creatures in the world, erroneously promoting female "autonomy"—understood as a synonym for rampant individualism—rather than celebrating feminine masochism, passivity, and submission (as any genuinely radical critic surely should do).

Whether this is an accurate description of feminists, even of feminists of the "Anglo" denomination—who have in recent years been the objects of so much progressive-critical rancor that one gets the impression that they, rather than heteropatriarchy, are women's greatest enemy—is beyond the purview of this book (and a question I plan to take up in another project). But let us, for a moment, assume that female "autonomy"—a woman's capacity to make basic decisions about her life, such as whether or not she wants to marry, whether or not she wants to go to school, or whether or not she wants to have an abortion—is a core feminist concern. Are you, Jack Halberstam, seriously telling me that feminists should replace this agenda by one that promotes female self-destruction, including self-cutting? Apparently you are, given that you align feminism with "masochistic passivity" (2011, 131), "the art of sacrifice" (138), and "a spiral of pain and hurt" (144), announcing that "cutting is a feminist aesthetic proper to the project of female unbecoming" (135).

What the fuck? That is what I wrote on page 135 of *The Queer Art of Failure*. It seems to me that when feminism becomes defined as a matter of "female unbecoming," let alone of self-cutting, patriarchy truly has won. Though I understand how the challenges that Saba Mahmood (2011) and Gayatri Spivak (1988) have leveled against the idea that (Western) feminism should invariably promote (non-Western) female agency allow Halberstam to arrive at this vision of feminism, he pursues the critique to a place that the other two thinkers might hesitate to endorse. Mahmood, for example, writes in the preface to her analysis of the Egyptian women's piety movement—which Halberstam draws on—that her "point is not that the program of ethical self-cultivation pursued by the piety movement is 'good' or conducive to establishing relations of gender equality, or that it should be adopted by progressives, liberals, feminists, and others" (2011, xii). Likewise, I doubt that Spivak's objective in asking Western feminists to consider the complex reasons for which Indian widows might choose to commit suttee rather than to agitate for "autonomy" was to argue that feminists should model *themselves* after such widows. Halberstam, in contrast, appears to sketch the connection between feminism and masochism based on the dubious assumption that because feminism has to do with women, it automatically also has—or should have—something to do with masochism.

Halberstam may believe that, in making his argument about shadow feminism, he is undermining the sovereign humanist subject. But this ignores the fact that the humanist subject—*explicitly* coded as male (and straight)—has always relied on the image of the nonsovereign female (non)subject as its "natural" counterpart, so that Halberstam's "feminism" ultimately amounts to nothing more than heteropatriarchal business as usual. He is more or less telling feminists that they should accommodate—even embrace—the image of femininity produced by heteropatriarchy, which is, essentially, akin to telling antiracists that they should accommodate—even embrace—the denigrating image of racialized subjects produced by white supremacists.

Irigaray and Cixous may have gotten away with their metaphorical usage of "feminine" irrationality. And as I disclosed in chapter 3, I am willing to give Edelman the benefit of the doubt with regard to his "figure" of sinthomosexuality. But I cannot extend the same courtesy to Halberstam because his depiction of femininity and feminism does not come across as in the least bit metaphorical or figural: it is essentializing (toward femininity) and hostile (toward feminism other than the kind that remains content to lurk in the shadows)

Moreover, what makes Halberstam's argument doubly disturbing is that he approaches the theme of female masochism from the position of a voyeuristic witness: "We might . . . cast female masochism as the willing giving over of the self to the other, to power; in a performance of radical passivity we witness the willingness of the subject to actually come undone, to dramatize unbecoming for the other *so that the viewer does not have to witness unbecoming as a function of her own body*" (2011, 140; emphasis added). This wording is chilling: Halberstam positions himself as an observer who does not have to witness unbecoming in his own body because the female masochist generously dramatizes it through her "feminine" body, a body that is willingly—if passively—given over to the other and therefore "undone." One can only wonder about the fantasy of femininity as a site of masochistic unbecoming that is here activated by a queer critic who has chosen, in his previous work, to paint robust portraits of queer masculinity. I patiently read Halberstam's (1998) celebration of phallic (bullish) female masculinity in the book by that name despite the implicit disparagement of femininity that it contained because I understood that there were good theoretico-political reasons for its basic premise. But I am balking at his attempt to dump his fantasy of "feminine" masochism on those of us with "feminine" self-presentations or on "our" (erroneous because too arrogant in its attempt to defeat heteropatriarchy) feminism.

Halberstam's fetishization of feminine unbecoming takes on an even more troubling valence when one realizes that it is aimed primarily at brown female bodies. For instance, in the context of discussing visual art by female artists of color, Halberstam adds "disappearance" to the virtues of his shadow feminism, praising the landscapes of J. A. Nicholls for presenting "queer femininity as startling absence" (2011, 142). Kara Walker's work, in turn, according to Halberstam, represents "femininity as a blurring of the female form with the natural landscape and as a violent cutting out of the figure altogether" (142). Halberstam admires the work of these artists—as well as Yoko Ono's "Cut Piece"—for enacting a radical passivity that cleaves "to that which seems to shame or annihilate" so that, in the end, there are no female subjects in these works, but merely "gaping holes, empty landscapes, split silhouettes—the self unravels, refuses to cohere, it will not speak, it will only be spoken" (144).

One is reminded here of the basic feminist observation that women in heteropatriarchal society do not speak but are spoken (to). As to why this—along with the disappearance, absence, and "violent cutting out of the [female] figure altogether"—should become our new feminist ideal is a little difficult to grasp. It seems to me that, in this particular instance, as in so many others, the critique of the autonomous humanist subject misfires, creating the kind of collateral damage that seems unacceptable: the "war" against "the subject" does not, in my view, justify this particular battle.

Moreover, it seems to me that the art of Nicholls, Walker, and Ono is, among other things, a critical commentary on the silencing (and "cutting out") of femininity in patriarchal culture—a commentary that it, furthermore, takes a degree of agency to produce. To recast it as an endorsement of female disempowerment seems odd to say the least, given that offering a critical commentary on, say, abjection is not the same thing as condoning abjection. Quite the opposite, a critical commentary on abjection is often an attempt to call attention to a problem that needs addressing. On the whole, there is something—dare I say it?—"psychoanalyzable" about Halberstam's struggle to come to terms with femininity as what needs to be banished, as what needs to unravel, destroy itself, annihilate itself, and reduce itself to "a gaping hole." When the prescription of feminine masochism comes from a critic who shows no intention of adopting either femininity or masochism as a personal mantle, it pushes the burden of nonsovereignty onto bodies that have always been asked to carry it.

7

Halberstam's tribute to female masochism is a case in which the queer rhetoric of bad feelings becomes so excessive that it misses its mark, generating a conservative—profoundly heteropatriarchal and racist—effect. I have noted at various points in this book that it is the urge to ritualistically slay the sovereign subject that tends to produce such a hyperbolic pitch: the critic raises his or her knife even though the target has already bled to death.

This problem emerges particularly strongly in situations where the rhetoric of bad feelings becomes prescriptive rather than descriptive, as is the case with Halberstam: unlike Love, who analyzes queer shame as an affective reality that persists across historical time, or Eng, who analyzes melancholia as an Asian American racial formation, thereby illustrating the painful psychic predicament of those who have been dispossessed, Halberstam suggests that in order to be "good" (genuinely progressive rather than merely liberal) political subjects, feminists—and perhaps even all "feminine" women—*should be masochistic, passive, submissive, and so on*; as opposed to Love and Eng, who describe psychic phenomena of abjection in the hope that one day these phenomena might be superseded, Halberstam elevates abjection into a politico-ethical *goal*, suggesting that any feminist, any woman, who aspires to autonomy instead is not a "real" feminist but merely a puppet of the hegemonic system that produces dreams of unassailable sovereignty.

Frankly, I do not think that it is a coincidence that this sliding from description to prescription takes place in the context of feminism (and femininity) specifically: as I have asserted, queer theory tends to naturalize "feminine" abjection in ways that it does not naturalize other forms of abjection, with the result that it asks "feminine" men and women—who are furthermore also often racialized—to showcase abjection for the rest of the field. Masculine gay men seem to find it easier to flirt with "feminizing" abjection than masculine lesbians, perhaps because they are less worried about descending into femininity permanently; as I observed earlier, they can sometimes even turn the abjection of femininity into a badge of honor. But this in no way alters queer theory's overall coding of femininity as "naturally" abjected (masochistic).

It is true that bad feelings can be politically subversive because they weaken the subject, thereby undermining its capacity to participate in the pragmatic ethos of productivity and cheerfulness that characterizes neoliberal capitalist society. At the same time, when the idiom of bad feelings becomes as indiscriminate as Halberstam's queer art of failure—which implies that every form of failure, including women's failure to exist, represents a queer victory—something of its theoretico-political power has been lost. Moreover, though bad feelings can compromise the happiness scripts of neoliberal capitalism, they can also be instrumentalized by capitalism, for—as I have conceded—capitalism is impressively adroit in turning attempts to resist its power into raw material for this very power.

Todd McGowan captures this dynamic perfectly when he argues that capitalism manages to transform every limit to its vitality into a new tool of revitalization, so that, for instance, the rebellious attire of those who have been pushed to the fringes of the capitalist order becomes the latest fashion craze, allowing the garment industry to reap unprecedented profits. As he argues:

What doesn't fit is just as necessary to the perpetuation of capitalism as what does. . . . To take the most obvious example, the style of baggy pants did not emerge in the Upper East Side of New York or from Paris but from street gangs. But it quickly spread to clothing production and provided untold millions in profit for manufacturers who undoubtedly scorned (and didn't socialize with) the gang members who started the trend.

(2016, 168)

These gang members, McGowan concludes, are every bit as integral to the capitalist system "as Donald Trump and Bill Gates" (168). It is demoralizing to realize that the same logic can be applied to bad feelings such as depression and anxiety: though these feelings can dampen a person's productivity, capitalism has found ways to make an immense profit from them anyway through the marketing of antidepressants, tranquillizers, psychotherapy, and self-help books. Likewise, "feminine" masochism may be Halberstam's solution to the flaws of liberal feminism but such masochism is widely marketed on the Internet, not only in mainstream pornography but also on social networking sites where young women compete to display their bleeding, anorexic, or otherwise suffering bodies to anyone who gets off on such bodies. Female self-cutting has even been incorporated into the plotline of the popular television show *The Affair*.

This way of looking at things poses a serious challenge to many of the queer strategies of opting out that I have outlined in this book. Even the disruptive power of desire that I have offered as a possible antidote to neoliberal conformity and efficiency can be folded back into the capitalist economy, as happens when Hollywood movies and mainstream television shows make a satisfying spectacle of the destabilizing effects of desiring in counterhegemonic ways. What is a more successful entertainment trope than a character whose "inappropriate" (or disappointed) desire destroys the fabric of his life, sending him into a crisis, and often even—usually temporarily—casting him into the role of a social pariah? From this viewpoint, capitalism knows how to turn even the truth event of love as Badiou (2001, 2012) has theorized it—love as an event that causes the kind of existential havoc, the kind of swerve in the usual course of life, that makes it impossible for the lover to keep living as he previously has—into a media display.

In acknowledging this quandary, I do not mean to retract what I have proposed about the subversive potential of counterhegemonic desire. Nor am I saying that there is no politico-ethical value to talking about bad feelings: as should be clear, I find the accounts of Muñoz, Eng, and Love constructive. Yet I am also feeling somewhat cautious about the pronounced emphasis on bad feelings within recent progressive theory, including queer theory. These days, so many critics—myself included—like to talk about bad feelings that it almost feels like bad feelings have become the virtuous feelings of critical theory (as I noted in the introduction, the bad feelings of queer theory have become its "good"—desirable—feelings). What worries me about this is that bad feelings can become a way for relatively privileged Western intellectuals to assume that they are doing something politically or ethically useful when in fact absolutely nothing is changing in the world: ruthless capitalism runs unchecked across the globe while we keep feeling sad and talking about the politico-ethical merits of feeling sad; feeling—in this case, feeling sad—becomes our sole way of dealing with questions of social justice.

The fetishization of bad feelings can obscure the fact that they do not necessarily transform anything, that they can even have a deeply depoliticizing impact. Consider Butler's (2004, 2009, 2012; Butler and Athanasiou 2013) ethics of precarity: according to this model, ethics arises from our capacity to empathize with the suffering of others, particularly from our ability to grieve the other who has in one way or another been violated; essentially, Butlerian ethics is based on the idea that our ability to feel bad about the fate of others will move us to act in support of these others. From a certain viewpoint, this is not very different from the Christian–humanitarian ethics that has long dominated mainstream ethical discourses in the West: it is because we recognize that the other is just as precarious, just as woundable, as we are that we are motivated to protect this other; if we can get to the point where the other's grief becomes our grief, then the other's outrage about her oppression also becomes our outrage, with the consequence that we may be willing to overlook the differences between ourselves and the other to intervene on behalf of this other.

There are alternative ways to arrive at the same conclusion, including our rational assessment (rights-based or not) that the other has been unjustly treated. But Butler is correct in suggesting that there is something viscerally powerful about the grief we feel when the other's vulnerability, particularly the other's bodily vulnerability, has been exploited. Accounts of genocide, torture, and rape, for instance, tend to move us even when we have no personal connection to the victims, which is precisely why Butler's call for a rethinking of grievability as a foundation for alleviating the power imbalances of the global order strikes a chord, why it is hard to deny her basic insight that there might be "something to be gained from grieving, from tarrying with grief, from remaining exposed to its unbearability and not endeavoring to seek a resolution for grief through violence" (2004, 30). Yet it is also possible that the rhetoric of grief functions as a distraction from political and economic solutions to global problems: to the degree that it allows us to experience ourselves as benevolent ethical subjects, subjects who are capable of feeling the appropriate remorse about the affliction of others, it can thwart political action; when feeling bad becomes a political intervention in its own right, no further intervention is deemed necessary.

Furthermore, inasmuch as progressive theory takes the deeply traumatized subject as its model for what subjectivity, *as such*, consists of—as I have remarked it tends to do—it risks losing track of the fact that some subjects are much more traumatized than others. On the one hand, affect theorists such as Ahmed, Berlant, and Cvetkovich have hugely enriched our vocabulary of bad feelings. On the other, it may be difficult to cast trauma as an ordinary, everyday occurrence, as Cvetkovich (2003, 2012) to some extent does, without in some ways watering down the very notion of traumatization.

I do not mean to suggest that Cvetkovich is mistaken in trying to deconstruct the distinction between acute, highly visible forms of traumatization and more subtle—and therefore often less visible—forms of traumatization. For instance, she is right to call attention to the continuities between, say, rape and more ongoing scenarios of sexism and sexual abuse. I am also moved by her personal narrative of middle-class depression in *Depression*. It is valuable to understand the ways in which even bourgeois subjects can fracture under the pressure of the neoliberal capitalist performance principle and its related utilitarian endeavors; it is valuable to see the paralyzing effects of late capitalist modernity on lives that, in principle, "should work." Moreover, Cvetkovich is surely right to interpret depression as an affective predicament that is often socially induced and therefore not reducible to a private pathology. In this sense, her project shares a great deal with Eng's endeavor to read racial melancholia as a depathologized structure of feeling that arises from collective rather than purely individual circumstances.

My graduate students have also profited immensely from Cvetkovich's analysis of the connection between the pressures of the neoliberal academy and depression, coming to recognize the ways in which their malaise emerges, in part at least, from a corporate academic culture characterized by immense competitiveness. At the same time, Cvetkovich's efforts to capture "the everyday life of trauma" (2003, 20), the way trauma structures life within modern capitalist societies, risks rendering the concept of trauma so capacious that it becomes virtually meaningless. That is, I am not entirely sure that trauma and capitalist modernity can be argued to be "mutually constitutive categories" (17), for I am not convinced that we live in a moment of history that is somehow *uniquely* traumatizing; I am not convinced that life under modern neoliberal capitalism is intrinsically more traumatizing than, say, life during the Middle Ages (let alone during the Middle Passage).

8

The conviction that life under modern neoliberal capitalism is uniquely traumatizing—that things have never been as bad as they are now—has become one of progressive theory's darling ideas. This stance can be traced back to Foucault's *The Birth of Biopolitics* (1978-1979), which posits that the rise of (neo)liberalism—which regards the individual's "freedom" as its highest value—is accompanied by forms of biopolitical regulation that compromise the subject's freedom all the more insidiously because they are largely undetectable. As Foucault explains, the paradox of (neo)liberal governmentality is that the only way it can produce "freedom" is by micromanaging the context within which the subject can be "free." On the one hand, "Liberalism formulates simply the following: I am going to produce what you need to be free. I am going to see to it that you are free to be free" (63). On the other, this production of freedom demands a high level of "organization of the conditions in which one can be free," with the result that it "entails the establishment of limitations, controls, forms of coercion, and obligations relying on threats, etcetera"; liberalism, in short, introduces "additional freedom through additional control and intervention" (63–64, 67).

Foucault goes on to elaborate on the various ways in which liberalism constrains individuals in order to (seemingly) uphold their freedom, touching, among other things, on the rise of a political culture that emphasizes the dangerousness of everyday life, a culture that encourages hypervigilance on the part of individuals who perceive themselves to be in constant danger. One can see how this idea resonates with contemporary theoretical insights about the centrality of terror in Western political discourse as well as with Tim Dean's (2009) discussion of the increasing management of health that characterizes our society (see chapter 1). Generally speaking, Foucault is convincing in his analysis of the biopolitical forces of regulation that bring the liberal *homo economicus*—a creature that applies the logic of entrepreneurship to every aspect of its life—into existence.

I do not object to these general outlines of Foucault's argument, which have become as commonplace in queer theory as they are in progressive critical theory, broadly understood. But where I part ways with Foucault is when he states:

Mechanisms of economic intervention have been deployed to avoid the reduction of freedom that would be entailed by transition to socialism, fascism, or National Socialism. But is it not the case that these mechanisms of economic intervention surreptitiously introduce types of intervention and modes of action which are *as harmful to freedom as the visible and manifest political forms one wants to avoid*?

(1978–1979, 69; emphasis added)

Foucault here suggests that the economic constraints of liberalism are just as bad as the political constraints of overtly repressive regimes such as fascism, that the restrictions on freedom that liberalism undertakes in order to "protect" freedom—in order to avoid the reduction of freedom that would result from a transition to nonliberal systems such as fascism—are just as harmful as the restrictions of fascism would be.

That Foucault includes socialism in his list of alternative systems may complicate matters somewhat, but what I want to focus on is the absurdity of arguing that people living in (neo)liberal democracies are as oppressed as people living in a fascist political system. More specifically, what interests me is what happens when progressive critics, including queer theorists, apply this line of thought to contemporary global politics. Usually they follow Foucault's reasoning about biopolitical control being so pervasive and deeply rooted that it determines every aspect of our being. This in turn all too easily results in the—to me, utterly nonsensical—notion that those of us in the Western world are up against the most repressive regime of human history, that disciplinary power has never been as all-encompassing as it is during our own era.

Wendy Brown's critique of the "choices" that Western women appear to have in comparison to some of their non-Western counterparts is representative of the trend I am referring to. In *Regulating Aversion*, Brown asks:

What makes choices "freer" when they are constrained by secular and market organizations of femininity and fashion rather than by state or religious law? Do we imagine the former to be less coercive than the latter because we cling to the belief that power is only and always a matter of law and sovereignty, or, as Foucault put it, because we have yet to "cut off the king's head in political theory?"

(2006, 189)

Brown asks these questions in the context of arguing that the biopolitical control that motivates American teenage girls to favor skimpy clothing—what Brown calls "the nearly compulsory baring of skin" (189)—is just as oppressive as the veiling of women in some Islamic societies. The matter is debatable and finally, for me, comes down to whether women in either system have the right (and practical capacity) to exit its demands, as American teenage girls arguably have more strongly than women in societies where religion mandates veiling as a compulsory part of female attire: American teen girls will not be banished from the streets for wearing loose pants and a turtleneck instead of a miniskirt and a bra-top. Nevertheless, I am willing to concede that the distinction between biopolitical manipulation and religious law blurs in this instance.

However, I balk at Brown's attempt to suggest—later in the same chapter of *Regulating Aversion* (2006, 196–199)—that the biopolitical forces that drive Western women to seek out cosmetic plastic surgery are no worse (or at least not much worse) than the more visible forms of heteropatriarchal control that, say, cause some women in some non-Western societies to undergo female genital mutilation (FGM). I understand Brown's impulse to protect non-Western societies against the charges of "backwardness" by asserting that Western cultures are just as heteropatriarchal as non-Western cultures. I am aware that in the same way that queer exceptionalism can portray the Western queer subject as uniquely free, the West, including the American government, has co-opted feminism in the service of claiming that the West is "exceptionally" egalitarian and respectful of its women. At the same time, it feels to me that in leveling the distinction between biopolitical control and overt cultural or religious restrictions, Brown is, at least in the context of plastic surgery, activating a hyperbolic discourse about the oppressiveness of biopolitics. After all, my refusal to get a boob job will not bar me from participating in collective life; it may cost me a few dates—and not just with men—but it will not render me a social outcast. Nor will it rob me of the capacity for sexual pleasure, as some of the more extreme forms of FGM do.

My response to claims such as Brown's—which are common in contemporary feminism, particularly queer feminism—is always the same: I would rather live in contemporary America, where my (female) subjectivity is manipulated by a host of biopolitical forces, including a culture industry that brainwashes me to obsess about my attractiveness, than in nineteenth-century England, where I would have been the legal property of my father or husband. In other words, there is, for me, a big difference between "sovereign" power that robs people of basic rights on the one hand and biopolitical control that guides us to certain life choices, including the happiness narratives that Ahmed analyzes, on the other. If we deny this difference, we end up suggesting that the changes in Western women's lives since the nineteenth century mean nothing; we end up implying that things like women's right to vote, work, go to school, get a divorce, and get an abortion—and, yes, to wear skimpy clothing if they happen to feel like it— have no value whatsoever.

Let me be precise: I agree that, globally speaking, our current capitalist system is perhaps the most oppressive political and economic system the world has ever witnessed; I agree that the ruthlessness with which Western capitalism exploits the resources, including the human resources, of the non-Western world is deplorable (though I am not certain it is worse than the exploitation of African Americans during slavery). However, I do not think that the biopolitical management of Western subjects—who tend to be the beneficiaries of global capitalism even when they oppose it politically— renders such subjects the most afflicted people in the history of the world.

Nor do I believe that secular Western women are just as controlled as women who live in societies that place overt legal and religious restrictions on women's equality. They are also not as tightly controlled as Western women living in deeply Christian communities. Progressive critics who argue that there is no difference between secular and religious forms of control, and who posit that (secular) legal rights are meaningless in the face of biopolitical control, appear to have forgotten about the staggering constraints that Christianity has historically placed on women and female sexuality. As Diane Enns writes with a refreshing degree of raw feminist sentiment: "Arrogance is the gift of a male God, passed down through the generations from father to son. Christianity inherited the prejudices of Greek philosophy against the body, against woman, against the world of the here and now" (2016, 26–27).

Because I agree with Enns, I have never been persuaded by the currently popular line of progressive reasoning that—fanned by Carl Schmitt (2005), Derrida (2005), and Agamben (2011)—insists that Western secularism is merely Christianity in disguise; though I agree that there are continuities between Christianity and modern secularism, I do not want to lose track of the fact that a great deal has also changed for the better. Nor can I see any way to absolve other monotheistic religions, such as Islam, of the charge of heteropatriarchy.

Attempts to do so usually arise from a laudable wish to defeat Western imperialism. But they frequently end up sounding like apologies for non-Western heteropatriarchy, like Brown's commentary on FGM arguably also does. In such instances, where the anti-imperialist struggle trumps the feminist struggle, the Western progressive, sadly, breaks rank with non-Western women (and men) who would like to see practices such as FGM abolished; she casts her lot with non-Western male elites—and the traditions that sustain these elites—rather than with feminist and other progressive efforts to defeat such elites. The illogical effect of this is that the very same critic who believes that marginalized Western subjects should opt out of hegemonic culture ends up implying that marginalized non-Western subjects—including women—should *opt into* their respective cultures in the name of cultural preservation.

I mentioned in the previous chapter that, from a biopolitical perspective, "rights" are merely a ruse of disciplinary power: a means of interpellating potentially unruly subjects into the normative fabric of the dominant social order. This attitude is obviously at the heart of the queer theoretical critique of gay marriage that I have outlined. But queer theory, including queer feminism, can overstate the oppressiveness of biopolitics to the degree that it disregards the various ways in which rights can be mobilized in the service of social justice.

Interestingly, Brown herself recognizes the problem in *Edgework* (2005), which was published just a year before the arguments I have just summarized. In this earlier text, Brown delineates the tension between critical legal theorists who—like many queer theorists—see rights legislation as a means of increasing state control over individual lives on the one hand and critical race theorists who view equal rights as a means of displacing culture- and tradition-bound forms of injustice on the other. As Brown explains, "While critical legal theorists tend to regard rights as entrenching and masking inequality, many critical race theorists have figured rights as vital symbols of personhood and citizenship, as the very currency of civil belonging in liberal constitutional orders" (125). Brown continues as follows:

> More interesting than brokering this debate in terms of the relative validity of arguments is recognizing what each argument makes visible that the other does not. The neo-Marxist perspective of the critical legal theorists emphasizes the convergence of formal legal equality with the tendency of other liberal capitalist discourses to naturalize class inequality and the social powers constitutive of class, including those powers conferred by legal rights. The histories of slavery and the civil rights movement out of which arises the critical race theory position, in contrast, emphasize the extent to which rights discourse historically has designated who does and does not count as a member of human society: if rights signal personhood, then being without them is not merely to be without a concrete asset, but to lack the less tangible but equally essential degree of civic belonging they confer.
>
> (125–126)

While the critical legal theoretical stance renders visible the role of rights legislation in perpetuating class injustice in liberal capitalist societies, the critical race theoretical stance emphasizes the value of rights in countering racist practices of marginalization and dehumanization. As Brown notes, the matter is further complicated by the fact that often these two forms of injustice impact the same subject, by the fact that class and race inequalities tend to converge. Brown goes on to assert that the same contradiction operates in the context of gender, "where both socio-economic deprivation and dehumanization operate as part of what constitutes women as such" (2005, 126). As a result, "clearly women need the 'rights of man' in order to establish their place in humanity, yet, as countless feminist theorists have also pointed out, these same rights will not only fail to address but will mask many of the substantive ways in which women's subordination operates" (126).

Even though Brown is (justifiably) skeptical of the ability of legal rights to address either racism or sexism, she here recognizes that "clearly women need the 'rights of man' in order to establish their place in humanity." In *Regulating Aversion*, in contrast, she seems to suggest that since we cannot stop cosmetic surgery in the West, it would be hypocritical (not to mention imperialist) to try to make non-Western FGM illegal. To me, this is like saying that because we cannot stop racist employment practices, we might as well go back to (legal) segregation. Obviously, "rights" are a partial solution at best. But pushing the critique of biopolitics so far as to propose that rights are invariably an insidious form of neoliberal governmentality implies that there was no point to abolishing slavery (because, look, it did not end racism) or that there was no point to women's suffrage (because, look, it did not end sexism).

In my more cynical moments, I suspect that the moaning that Western progressives do about how everything sucks in the West—their complaints about biopolitics, bad feelings, and cosmetic surgery—can be a way to avoid feeling guilty about the fact that many Western lives, particularly the lives of those who can afford cosmetic surgery, do not actually suck that much. This is not to deny that there are plenty of severely marginalized subjects in the West. But the complaining I see about biopolitical control, middle-class precariousness, cruel optimism, feeling depressed, feeling anxious, feeling ashamed, and feeling pressured to go under the plastic surgeon's knife does not usually apply to such subjects.

I am not saying that we should stop being critical of biopolitics. But I think that we should be aware of the possibility that the intensity of the critiques that have recently been leveled against it may be yet another version of what Sedgwick diagnosed as a paranoid hermeneutics of suspicion: an interpretive practice that distrusts the surface of things, actively digs for hegemonic intent, and flees from all surprises because the worst that could happen would be for the critic to be duped by ideology. This approach easily finds tyranny even in places that are relatively devoid of it.

Speaking personally for a moment, I can honestly say that—despite my bouts of depression, anxiety, exhaustion, and other middle-class insecurities—I am not an oppressed subject in the same way as I was when growing up in poverty. This may be why I experience some of progressive theory's incessant grumbling regarding biopolitics and other modalities of hegemonic power as a bit self-indulgent. One might even wonder whether queer theory's pronounced rhetoric of failure, abjection, masochism, depression, and general neoliberal malaise might not, on some level, be a means of overcompensating for the relatively high institutional success that it has enjoyed since 1990.

Another way to express the matter is to say that progressive theory's hatred of the sovereign subject can lead to an insistent identification with the role of the passive victim: because agency, autonomy, and responsibility have been maligned to the point that they are entirely unpalatable as personal attributes, critics are looking for "proof" of paralyzing victimization even in the contexts of lives that are arguably fairly comfortable. Because the last thing anyone wants to be is an empowered "individual"—such a creature having been declared the epitome of evil—everyone is trying to find ways to be a sufferer, a wounded being whose existence is threatened by a whole host of invisible biopolitical forces. That these forces are invisible is convenient because when there is nothing concrete to attack, the discourse of victimization can run in circles ad infinitum: we may not know exactly what the problem is but we know it could hardly be worse. Unfortunately, when everyone is a victim, no one is.

Ironically, in the background of all this complaining hovers the very idea that queer theory has been so critical of, namely, that a perfect world—in this case, a world without bad feelings, a world without any form of biopolitical manipulation—might one day materialize. As McGowan (2016) points out, this is how even anticapitalist theoretical approaches end up replicating capitalism's promise of eventual fulfillment, of a future with no lack, scarcity, limitation, or regulation; the very conviction that everything sucks implies that a solution is hiding somewhere in the midst of all the confusion, that with the right kind of exertion (the right kind of critical acumen) we might be able to arrive at a place where things would no longer suck. Of course, like capitalism, progressive theory would instantly collapse if such a place were ever to actually be found.

As a consequence, at least when it comes to bad feelings, we might benefit from recalling the Lacanian formulation I have already resorted to a couple of times: there is no Sovereign Good. Though many of our bad feelings are generated by an unjust world—and hence open to theoretico-political intervention—a degree of feeling bad defines the human condition. The harshness of this conclusion may explain why Lacanian analysis never thrived in happiness-saturated America. Fair enough. I can see why most people would rather go to a therapist who promises to make them feel better than one who tells them that she is going to reconcile them to their castration, including the fact that they will be likely to always feel a bit shitty. But is it possible that even American progressive critics cannot quite shed the idea that bad feelings represent a deviation from life rather than life itself?

9

Lacan's pronouncement regarding the lack of Sovereign Good does not mean that he offers no tools for thinking about bad feelings from a political and ethical perspective. Indeed, we have already seen that he regards Antigone's bad feelings as a platform for a politico-ethical intervention. But what is perhaps more interesting in the present context is what he suggests about the subject's traumatic encounter with the bad feelings of others. To grasp what I mean, it helps to recollect that when Lacan flatly rejected the Judeo-Christian injunction to "love thy neighbor," he stressed that the neighbor is "by its very nature alien, *Fremde*" (1959–1960, 52). The neighbor, in short, is too weird, too uncanny, to be lovable. This leads Lacan to articulate our ethical predicament as follows: "One would have to know how to confront the fact that my neighbor's *jouissance*, his harmful, malignant *jouissance*, is that which poses a problem for my love" (187).

Lacan therefore proposes that ethics does not ask that we love our neighbor—for we cannot—but rather that we come to terms with her characteristic approach to jouissance, with a jouissance that we may well experience as harmful or malignant. As Eric Santner explains, Lacanian ethics "means exposure not simply to the thoughts, values, hopes, and memories of the Other, but also to the Other's touch of madness, to the way in which the Other is disoriented in the world, destitute, divested of an identity that firmly locates him or her in a delimited whole of some sort" (2001, 81–82). That is, the other's disconcerting indecipherability does not arise only from the fact that her thoughts, values, hopes, and memories are different from ours but also from the fact that she is alien to herself—divested of a stable, clearly delineated identity—in the same way as we are to ourselves. This is why ethics, according to Santner, must confront the other's unique madness and existential confusion, "the always contingent . . . and, in some sense, demonic way in which he contracts a foothold in Being" (78).

In slightly different terms, when we discard the idea that we can learn to love our neighbor, ethics becomes a question of how we might be able to meet the other as a "real" entity rather than merely as a symbolic or imaginary construct. Žižek conveys the matter as follows:

We need the recourse to performativity, to the symbolic engagement, precisely and only insofar as the other whom we encounter is not only the imaginary *semblant*, but also the elusive absolute Other of the Real Thing with whom no reciprocal exchange is possible. In order to render our coexistence with the Thing minimally bearable, the symbolic order qua Third, the pacifying mediator, has to intervene . . . if the functioning of the big Other is suspended, the friendly neighbor coincides with the monstrous Thing (Antigone).

(2005, 144)

In our usual interactions with the other, we have recourse to symbolic structures of performativity and imaginary structures of identification: on the symbolic level, we relate to the other as a creature of signification and meaning production; on the imaginary level, we relate to the other as a fantasy object—or as a mirror image—that offers ego gratification. If this were the sum total of our relationship to the other, ethics would be easy, for we are usually relatively trained in the arts of communication and identification. Unfortunately, the other is also a "real" entity, an entity filled with monstrous jouissance, the kind of jouissance that bars communication and identification alike; the other as "real" does not make any sense.

From a Lacanian standpoint, this is where ethics must begin: the "real" ethical question, Lacan suggests, is not how we might manage to love our neighbor as someone we can communicate and identify with—as someone we can invite to our barbecue—but how we relate to the other as a bearer of jouissance, as someone whose pleasure and suffering cannot be processed through our symbolic or imaginary filters. On this understanding, an ethics that merely (benevolently) tolerates the other as a symbolic or imaginary entity is not strong enough, for it balks in the face of difference that feels too radically different. As long as communication and identification are possible, empathy—and the ethical response that may arise from empathy—is relatively simple. But when communication and identification fail, so does, all too easily, empathy. Such situations can give rise to deep ethical ambivalence.

This is why, from a Lacanian perspective, ethical paradigms based on empathy, such as Butler's ethics of precarity, fail to fully capture the ethical conundrum presented by the other. Simply put, whenever our symbolic and imaginary supports collapse, the other risks becoming overly proximate in its grotesque jouissance, thereby effectively neutralizing our capacity to empathize with its vulnerability. Is this not often, for instance, the Western liberal subject's response to the Islamic suicide bomber whose death-driven jouissance is, precisely, deemed too abhorrent to be tolerable?

The Butlerian response of feeling bad for the other—of grieving the other—is here challenged by the necessity of figuring out how to cope with the extremely bad feelings of this other, the kinds of bad feelings that are, precisely, deemed harmful and malignant (in being primarily destructive).

Articulated in less dramatic terms, Lacanian ethics asks us to relate to the utter singularity of the other as an entity who, like us, is fanatically driven to the traumatic groove of its drive destiny (its repetition compulsion). If there is any space for identification in this scenario, it takes place on the level of acknowledging that the other is just as crazy, just as irrational, as we are; what we identify with are not specific (symbolic or imaginary) attributes of the other but the fact that, like us, the other cannot fully control its destiny (but is rather to some extent controlled by this destiny, its singular "fate in the real").

By this I do not mean that we have no say over our destiny; in my earlier work (see Ruti 2013, 2015b) I have revealed that I am not persuaded by lines of reasoning—such as the one Butler follows in *Giving an Account of Oneself* (2005)—that suggest that our inner opacity, including our predicament of being motivated by unconscious passions, makes us incapable of taking responsibility for our actions. My point is merely that the other's jouissance, including its suffering, can render it so uncanny that we find it impossible to identify with it in the usual sense of the term, and that when this happens, the only thing that unites us with the other is our awareness of our own (comparable) uncanniness. More generally speaking, in post-Lacanian theory, Lacan's reflections on the other as "real," as an "alien" entity that ruptures the (always fantasmatic) coherence of our social world, have been recast as a political query about how we can ethically relate to what is most terrifying, overwhelming, off-putting, or repellent about the other. That is, the main ethical concern is no longer how we might manage to recognize others as our equals even when they hold different values—how we might build a viable "human" community out of radically divergent opinions and outlooks—but rather how we are (or are not) able to meet the seemingly "inhuman" (real) aspects of the other.

10

What is most innovative about the version of Lacanian ethics I have just delineated—which is quite different from both the ethics of the act and the ethics of desire that I have discussed throughout this book—is its emphasis on the idea that a properly ethical attitude must risk our symbolic and imaginary supports, must risk an encounter with the unsettling "real" of the other's being. On this view, ethics is no longer merely a matter of prudent interpersonal negotiations within the symbolic and imaginary registers but asks us to withstand the other's intrinsic strangeness. Within queer theory, an example of this approach can be found in Tim Dean's attempt to make a case for cruising as a relational modality that does not strive to domesticate the other's strangeness but rather relishes it as a source of erotic energy.

In his analysis of cruising, Dean asserts that it is neither the self nor the stranger who requires protection in the encounter between self and stranger but the stranger's otherness (his strangeness): "My 'getting to know him'—my genial effort to make the stranger more familiar—is partly what his otherness needs protection from" (2009, 179). Though Dean acknowledges that the encounter with the other is not invariably traumatizing, that it can also be pleasurable, he follows the Lacanian logic I have outlined in stressing that ethics demands an openness to the potentially traumatizing aspects of the other. Berlant and Edelman (2014) are getting at something similar when they argue that what persists after we separate sex from the optimistic fantasies of healing and self-actualization that tend to surround it is a destabilizing encounter with alterity that might be difficult to bear. I have admitted that I find the idea that the other's sexual proximity is "unbearable" somewhat unconvincing; it feels like an exaggeration. But I am willing to concede that it can (sometimes) be disconcerting.

Like Lacan, Dean suggests that an ethics based on recognition—an ethics based on the idea that we empathize with those we can identify with—does not go far enough, that ethics entails taking an interest in others even when we do not recognize ourselves in them, even when we cannot see anything of ourselves in them. This is why Dean's alternative to the usual "politics of identification" is "an impersonal ethics in which one cares about others even when one *cannot* see anything of oneself in them" (2009, 25). Dean aligns his impersonal ethics with the psychoanalytic practice of nonjudgmental listening, explaining that "the psychoanalytic rule of free association—'that whatever comes into one's head must be reported without criticizing it'—requires a suspension of judgment that permits different forms of thinking to emerge"; "the clinical practice of analysis depends on not pathologizing *any* desire" (2009, 28–29).

We know that analysis has not always lived up to this ideal, that in relation to nonnormative modes of sexuality in particular, it has frequently reverted to pathologizing judgments. But one might say that whenever this happens, the analyst is no longer doing analysis proper but lapsing into some other form of "therapeutic" practice. A competent analyst, after all, is trained to suspend judgment. Such an analyst does not deny that countertransference occurs. But she is self-aware enough to catch herself when it emerges. In the same way that the analysand may over time learn to detect the unconscious habits through which the repetition compulsion shapes her existence, the analyst becomes—should become—skilled at recognizing the intrusion of countertransferential judgments. If she fails at this, she fails at analysis.

At first glance, Dean's ethical approach may seem antithetical to the one Leo Bersani builds in his dialogue with Adam Phillips (Bersani and Phillips 2008): where Dean stresses the importance of caring about even those who seem entirely different from the self, Bersani wants to replace an ethics of difference by an ethics of sameness, proposing that if we refuse to approach others through the lens of their psychological particularity, or through categories such as race, ethnicity, gender, or nationality, we will discover that what is different about them is "merely the envelope of the more profound . . . part of themselves which is our sameness" (86). But the divergence of these visions turns out to be merely apparent in the sense that both promote impersonal ethics as an alternative to an ethics based on identification, Dean by urging us to care beyond difference, and Bersani by urging us to brush difference aside altogether (not coincidentally, caring beyond difference might amount to the same thing as brushing aside difference).

If the visions of Dean and Bersani ultimately converge, it is because both thinkers recognize what I alluded to earlier, namely that the demand for identification easily produces the opposite impulse to vehemently disidentify from what seems too different (monstrous). As Bersani explains, inasmuch as the ego is driven to bolster its power and narcissistic satisfaction by pitting itself against the rest of the world, it tends to turn every site of difference—every attribute of the other that it cannot easily identify with—into an enemy; the ego's need to demarcate and uphold the purity of its boundaries by excluding what defeats its capacity for identification becomes an excuse for murderous violence. The only antidote to this, according to Bersani, is an ethics predicated on "a universal relatedness grounded in the absence of relations, in the felicitous erasure of people as persons" (Bersani and Phillips 2008, 38).

If Dean tells us to take a nonjudgmental attitude toward those characteristics of others we cannot identify with, Bersani asks us to ignore these characteristics altogether; he asks us to stop fretting over difference, over people's idiosyncratic personalities, and to focus instead on what he calls their "virtuality" (the potentiality within them). This virtuality is what we share with others in the sense that, like them, we are always in the process of reaching toward an ideality of some kind; like others, we are constantly in the process of becoming something that we, at present, are *not* (but have the potential to become). Essentially, Bersani posits that we should identify with whatever is still absent—merely virtual—rather than already present in others so as to bypass the ego's tendency to become hostile toward presences that are perceived to be inassimilable to its economy and therefore threatening.

This does not mean that narcissism is erased but merely that it is rendered "impersonal": what the ego cathects to in the other is not its beautiful "content" (existing attributes) but rather its "form" as a container of virtuality (potentiality). This core idea here is analogous to the one I presented earlier regarding the other's uncanniness: Lacanian ethics does not ask us to identify with the specifics of the other's uncanniness but rather to acknowledge the equally disturbing presence of our own uncanniness, so that, again, it is not the (personal) content but the (impersonal) form of uncanniness that matters.

Dean likewise emphasizes the impersonality of his ethical paradigm, using terms that explicitly echo Bersani's call for a "felicitous erasure of people as persons." As Dean states, "I describe this ethics as 'impersonal' because it entails regarding the other as more than another person: it is not a question of discerning that 'sex-crazed killers' are people too but of basing ethics on the *failure* to identify others as persons and of seeing how otherness remains irreducible to other persons, as well as to social categories of difference" (2009, 25). In their distinctive ways, both Dean and Bersani thus advocate an indifference to difference, replacing the personal with the impersonal as a foundation of ethics.

It is interesting to consider the resonances between this ideal of impersonality and the centrality of anonymous sex to some gay male subcultures.

But I am even more interested in the fact that both Dean and Bersani seem to support the Lacanian insight that ethics based on identification does not go far enough. As Dean observes, "Enlarging my estimation of others until they seem as worthy of consideration as I seem to myself represents, in fact, a diminishment of otherness" (2009, 25). This is precisely Lacan's point about the ethical injunction to love thy neighbor: this injunction domesticates the other's alienness, with the consequence that when this alienness resurfaces, "love" washes away in a flood of aggression.

This formulation allows me to elaborate on the fleeting reference I made to Butler's ethics of precarity earlier in this chapter, for the difference between the impersonal paradigm that Dean and Bersani advocate and Butlerian ethics is this: if Butler places her faith in our capacity to empathize with the vulnerability of others—if her ethics remains an ethics that appeals to us as persons on behalf of other (suffering) persons—Dean and Bersani turn to the inhuman because they believe that our empathy is likely to falter the moment the other person no longer appears fully human, the moment the other person no longer meets our definition of what it means to be a person. This does not mean that Dean and Bersani are out to destroy "the subject" in the way that I have mocked at various points in this book. Rather, they start from the premise that the subject always includes seemingly "inhuman" intonations: intonations that render it too "real" in the Lacanian sense.

Simply put, like Lacan, Dean and Bersani are looking for ways to transcend the hostility that arises when the other ceases to make (symbolic and imaginary) sense. Or, to express the matter in yet another way, if Butler believes that it is possible to render the notion of the human capacious enough to include everyone, Dean and Bersani, like Lacan, assume that this attempt will inevitably fail, that some people will always fall outside the definition of the human. This is what leads Dean and Bersani to the trope of impersonality.

Notably, it also leads them to present universalist paradigms that challenge the ethical relativism characteristic of much of progressive theory. In marked contrast with multiculturalist and other difference-based accounts, both thinkers urge us to cut through the morass of differences— the countless attributes that separate us from others and that can cause us to regard others with a degree of suspicion—so as to focus on what we share with others: the inhuman frequencies of human life that often render us frighteningly awkward. Dean locates this inhumanness in the strange-ness of both self and other. Bersani locates it in virtuality. These notions, in turn, are related to other Lacanian (or psychoanalytic) terms that I have used in this book: jouissance, uncanniness, out-of-jointness, the repetition compulsion, and so on.

The biggest danger of universalizing visions such as these is the same as with Edelman's fixation on the subject's constitutive lack-in-being, namely, that their emphasis on shared modalities of awkwardness might interfere with our capacity to see how some subject positions are much more bur-dened by such awkwardness—and thus much more difficult to navigate—than others. At the same time, the realization that the other is "like" me not in the sense of having the same (human) attributes as me but in the sense of being just as riven by (inhuman) awkwardness as I am, and therefore just as perpetually at a loss with regard to how it is supposed to fit into the world as I am, might allow for more generous modes of connection across seem-ingly insurmountable divisions. Indeed, though Dean and Bersani, like Edelman, theorize from a Lacanian perspective, they manage to unearth yet another reason why Edelman's plea for self-shattering negativity rings so hollow: in shifting their focus from the self's jouissance to the jouissance of the other, they illustrate a serious limitation of politico-ethical visions based on destructiveness, namely, that it is inconceivable that destructive-ness would be an adequate response to someone else's (inhuman) awk-wardness. Destructiveness as a politico-ethical attitude works in relation to normative structures of power: like Benjaminian divine violence, it coun-ters the brutality of institutionalized dominance by anarchic violence. But this cannot be our response to those who are struggling to make a "human" life out of elements that sometimes seem inhumanly awkward.

It seems to me that Dean and Bersani are right to assume that an ethics of empathy only goes as far as empathy itself does, which is why it can be unacceptably erratic, too easily derailed by lapses of empathy (and there will always be lapses—even Butler cannot prevent these). As a result, an impersonal universalism that cuts through differences may be the only viable alternative. I know that this is a hard thing for posthumanist theory, including queer theory, to admit. But it feels like we have exhausted—tried and found wanting—our other options: rampant relativism, inter-personal recognition, empathetic identification, grieving the other, feeling bad about the impotence of our mourning, destroying ourselves for the sake of the other, and so on.

The longer I ponder the contours of contemporary ethics, the more convinced I become that impersonality and universalism—and perhaps even universal models of justice—are worth a second look. Don't get me wrong: I do not want to return to Western metaphysics, for its impersonality and universalism were never genuine; its so-called impersonality and so-called universality were used to promote the interests of the powerful. But impersonality and universality—like subjectivity, autonomy, and rationality—are not the property of Western metaphysics. They *can* be thought along different lines. One of the many things I appreciate about the work of Lacan, Dean, and Bersani is that they have begun this process of thinking impersonality and universality anew. For now, it's just a start. But it's something.

CONCLUSION

A Dialogue on Silence with Jordan Mulder

During the process of drafting this book, I received a term paper on the politico-ethical potential of silence from one of my graduate students, Jordan Mulder, who was enrolled in my seminar on Marxism and psychoanalysis. Jordan's paper both spoke to me personally and struck me as relevant to the themes of this book. I consequently asked for his permission to use selections from the paper to create a dialogue between the two of us. Through some back and forth between us, we generated the text that follows. I hope that it serves as a fitting conclusion to my analysis of the queer ethics of opting out.

JORDAN MULDER: Lacan writes in the *Écrits* that, "whether it wishes to be an agent of healing, training, or sounding the depths, psychoanalysis has but one medium: the patient's speech" (1966, 206). It seems to me that this valorization of speech as the "one medium" of psychoanalysis raises quite forcefully the problematic of the silent subject, the subject who slips into silence, who refuses to speak. Does such a subject become, as Kirsten Hyldgaard proposes, "an empty, passive canvas for the brush-strokes of the Other?" (2003, 240). Put differently, does silence involve an automatic acquiescence to the misrecognitions of the Other? Or can it perhaps be read as a form of resistance, as a refusal to open one's interiority to the interpretive, probing attitude of the Other (or other)?

MARI RUTI: Your questions intersect in interesting ways with the queer ethics of opting out I have outlined in this book. In the course of my discussion, I have touched on various modalities of opting out, such as the suicidal ethical act, desubjectivation, failure, and bad feelings such as melancholia and depression. Silence could be said to resonate with each of these modes of resisting the neoliberal creed of success, good performance, and cheerfulness, including the dominant happiness scripts that Sara Ahmed discusses: like the ethical act and desubjectivation, silence can destroy—or at least damage—the subject's viability as a symbolic entity, particularly in social situations where speaking, even speaking up, is expected; like failure, it can render the subject an outcast, a creature who may be physically present yet not (success)fully a member of the social group; and like bad feelings such as melancholia and depression, it can signal the subject's withdrawal from the usual preoccupations of life. In a way, it is a means of uttering the defiant *No!* I have analyzed without actually uttering it. From a Lacanian perspective, what you say about silence being a refusal to open one's interiority to the interpretive, probing attitude of the Other (or other) could be said to be a sign that the subject has learned not to heed the desire of the Other, which in most social situations, especially ones involving authority of any kind, elicits the subject's speech (active participation). Yet you also raise the possibility that silence can be appropriated by the Other, that when the subject does not speak, it offers itself as a passive canvas for the misrecognitions of the Other. Essentially, you wonder whether silence is a form of resistance or acquiescence. Perhaps it can cut both ways, as for instance masochism also does: masochism can imply resistance when enacted by certain subjects—say, men who are expected to stay on top, literally and figuratively—but it can imply "business as usual" when enacted by, say, straight women in relation to their empowered male partners.

JM: From a Lacanian viewpoint, silence raises some complicated questions about resistance. For example, is speech positioned against the drives, from which nonlinguistic urges—albeit ones already affected by language—emerge? If so, is silence better in contact with the disruptiveness of the drives, which, retaining vestigial attachments to certain infantile "cathexes," always threaten to mobilize nonnormative processes of regression? Perhaps. But how then do we explain Lacan's primarily negative view of silence, which classifies it as something to be eliminated? If his goal was the subversion of the Other's hegemony, would not silence offer an excellent starting point? From a loosely Marxist position, one could even argue that silence is able to facilitate positive solidarities by allowing the silent subject to disavow existing models of subjecthood. Marxist theories of solidarity require that one remain, to a certain extent, alienated from the normative social order, if only so that one can encircle back around to others and form new forms for political cohesion through that shared experience of alienation. Silence, on this view, becomes a gesture of nonparticipation and disobedience that posits the terms of dialogue themselves as skewed, predirected, and compromised—as, essentially, nondialogic; silence becomes a way to expose the fact that the language, the discourses, and the axioms in which one moves are always already aligned against the self.

MR: Although you are critical of Lacan's tendency to imply that silence indicates the patient's resistance to transference, and that it should therefore be transcended in the analytic setting, I believe that much of what you say is actually in sync with his general outlook. On the one hand, Lacan, like all analysts, was forced to work with the analysand's speech; it is hard to free associate without saying anything. On the other, the analyst's own (relative) silence implies that silence is a powerful means of communication. Julia Kristeva (1987, 1997) has perhaps been more attentive to the significance of silence on the patient's side than Lacan was, choosing to listen to the gaps in speech as much as to speech itself, and discovering there, precisely, the pulsation of the presymbolic drive that you refer to. Kristeva believes that it is only when this drive meets up with the signifier—energizes the signifier from within, as it were— that the signifier remains innovative. As I argued in the context of my account of Lacan's reading of James Joyce, I believe that Lacan came to the same conclusion toward the end of his career. But more pertinently for our discussion, I would assert that even if Lacan failed to say so, silence can function as a tool of rebellion in the clinical setting. Recall that the purpose of analysis, for Lacan, was to allow the patient to arrive at the point where he or she does not give a damn about what the Other wants; analysis "works" precisely when the patient finally utters her *No!* or *Enough!* to the desire of the Other. It seems to me that, within the walls of the analyst's office, silence may be a more effective way of uttering such a *No!* than aggressive speech. After all, to the degree that speech is what the analyst wants from the patient, even aggressive speech is a bigger concession to the analyst's desire than silence. I remember that the most meaningful moment of my own Lacanian analysis was when I lay on the couch for fifty minutes without saying a word. For perhaps the first time in my entire life, I was not trying to please the Other. Fortunately, my analyst was smart enough to recognize the significance of this moment. She was a true Lacanian in the sense that she respected my ability to resist her desire. As a consequence, this was a real turning point in the analysis, essentially facilitating its termination in terms that felt constructive to me. It also strikes me that there is a strong correspondence between the Lacanian attitude of dissociating oneself from the Other's desire and what you say about alienation—the subject's rejection of "existing models of subjecthood"—being important for a Marxist theorization of political solidarity. You suggest that silence can function as an index of productive alienation in the Marxist sense. I think that this is not incompatible with Lacan's general understanding of political resistance, even if it might complicate the analytic process. Earlier in this book, I quoted Žižek's observation that "alienation *in* the big Other is followed by the separation *from* the big Other" (Butler, Laclau, and Žižek 2000, 253). Simply put, alienation leads to separation (to the *No!*). It seems to me that Marxism and Lacan share this insight.

JM: This is interesting in light of the fact that, in our current neoliberal society, organized around the fantasy of an informed electorate of autonomous individuals, having a "voice" is seen as a prerequisite of participating in political decision making. Insisting that everyone has (or should have) a voice is a way to guarantee that society remains appropriately liberal, appropriately enfranchised, and appropriately—in an amusing paradox, since speech is inconceivable without some notion of dependence on an other who will respond and stimulate various responses in you—individualistic.

MR: This is exactly why silence could be read as intrinsically defiant. In mainstream terms, it would be likely to be coded as a sign of political complacency, but from the perspective of the ethics of opting out I have delineated in this book, it could be argued to be a means of withdrawing from a social world organized around the ideal of the autonomous individual. Though I have in this book raised reservations about the mind-numbing repetitiveness with which progressive theory keeps assaulting the sovereign self, I agree with you that insofar as neoliberal capitalism relies on the fantasy of such a self, a degree of intervention might be necessary to keep this fantasy from determining the existential paths of even those who keep falling short of it. In this context, silence, like melancholia and depression, functions as a sign of the subject's refusal to enact the rituals of sovereignty, thereby pointing to alternative modes of dwelling in the world.

JM: Our society of course respects silence in ritualized, obligatory ways: we call for moments of silence after tragedies such as 9/11, or on memorial days, to command introspection and to perform memorialization but perhaps also to superstitiously appease the spirits of soldiers whose sacrifices now amount to having assured for us, their fellow citizens, a higher standard of living—the privilege to work not in a factory making products but in an office designing them. We enjoy adopting briefly, even flirtatiously, that special kind of silence that sentimental and national causes require us to perform with all the conspicuous sincerity of a pantomime—in the wake of horrible events, our grief is best and most safely expressed in caricature, the trauma in question well secreted behind the still bodies of a tableau.

MR: You are talking about the ways in which silence can be instrumentalized for nationalist purposes. On the one hand, moments of silence communicate that we are decent human beings capable not only of mourning our losses but also—and this is what makes Judith Butler (2004) justifiably angry—of knowing which losses are worth grieving and which are not. On the other, such moments surreptitiously communicate the very opposite message, which is that it is time to brush ourselves off and get back to the sway of everyday life, including the sway of producing and consuming that is the linchpin of neoliberal capitalism. In other words, the "moment" of silence places the emphasis on the passing, short-lived quality of our acts of mourning. As I have proposed in this book, our collective order is hostile to prolonged grief because such grief paralyzes our capacity to make a contribution to its economy. At the same time, it needs signs of grief to assure everyone that we have not lost our basic humanity. Moments of silence function as the perfect compromise: we are allowed—nay, told—to grieve yet we are simultaneously being told that we should do so expediently; the moment should not extend itself to become a way of life.

JM: Silence can also be used fetishistically to separate the agentic neoliberal subject from its others, to signal the utter otherness—or backwardness—of the other. For instance, movie screens abound with hard-partying Western tourists who, in their sojourns through the developing and rural worlds, encounter stock figures like the "Oriental" monk or the chaste French nun. The contrived fish-out-of-water plots of these films necessitate that such figures embody, through their silence, the mystique of the old world. This mystique functions as the backdrop for the ability of the protagonists to redefine themselves through their comic struggles to come to terms with alterity. In this sense, many contemporary comic travel films are rewritings of *A Midsummer Night's Dream*, albeit with modern-day tropes of racialized domination plugged in. One can think, for example, of *Vicky Cristina Barcelona*, *The Hangover Part II*, *The Best Exotic Marigold Hotel*, and *Sex and the City 2*. In the process of a dalliance with their stereotyped, thinly allegorized alter egos, the Western heroes of these movies wrestle something useful—modern subjecthood—back from a force so stupid in its anachronism that it has tipped over into an uncanny mysticism; the muted figures of otherness might hold the key to subjectivity but the heroes do not know what to do with it. As a result, a liberal competence—which knows how to transform otherness into intelligibility—must neutralize the threat posed by the silent other. The finale to such films often involves the monk or nun throwing away their vow of silence completely, perhaps (if a monk) to reveal a newfound allegiance to a culture of constant productive exchange, for instance, to the globalized community of interconnected speaking subjects, or (if a nun) to declare love for the film's protagonist. In such gestures, neoliberal society successfully confronts its silent other, strangling speech from it through a process no less imperious than the practices of interrogation that confront similarly ethnicized and theologized suspects charged with dreaming up plots of world domination.

MR: You have put your finger on the role that silence plays in the fetishistic production of the exotic other who, by virtue of its unwillingness (or incapacity) to participate in the vocal world of neoliberal agency, functions both as an object of desire and as a site of tremendous anxiety for the urban Western subject. Insofar as this other does not communicate, it creates an obstacle to the subject's capacity to grasp its meaning, thereby giving rise to the kind of Orientalist, racialized, or class-based desire you depict; desire, as every Lacanian knows, operates on the logic of distance so that it is exactly the other who exasperates the subject with its elusiveness that is also the object that the subject most covets. In this book, I have analyzed the kind of desire—desire that meets up with the jouissance of the drive—that short-circuits this predatory dynamic, arguing for the ethical potential of desire that refuses to surrender its most cherished objects even when this refusal costs the subject some of its social viability or comfort. But there is no doubt that most of the desire that we see in the world does not contain such ethical potential but instead follows the trajectory of conquest that you describe. Orientalist desire, as Edward Said (1979) theorized it, constructs the exotic other in part on the basis of its silence (or silencing): it is precisely to the extent that the other remains silent—or is silenced—that the Western subject can project upon it its orientalizing fantasies, including the old world mystique you mention. The Eastern other, in particular, is often defined primarily by its silence and the enigma that this silence generates. In this sense, the Eastern other always already functions as an enigmatic signifier—in Jean Laplanche's (1999) sense—for the Western subject, as Homay King (2010) has brilliantly demonstrated. This can lead to a fetishistic worship, which we see, for instance, in the popularity of Buddhist meditation in the United States. But it can also generate the deep anxiety that the Western rational subject feels in relation to the unknowable, particularly the other who seems to actively withhold its meaning. Unfortunately, the all-too-common coping mechanism for this anxiety is aggression directed toward the other so that the other is either forced to speak—to divulge its alien meaning, as you mention—or eradicated altogether, rendered definitively mute. Either way, the threat posed by the other's enigma is defused, allowing the neoliberal subject to declare the victory of rationality—the will to know—over the uncanny mysticism of silence.

JM: If we flip things from the silent object to the silent subject, what interests me is the possibility that the silent subject might, in Lacanian terms, be trying to draw nearer to the lost primordial object (the Thing) by relinquishing the linguistic tools that originally interposed between the subject and that object. Lacan writes, "Since there is this damned system of the signifier, such that you have not yet been able to understand either how it came to be there, how it came to exist, what purpose it serves, or where it is leading you, it is what leads you away" (1955–1956, 54). In other words, it is language that distances me from my object. This may in turn give rise to the fantasy that if I cease to use language, if I fall silent, I may get closer to the object and may even recover it. Such a fantasy illustrates my immense foolhardiness in relation to my object: I am the gullible, pathetic subject whose irrational fixation on the object has become crippling. My task is to learn to desire less intensely. And it is also to learn to direct my desire outward, away from the lost object and toward empirical objects that I have some chance of enjoying because at least they—unlike the lost object—exist.

MR: Among other things what you are describing is the predicament of the melancholy lover who is unable to direct his desire to new objects because he is unable to break his cathexis to the one he has lost. But you are also getting at the key distinction between the object cause of desire and the object of desire that is central to Lacanian theory. The object cause of desire—the Thing—is what causes us to desire whereas the object of desire is what we reach toward in order to satisfy our desire. The gap between these two objects—the object cause of desire and the object of desire—is why no empirical object can ever fully satisfy our desire; what we are after is the original object cause of desire, the Thing, and in comparison the objects of desire that we discover in the world will always pale in comparison. This is one reason we often engage in elaborate efforts to beautify our object of desire, to bestow upon it every possible perfection in the (unconscious) hope that, in so doing, we will bring it closer to the Thing. This explains the dynamic of fetishization and idealization. Incidentally, Todd McGowan (2016) argues that it is precisely the gap between the object cause of desire and the object of desire that sustains capitalism's capacity to instill in us the hope that our desires will one day be fully met, that drives us to move restlessly from one object of desire to the next in pursuit of the perfect object that would finally bring our desire to an end by offering us complete satisfaction. This applies as much to mundane objects such as televisions, phones, and cars as to lovers; as soon as we acquire such objects, we recognize that they do not bring us the satisfaction we are after, with the result that we start hankering for an improved model: a bigger television, a sleeker phone, a faster car, or a more attractive lover. Even when we are eating a particular brand of ice cream, we may on some level be wondering whether a different brand might be more satisfying. That said, what you are also gesturing toward is the fidelity to the object that the subject displays when it is not willing to cede on its desire even when the external world is telling it that its desire is irrational. You portray the object cause of desire—rather than the object of desire—as the site of such fidelity. My point in this book has been that an ordinary (empirical) object of desire can become the recipient of such fidelity insofar as it seems to contain an echo of the object cause of desire (the Thing). That is, I have tried to find a way to explain how mundane objects sometimes come to embody what Lacan calls "the dignity of the Thing," why it is that we tend to deem specific objects as irreplaceable. What you say about the signifier leading us away from this type of desire, and about silence perhaps consequently facilitating our capacity to feel it, is thought provoking. One way I can relate our ideas is to point to relationships that feel uniquely meaningful exactly because they do not require constant conversation to thrive—relationships that weave silence into the intricate fabric that connects the individuals in question. That said, you are absolutely right that silence—which can take the form of melancholia—often accompanies a subject who has been torn down by an "impossible" desire, the kind of desire that cannot receive a response. The crypt of silence that such a subject fashions around the lost object testifies to the painful unavailability of the object, whether the Thing or the worldly object that seems to transmit something of the Thing's aura.

JM: One sign that silence can enfeeble the self is the unease that often attends being silent. To be silent is often to be anxious, especially and most obviously when one is in talkative company, when one feels the familiar, slowly mounting pressure to contribute that, for the *really* silent person, remains unheeded; to be silent is to be anxious especially and most obviously during those times of nonspeaking when one suddenly finds all the surrounding bustle of activity impossibly foreign in nature, inexplicable in purpose, a theater put on for an audience in which one's presence is an accident—uncanny, in short.

MR: One reason your treatise on silence struck me so forcefully is that I am intimately familiar with the predicament you describe: the anxiety that can accompany silence in contexts where it stands out as an anomaly. This is why I never, in classroom settings, call on silent students unless they give me some sort of a sign that they want to speak: having once been such a student myself, I know the panic of the moment when the Other—in this case, the professor—demands speech. But such panic can accumulate slowly as well, as is the case when the semester rolls by and you remain the only utterly silent student in the seminar room. You see the plea in the professor's eyes. You sense the discomfort of the other students. You want to respond to the plea and to dissolve the discomfort. This is an instance where your silence is not a form of rebellion, where you are still desperately trying to meet the desire of the Other. But you know that you are going about it all wrong, that you are not giving the Other what she wants. And if you ever say anything, suddenly all eyes are on you, and *now things really are terrifying*, so you start to blush and stammer. This is a moment when the jouissance of the real fractures your—already fragile—symbolic edifice. Now that I find myself on the other side of this scenario—now that I am the (sometimes excessively) talkative professor facing the silent student—I know that, in such situations, there is usually a great deal of good will in the room coming from the professor and the other students: we want the silent student to say something, anything, and we do not care how well it comes out; we just want this student to feel like he belongs. But of course this is *not* how the student usually feels—this much is obvious to anyone witnessing his efforts to step out of the vault of silence that protects him.

JM: Still, there is no need to view silence as a form of suffering broadly construed: if suffering were all it provided, there would be no purpose to silence but only pain for its own sake. As you imply earlier, anyone who has fallen into thoughtful silence in the company of a close friend, and has, upon returning to consciousness a moment later, seen that one's private reveries were not only forgiven but entirely unnoticed, can attest to the unique forms of affection present in a relationship when silence is considered acceptable.

MR: Yes, this is exactly what I meant earlier when I implied that some relationships are enriched by silence.

JM: But then there are instances in which the anxiety that attends silence does not derive from a position of discomfort with the failure to fulfill a social command but arises instead from the inability to find the right words, or any words at all—the inability, in effect, to know the right thing to say. In such cases, silence indicates such an acute disconnection from the community at large that the very linguistic cues that signal membership are lost: you assume an unusual position of insight; you become a visitor to a country whose language you do not know how to speak but, still, can hear (and understand). If, as Lacan argues, the psychotic is "ignorant of the language he speaks" (1955–1956, 12), the silent subject is ignorant of how to speak the language he already knows. Yet from such a space of ignorance the silent subject might be able to form bonds that are not premised on the condoned, existing forms of social interaction—provided, of course, that he is able to articulate them. In other words, silence can be the beginning or the outward sign of a social relation that is fundamentally alternative in nature, one that does not require exchange to affirm it; or, more precisely, silence can facilitate the kind of exchange, if it can still be called exchange, that more closely resembles a communion of souls, the extra- or prelinguistic position beyond (binary) difference that much of (for example) feminist theory has struggled to envision as an antidote to the usual dynamic where one party dominates the other or assimilates the other into the self (reduces difference to the Same, as Irigaray might put it).

MR: You express appealingly the potential that silence offers for alternative kinds of social bonds. It is striking that I can only really imagine this type of "communion" in the context of romantic relationships. This is what Irigaray also does in *To Be Two* (2001), which is, among other things, a treatise on the kind of eros that does not reduce difference to the Same—that allows the two to remain "two." Other kinds of relationships seem to rely more heavily on symbolic mediation. This of course is the source of both the discomfort caused by silence in most social settings and its potential as a tool of opting out of the normative demands of sociality.

JM: It is worth emphasizing that, from the point of view of language—the point of view of normative sociality—silence is always already primarily negative: the silent subject refuses something, denies the other an agreed-upon part of the social pact, reneges on a desirable form of intersubjective commitment. Here it is instructive to return to the distinction between the psychotic and the silent person. Psychosis is a malfunction in language (and only thereafter a disorder in subjectivity, insofar as subjectivity is predicated on language); it is an employment of language that ends up unintelligible. Recall that the central feature of the symptom, broadly understood, is that it represents an attempt at expression, lnguage.

at assembling a self-cure that, no matter its level of convoluted detour, works out illicit desires within an acceptable social frame and requires treatment only when the expression of such desires becomes socially debilitating. The psychotic symptom in particular, in being a matter of scrambled speech, erects no barrier against language; in its twisted way, it still cooperates with language. The other may detect a desire for acceptance within even the most delusional psychotic because psychosis, as a failure of language, accepts as its implicit precondition the effort to use language. In contrast, silence seems anomalous (mysterious) because the other can divine that the silent subject does possess at least a passable facility with speech and yet, for reasons impossible for the other to determine without making assumptions, does not make any use of it (or, at least, any valuable use: there are always moments when the silence breaks, but they are fleeting; they are the rationed-out foodstuffs evidencing the dwindling reserves . . .).

MR: This is why silence can so easily become an enigmatic signifier. This may also be why silence is sometimes read as being manipulative. Because silence carries ambiguity—the lack of clear meaning—it can make its recipient apprehensive, and perhaps even wound her. Consider, for a moment, our culture's stereotype of the silent straight guy. Sometimes this man's silence is assumed to signal his emotional incompetence: he is not able to communicate because "being a guy" means he does not know how to express himself. I do not have much patience with this line of reasoning because, in naturalizing the taciturn man, in resorting to an essentialist understanding of gender difference, it absolves certain kinds of men of responsibility for the kind of behavior that many straight women—particularly their intimate partners—experience as hurtful. The alternative, then, is to read this man's silence as a manipulative act, as a power play designed to fluster its recipient. In such contexts, silence becomes a weapon in the gendered warfare of modern society, as is the case when a man tells his girlfriend that nothing is wrong when obviously something is bothering him. Withholding speech, in other words, can signify domination: the one who says less wins the emotional game, which is exactly why self-help guides aimed at straight women—which I have criticized in earlier work (see Ruti 2011a, 2011b, 2015a)—advise women to meet men's silence with silence (don't call back, don't respond to emails, and so on). Straight women are essentially being told to use silence to empower themselves by fanning the kind of desire that, as we have established, arises from the other's enigma. I know that such gendered dynamics are far from what you are talking about. But they should perhaps figure into our attempts to think about the countercultural potential of silence. In what situations, and for whom, does this potential remain a genuine potential?

JM: In the scenario you describe, the straight man steps right into the role that the symbolic order has created for him (well before his birth), and more than this he articulates in his half-grunted monosyllables, with hypnotic eloquence, the lazy verbal passivity that he freely commands, conveying with hard-won half-smiles and chin-jerks which valiant attempt to engage him he is less repulsed by. This is quite different from the action of the silent subject who retreats into silence—or refuses to emerge from silence—as a way of countering the demand to submit to language as the cornerstone of the Other's hegemony. Lacan argues that our submission to language is the precondition of our subjectivity, of our coming to be as subjects-of-lack capable of meaning production. Insofar as the silent subject remains a divided subject, a subject of lack, he cannot escape this submission any more than his more talkative counterparts. However, the silent subject is anomalous in refusing to "get over" the harsh imposition of this injunction to adopt language; this subject appears jealously fixated on and resentful of the moment in its prehistory when it was forced to cut itself off from pre-Oedipal self-presence. The silent subject every day seeks to repeat this moment in which the Law vanquishes the self, hoping to obtain a victory from the conflict. Consequently, it recoils from those situations in which the command to speak is issued, for these faithfully replicate the formative submission to the code of language. Silence in this way might constitute an ambivalence or resistance to one's very constitution as a subject, a stubborn but steadfast compulsion to reenact the traumatic originary instance of language's assertion (the unconscious hope being that in sidestepping the assertion, one is able to undo the trauma).

MR: Your depiction of the silent subject's resistance to its constitution as a subject, and particularly to official situations that replicate the structure of this constitution, shares parallels with the attempts of queer theorists to conceptualize an insubordinate subject who rejects at least some of the dictates of normative subjectivity. In a way, you are talking on the constitutive level—the level at which the signifier brings the subject into being as a speaking, yet divided, subject—about the kind of hesitation with the parameters of normative subjectivity that queer theorists have talked about in the context of queer subjects specifically. You describe the silent subject who recoils from the violence of the Other by opting out of the Other's signifiers. Queer theorists, in turn, describe alternative ways in which subjects—through defiant acts, failure, bad feelings, and so on—recoil from the same violence. Indeed, your reference to the silent subject's unwillingness to "get over" its constitutive wounding by language resonates with queer theory's unwillingness to "get over" the painful legacies of queer abjection. Does this mean that the silent subject is automatically the ally of the—often not so silent—queer subject?

JM: I would say yes in the sense that the silent subject's defiance, like that of the queer subject, tends to elicit the hostility of the surrounding world. It is not only that the silent subject irks the Other by its noncompliance to the rules of social interaction; it is also that the talkative subject who elicits—but fails to receive—a response from the silent subject can start to feel like an aggressor, even a sadist. In the latter situation, the talkative subject comes to view the silent subject as an enemy because this subject, in turn, makes it feel overly forceful. The talkative subject resents the silent subject for turning a seemingly innocent, commonplace interaction into a contest for domination. The silent individual becomes the enemy because he makes the talkative individual feel like a monster.

MR: You are referring to an intersubjective dynamic that shares parallels with the one Sara Ahmed (2010) calls attention to in the context of describing the queer child's relationship to her parents. Essentially, the problem is that the child's queerness can make the parents unhappy even when she is not actively doing anything to cause this unhappiness; it is the sheer fact of queerness—like the fact of silence—that feels uncomfortable to the parents, who consequently start to project their unhappiness onto the child, insisting that she must be unhappy (even if she happens to be perfectly happy). So in both instances, the problem is on the side of the Other's perception, on the side of the Other's gaze in response to a queerness or silence that is experienced as alien and therefore disturbing.

JM: The relationship of the silent subject to the Other's gaze is complicated. Normally, one is free to look at whomever is speaking. The silent subject invites no such gaze, and therefore constitutes the site (stain?) that one's eyes must pass over quickly and surreptitiously, putting forth a visible presence otherwise diffused. This can make the Other—the one who feels like his gaze might be excessively probing or intense—feel uncomfortable. At the same time, the silent subject may actually want to be noticed and looked at more desperately than anyone. Indeed, the silent subject invites the stare, if for no other reason than that she causes others to ask, What's her deal? What is she thinking? If speech serves as a command to be gazed at, silence serves as a lure for the gaze, regardless of its motives.

MR: This is something I think about a great deal with respect to silent students in the classroom. As a professor, I am in a bit of a bind: on the one hand, I know that if I do not allow my gaze to meet the eyes of the silent student, I may give her the impression of ignoring her, essentially communicating that she does not count, that I am not interested; on the other, I know that if I look at this student for more than a second, I might be read as aggressively demanding speech. Because neither is a palatable option, I try to strike some sort of a balance between looking and not looking. The point is that I am aware of the dynamic and—yes, as you say—slightly uncomfortable. In that sense at least, silence does indeed serve as a lure for the gaze.

JM: I would like to end by deliberating more explicitly on the political and ethical potential of silence. There are many actual argumentative positions silence may signify—and if these do not constitute actual positions, for "positions" may require a degree of reasoned elaboration that silence inherently refuses, then they are strategies designed to achieve an end outside the procedures of formal argumentation themselves. Silence, indeed, indicates a skepticism regarding these very procedures, a tacit critique that highlights the inherently compromised status of argumentation as such. In other words, silence implicitly proposes that to speak would be to capitulate in some essential way to the very corrupt coordinates that shape the contours of any speech, dialogue, or negotiation. It is in this sense that silence can been used to advance a political agenda. Consider, for example, the famous 1917 Silent Parade in New York, organized by W. E. B. Du Bois to agitate for antilynching legislation. As the historian Peter de Bolla remarks, the silence of the Parade facilitated "something like organized and conspicuous theater," displaying the protesters' "precarious psychological location between justified rage and creative restraint" (quoted in Miller 2009, 185). While the perceived passivity of the Silent Parade, and its ineffectiveness in spurring any legislative change, led many in the post-Reconstruction movement to become more militant—to tell America to *go to hell* as loudly as they could—its lack of legislative success (a nonresult, it should be noted, that it shared with many of the nonsilent protests that occurred in New York and across the country during the same time period) in no way reflects a mistake in its conception: it was designed not merely to achieve legislative change but also to upset the symbolic position into which the period consigned black subjects. As the words of the journalist James Weldon Johnson attest, in this respect the protest was quite victorious: "The power of the parade consisted in its being not a mere argument in words, but a demonstration to the sight": "The effect on the spectators was not wholly in what they saw, it was largely in the spirit that went out from the marchers and overpowered all who came within its radius. . . . When the head of the procession paused at 30th Street . . . I turned to Dr. Du Bois at my side and said, 'Look!' He looked, and neither of us could *tell* the other what he felt" (1995, 65–66; emphasis added).

MR: Essentially, the silent protest here functions as a nonviolent version of the *No!*—the Lacanian act—that I have analyzed.

JM: Indeed, one beneficial aspect of silent protests is that they rebuff incitements to violence. The refusal to respond to the heckles and shouts coming from white faces in New York tenement windows constrains the ire that might otherwise cause one to throw things at those windows. Conversely, when one refuses to respond defensively to the barbs and jabs designed to provoke and to bait, one also refuses to present those doing the barbing and jabbing with the excuse they require to escalate the confrontation into a violent struggle (a struggle that is then used as a pretext to crack down more harshly on such protests in the future). By forgoing the violent dimension of the act, silent subjecthood makes its dissent clear without allowing that dissent to reach the point of such fervor that it collapses upon itself. Silent protests never initiate the kinds of all-out physical conflagrations that have historically proven unsatisfactory: ineffective in comparison to nonviolent civil disobedience.

MR: You are presenting a very concrete example of how the act of saying *No!* can become a collective, rather than merely a private, act of defiance.

JM: What makes silent protests so effective is the way they perform a semblance of violence upon the self, almost as a direct substitution "in the real" for the more invisible, systemic, and symbolic violence of the structural inequalities to which they call attention. Extreme forms of self-inflicted violence can carry immense political consequences: among various unforgettable images of silent self-annihilation are those of Buddhist monks protesting the Vietnam War. Instead of uttering vehement declarations, these monks silently lit themselves on fire and did not scream as the flames leaped up their robes and bodies. Silence was an integral feature of the political statements that such self-immolations intended to make. The conflagration, when it arrived to conclude the period of silence that preceded it, took on the character of symbolic impositions themselves. The self-immolator exposed the symbolic for what it really is: the fire that consumes the self.

MR: This is the sense in which Edelman's account of the Lacanian act as a plunge into the jouissance of the real, or Foucault's account of desubjectivation, becomes tangible. It is precisely out of respect for these kinds of historical actions—and I am also thinking of Mohammed Bouazizi, whose "act" of self-immolation instigated the Arab Spring—that I have, in this book, been resistant to the easy rhetoric of self-annihilation—a rhetoric that remains purely figurative, that does not in any way touch, let alone destabilize, the subject professing it—that characterizes so much of progressive theory, including queer theory.

JM: There is a dark side, however, to silence used in political contexts. Consider the US government's refusal to "negotiate with terrorists": the United States elects to remain a silent body that merely acts, and whose action, moreover, is driven by affronted moralism. From the perspective of such moral outrage, issuing a verbal response would constitute an unacceptable concession. And it would also compel a recognition of the very foe whose right to exist the United States questions by refusing to speak to it. Silence is here the first condition for unilateral action, just as speaking is the first for diplomacy. Along related lines, one cannot forget the dogmatic vows of silence taken by monks in the Catholic Church. These compose the outward manifestation of a deeper structural prohibition on the right to question the hierarchical chain of authority. In addition, one cannot forget the damaging effects of such military policies as "don't ask, don't tell." In other words, silence can also indicate an institutional reluctance to publicly own up to structural violence. In such cases, the failure to verbally recognize difference functions as a way to preserve the status of that difference as difference, as a kind of illicit transgression so apparently destabilizing that it cannot even be granted symbolic legitimation through its acknowledgment in language.

MR: This is exactly why I have argued for the necessity of normative judgments regarding the "content" of various acts of opting out. I have proposed that in turning antinormativity into a new norm, queer theory all too easily loses the ability to distinguish between defiant acts that are ethical and others that are simply just destructive (violent). Among other things, I have posited that as much as queer theory rails against "morality," it cannot get around the fact that it needs some set of normative codes to draw the parameters of its ethics, including its assessment that heteropatriarchy is an oppressive system. You seem to be suggesting something similar about silence—that silence is not *intrinsically* progressive but can also be deployed for reactionary political purposes.

JM: Still, institutional manipulations of silence—instances where silence is used by the powerful to further disempower the powerless—should not be taken to entirely compromise silence as a political program. Undoubtedly, like the analyst's adoption of silence as a ruse to elicit self-revelation from the patient, the strategy of withholding recognition from marginalized groups remains a symbolic practice fully rooted within the discourse of the Other. In contrast, silence as an antihegemonic political program of resistance tries to upset symbolic—including political—categories themselves. As I have argued, silence, on a fundamental level, can be a means of eschewing condoned forms of symbolic subjectivity. That said, no silent person should automatically identify him- or herself as a radical subject; such narcissism should be assiduously avoided. Social anxiety—which is often as far as the silent person gets—does not equal social subversion. But in socioeconomic and political environments that have come to use speech as a lubricant for exchange, it is important to grapple with the fact that speaking as such can constitute a concession to the Law of the Other, and particularly, in our current context, to the laws that buttress neoliberal capitalism. Is it, indeed, even possible to think about notions like capitalist entrepreneurship without invoking some kind of a clichéd extroverted subject who goes about "networking," "making connections," and being verbally "dynamic"? Is it possible to view the traditional job interview, in which the interviewee is obligated to make disclosures about him- or herself to a silent, judging Other, as anything but a perversion of the psycho-analytic session, and perhaps even as its horrible eventuality? Has the prevailing culture unexpectedly modeled itself on a popular version of Freud's central insight—his emphasis, that is, on the value of speech as a transformative practice for the self? The advocate of silence as a form of political and ethical engagement must consider these possibilities. But past these—and past, too, the silent respites observed by Romantic poets, who hole themselves up in wooded solitudes far from the hustle of city centers; past the studious fascination with which people politely ignore one another on the street; and past, too, the self-aware misan-thropy of Žižek, who boasts of his disengagement from others in spite of his oratorical gifts and of the speech-like quality of his prose—past these, how should silence be articulated today?

MR: I will only add the line from Lacan about the role of the analyst as a kind of rubbish dump that you quote in your paper: "All day long in fact he has to endure utterances that, surely, are of doubtful value to him-self and even more so to the subject who communicates them to him" (1955–1956, 29).

REFERENCES

Agamben, Giorgio. 2011. *The Kingdom and the Glory: For a Theological Genealogy of Economy and Government*. Translated by Lorenzo Chiesa. Stanford: Stanford University Press.

Ahmed, Sara. 2004. *The Cultural Politics of Emotion*. London: Routledge.

——. 2006. *Queer Phenomenology: Orientations, Objects, Others*. Durham, N.C.: Duke University Press.

——. 2010. *The Promise of Happiness*. Durham, N.C.: Duke University Press.

——. 2014. *Willful Subjects*. Durham, N.C.: Duke University Press.

Allen, Amy. 2008. *The Politics of Our Selves: Power, Autonomy, and Gender in Contemporary Critical Theory*. New York: Columbia University Press.

——. 2013. "Feminism, Foucault, and the Critique of Reason: Re-Reading the *History of Madness*," *Foucault Studies* 16 (2013): 15–31.

Badiou, Alain. 2001. *Ethics: An Essay on the Understanding of Evil*. Translated by Peter Hallward. London: Verso.

——. 2005. *Being and Event*. Translated by Oliver Feltham. New York: Continuum.

——. 2012. *In Praise of Love*. Translated by Peter Bush. New York: New Press.

Barthes, Roland. 1977. *A Lover's Discourse: Fragments*. Translated by Richard Howard. New York: Hill and Wang.

Bataille, Georges. 1986. *Eroticism: Death and Sensuality*. Translated by Mary Dalwood. San Francisco: CityLights.

Benhabib, Seyla. 2006. *Another Cosmopolitanism*. Oxford: Oxford University Press.

——. 2011. *Dignity in Adversity: Human Rights in Troubled Times*. New York: Polity.

Berlant, Lauren. 2008. *The Female Complaint: The Unfinished Business of Sentimentality in American Culture*. Durham, N.C.: Duke University Press.

——. 2011. *Cruel Optimism*. Durham, N.C.: Duke University Press.

Berlant, Lauren, and Lee Edelman. 2014. *Sex, or the Unbearable*. Durham, N.C.: Duke University Press.

Bersani, Leo. 1995. *Homos*. Cambridge, Mass.: Harvard University Press.

Bersani, Leo, and Adam Phillips. 2008. *Intimacies*. Chicago: University of Chicago Press.

Bollas, Christopher. 1993. *Being a Character: Psychoanalysis and Self-Experience*. New York: Routledge.

Brown, Wendy. 2005. *Edgework: Critical Essays on Knowledge and Politics*. Princeton, N.J.: Princeton University Press.

——. 2006. *Regulating Aversion: Tolerance in the Age of Identity and Empire*. Princeton, N.J.: Princeton University Press.

Butler, Judith. 1990. *Gender Trouble: Feminism and the Subversion of Identity*. New York: Routledge.

——. 1993. *Bodies That Matter: On the Discursive Limits of "Sex."* New York: Routledge.

——. 1997. *The Psychic Life of Power: Theories in Subjection*. Stanford: Stanford University Press.

——. 2000. *Antigone's Claim: Kinship Between Life and Death*. New York: Columbia University Press.

——. 2004. *Precarious Life: The Powers of Mourning and Violence*. New York: Verso.

——. 2005. *Giving an Account of Oneself*. New York: Fordham University Press.

——. 2009. *Frames of War: When Is Life Grievable?* New York: Verso.

——. 2012. *Parting Ways: Jewishness and the Critique of Zionism*. New York: Columbia University Press.

Butler, Judith, and Athena Athanasiou. 2013. *Dispossession: The Performative in the Political*. New York: Polity.

Butler, Judith, Ernesto Laclau, and Slavoj Žižek. 2000. *Contingency, Hegemony, Universality: Contemporary Dialogues on the Left*. London: Verso.

Cixous, Hélène. 1975. "The Laugh of the Medusa." *Signs: Journal of Women in Culture and Society* 1 (3): 875–893. This translation was published in 1976.

Cobb, Michael. 2012. *Single: Arguments for the Uncoupled*. New York: New York University Press.

Cooper, Julia. 2016. "Melancholy Utopia: Loss and Fantasy in Contemporary American Literature and Film." PhD diss., University of Toronto.

Copjec, Joan. 2004. *Imagine There's No Woman: Ethics and Sublimation*. Cambridge, Mass.: MIT Press.

Cvetkovich, Ann. 2003. *An Archive of Feelings: Trauma, Sexuality, and Lesbian Public Cultures*. Durham, N.C.: Duke University Press.

——. 2012. *Depression: A Public Feeling*. Durham, N.C.: Duke University Press.

Dean, Tim. 2006. "The Antisocial Homosexual." *PMLA* 121:826–828.

——. 2009. *Unlimited Intimacy: Reflections on the Subculture of Barebacking*. Chicago: University of Chicago Press.

Deleuze, Gilles, and Félix Guattari. 1972. *Anti-Oedipus: Capitalism and Schizophrenia*. Translated by Robert Hurley. New York: Penguin. This translation was published in 2009.

Derrida, Jacques. 2001. *On Cosmopolitanism and Forgiveness*. Translated by Mark Dooley and Michael Hughes. New York: Routledge.

——. 2005. *The Politics of Friendship*. Translated by George Collins. New York: Verso.

——. 2006. *Specters of Marx: The State of the Debt, the Work of Mourning, and the New International*. Translated by Peggy Kamuf. New York: Routledge.

Duggan, Lisa. 2003. *The Twilight of Equality? Neoliberalism, Cultural Politics, and the Attack on Democracy*. Boston: Beacon.

Edelman, Lee. 2004. *No Future: Queer Theory and the Death Drive*. Durham, N.C.: Duke University Press.

———. 2006. "Antagonism, Negativity, and the Subject of Queer Theory." *PMLA* 121:821–822.

Ehrenreich, Barbara. 2009. *Bright-Sided: How Positive Thinking Is Undermining America*. New York: Picador.

Eng, David. 2001. *Racial Castration: Managing Masculinity in Asian America*. Durham, N.C.: Duke University Press.

———. 2010. *The Feeling of Kinship: Queer Liberalism and the Racialization of Intimacy*. Durham, N.C.: Duke University Press.

Enns, Diane. 2016. *Love in the Dark: Philosophy by Another Name*. New York: Columbia University Press.

Foucault, Michel. 1961. *History of Madness*. Translated by Jonathan Murphy and Jean Khalfa. London: Routledge. This translation was published in 2006.

———. 1978–1979. *The Birth of Biopolitics: Lectures at the Collège de France, 1978–1979*. Translated by Graham Burchell. New York: Palgrave Macmillan. This translation was published in 2008.

———. 1981–1982. *The Hermeneutics of the Subject: Lectures at the Collège de France, 1981–1982*. Translated by Graham Burchell. New York: Palgrave Macmillan. This translation was published in 2005.

———. 2000. *The Essential Works of Michel Foucault*. Vol. 3. Edited by James Faubion. New York: New Press.

Fraser, Nancy. 2010. *Scales of Justice: Reimagining Political Space in a Globalizing World*. New York: Columbia University Press.

———. 2013. *Fortunes of Feminism: From State-Managed Capitalism to Neoliberal Crisis*. New York: Verso.

Freud, Sigmund. 1914. "On Narcissism: An Introduction." In *The Standard Edition of the Complete Psychological Works of Sigmund Freud*, vol. 14, translated by James Strachey, 73–102. London: Hogarth Press. This translation was published in 1957.

———. 1917. "Mourning and Melancholia." In *The Standard Edition of the Complete Psychological Works of Sigmund Freud*, vol. 14, translated by James Strachey, 239–260. London: Hogarth Press. This translation was published in 1957.

Gramsci, Antonio. 2012. *Selections from the Prison Notebooks*. Edited and translated by Quintin Hoare and Geoffrey Nowell Smith. New York: International Publishers.

Halberstam, Judith. 1998. *Female Masculinity*. Durham, N.C.: Duke University Press.

———. 2006. "The Politics of Negativity in Recent Queer Theory." *PMLA* 121:824–825.

———. 2011. *The Queer Art of Failure*. Durham, N.C.: Duke University Press.

Halley, Janet. 2006. *Split Decisions: How and Why to Take a Break from Feminism*. Princeton, N.J.: Princeton University Press.

Halperin, David. 2007. *What Do Gay Men Want? An Essay on Sex, Risk, and Subjectivity*. Ann Arbor: University of Michigan Press.

Harari, Roberto. 2002. *How James Joyce Made His Name: A Reading of the Final Lacan*. Translated by Luke Thurston. New York: Other Press.

Holland, Sharon. 2012. *The Erotic Life of Racism*. Durham, N.C.: Duke University Press.

Huffer, Lynne. 2010. *Mad for Foucault: Rethinking the Foundations of Queer Theory*. New York: Columbia University Press.

——. 2013. *Are the Lips a Grave? A Queer Feminist on the Ethics of Sex*. New York: Columbia University Press.

Hyldgaard, Kirsten. 2003. "The Cause of the Subject as an Ill-Timed Accident." In *Jacques Lacan: Critical Evaluations in Cultural Theory*, vol. 1, *Psychoanalytic Theory and Practice*, edited by Slavoj Žižek. New York: Routledge.

Irigaray, Luce. 1974. *Speculum of the Other Woman*. Translated by Gillian Gill. Ithaca: Cornell University Press. This translation was published in 1985.

——. 2001. *To Be Two*. Translated by Monique Rhodes and Marco Cocito-Monoc. New York: Routledge.

Jagose, Annamarie. 2007. "Theorizing Queer Temporalities: A Roundtable Discussion." *GLQ: A Journal of Lesbian and Gay Studies* 13 (2–3): 177–195.

Johnson, James Weldon. 1995. *The Selected Writings of James Weldon Johnson: The New York Age Editorials*. Oxford: Oxford University Press.

King, Homay. 2010. *Lost in Translation: Orientalism, Cinema, and the Enigmatic Signifier*. Durham, N.C.: Duke University Press.

Kipnis, Laura. 2003. *Against Love: A Polemic*. New York: Vintage.

Kirshner, Lewis. 2004. *Having a Life: Self-Pathology After Lacan*. Hillsdale, N.J.: Analytic Press.

Kristeva, Julia. 1974. *Revolution in Poetic Language*. Translated by Leon Roudiez. New York: Columbia University Press. This translation was published in 1984.

——. 1987. *Black Sun: Depression and Melancholia*. Translated by Leon Roudiez. New York: Columbia University Press. This translation was published in 1989.

——. 1997. *Intimate Revolt: The Powers and Limits of Psychoanalysis*. Translated by Jeanine Herman. New York: Columbia University Press. This translation was published in 2002.

——. 2000. *Melanie Klein*. Translated by Ross Guberman. New York: Columbia University Press. This translation was published in 2001.

——. 2005. *Hatred and Forgiveness*. Translated by Jeanine Herman. New York: Columbia University Press. This translation was published in 2010.

Lacan, Jacques. 1955–1956. *The Seminar of Jacques Lacan, Book III: The Psychoses*. Translated by Russell Grigg. New York: Norton. This translation was published in 1993.

——. 1959–1960. *The Seminar of Jacques Lacan, Book VII: The Ethics of Psychoanalysis*. Translated by Dennis Porter. New York: Norton. This translation was published in 1992.

——. 1966. *Écrits: The First Complete Edition in English*. Translated by Bruce Fink. New York: Norton. This translation was published in 2007.

——. 1969–1970. *The Seminar of Jacques Lacan, Book XVII: The Other Side of Psychoanalysis*. Translated by Russell Grigg. New York: Norton. This translation was published in 2007.

——. 1972–1973. *The Seminar of Jacques Lacan, Book XX: On Feminine Sexuality, the Limits of Love and Knowledge*. Translated by Bruce Fink. New York: Norton. This translation was published in 1999.

——. 1975–1976. *Le Séminaire de Jacques Lacan, Livre XXIII: Le Sinthome*. Paris: Éditions du Seuil, 2005. All translations of this text are mine.

Laplanche, Jean. 1999. *Essays on Otherness*. Edited by John Fletcher. New York: Routledge.

Lear, Jonathan. 2000. "Introduction." In *The Essential Loewald: Collected Papers and Monographs*, by Hans Loewald. Hagerstown, Md.: University Publishing Group.

Levinas, Emmanuel. 1991. *Entre Nous: On Thinking-of-the-Other*. Translated by Michael Smith and Barbara Harshav. New York: Columbia University Press. This translation was published in 1998.

Love, Heather. 2007. *Feeling Backward: Loss and the Politics of Queer History*. Cambridge, Mass.: Harvard University Press.

Mahmood, Saba. 2011. *The Politics of Piety: Islamic Revival and the Feminist Subject*. Princeton, N.J.: Princeton University Press.

Marcuse, Herbert. 1955. *Eros and Civilization: A Philosophical Inquiry Into Freud*. Boston: Beacon. This translation was published in 1974.

McGowan, Todd. 2013. *Enjoying What We Don't Have: The Political Project of Psychoanalysis*. Omaha: University of Nebraska Press.

——. 2016. *Capitalism and Desire: The Psychic Cost of Free Markets*. New York: Columbia University Press.

Miller, Monica. 2009. *Slaves to Fashion: Black Dandyism and the Styling of Black Diasporic Identity*. Durham, N.C.: Duke University Press.

Muñoz, José Esteban. 1999. *Disidentifications: Queers of Color and the Performance of Politics*. Minneapolis: University of Minnesota Press.

——. 2006. "Thinking Beyond Antirelationality and Antiutopianism in Queer Critique." *PMLA* 121:825–826.

——. 2009. *Cruising Utopia: The Then and There of Queer Futurity*. New York: New York University Press.

Nietzsche, Friedrich. 1989. *On the Genealogy of Morals*. Translated by Walter Kaufmann and R. J. Hollingdale. New York: Vintage.

Perez, Hiram. 2005. "You Can Have My Brown Body and Eat It, Too!" *Social Text* 23 (3–4): 171–191.

Puar, Jasbir. 2007. *Terrorist Assemblages: Homonationalism in Queer Times*. Durham, N.C.: Duke University Press.

Ruti, Mari. 2006. *Reinventing the Soul: Posthumanist Theory and Psychic Life*. New York: Other Press.

——. 2008. "Why There Is Always a Future in the Future: The Antisocial Thesis in Queer Theory." *Angelaki: Journal of the Theoretical Humanitie* 13 (1): 113–126.

——. 2011a. *The Case for Falling in Love: Why We Can't Master the Madness of Love–and Why That's the Best Part*. Naperville, Ill.: Sourcebooks.

——. 2011b. *The Summons of Love*. New York: Columbia University Press.

——. 2012. *The Singularity of Being: Lacan and the Immortal Within*. New York: Fordham University Press.

——. 2013. *The Call of Character: Living a Life Worth Living*. New York: Columbia University Press.

——. 2015a. *The Age of Scientific Sexism: How Evolutionary Psychology Promotes Gender Profiling and Fans the Battle of the Sexes*. New York: Bloomsbury.

——. 2015b. *Between Levinas and Lacan: Self, Other, Ethics*. New York: Bloomsbury.

Said, Edward. 1979. *Orientalism*. New York: Vintage.

Santner, Eric. 2001. *On the Psychotheology of Everyday Life: Reflections on Freud and Rosenzweig*. Chicago: University of Chicago Press.

240

REFERENCES

Sayers, Philip. 2014. "Unhooking Oneself: Repetition and Drive in *White Teeth.*" Association for the Psychoanalysis of Culture and Society Annual Conference, October 18, 2014.

Schmitt, Carl. 2005. *Political Theology: Four Chapters on the Concept of Sovereignty.* Translated by George Schwab. Chicago: University of Chicago Press.

Sedgwick, Eve. 2003. *Touching Feeling: Affect, Pedagogy, Performativity.* Durham, N.C.: Duke University Press.

Silverman, Kaja. 2000. *World Spectators.* Stanford: Stanford University Press.

Spivak, Gayatri. 1988. "Can the Subaltern Speak?" In *Marxism and the Interpretation of Culture,* edited by Cary Nelson and Larry Grossberg. Champaign: University of Illinois Press.

Warner, Michael. 1999. *The Trouble with Normal: Sex, Politics, and the Ethics of Queer Life.* New York: Free Press.

Žižek, Slavoj. 2001. *Enjoy Your Symptom! Jacques Lacan in Hollywood and Out.* New York: Routledge.

——. 2005. "Neighbors and Other Monsters: A Plea for Ethical Violence." In *The Neighbor: Three Inquiries in Political Theology,* by Slavoj Žižek, Eric Santner, and Kenneth Reinhard. Chicago: University of Chicago Press.

——. 2012. *Less Than Nothing: Hegel and the Shadow of Dialectical Materialism.* New York: Verso.

Zupančič, Alenka. 2000. *Ethics of the Real: Kant, Lacan.* London: Verso.

——. 2003. *The Shortest Shadow: Nietzsche's Philosophy of the Two.* Cambridge, Mass.: MIT Press.

INDEX

abjection, 2, 3, 4, 16, 110, 139, 170, 177–178, 186, 192–193, 203, 228
adoptees, transnational, 184–185
Adorno, Theodor W., 60, 70
affect theory, 5–6, 9, 126. *See also* Ahmed, Sara; bad feelings; Berlant, Lauren; Cvetkovich, Ann
Against Love: A Polemic (Kipnis), 23
Agamben, Giorgio, 201
agency, 40–41, 49–50, 56, 64, 86, 117, 126
Ahmed, Sara, 6, 169; and fetishization of mobility in Western queer culture, 31–32; and gay marriage, 17–20; and happiness scripts, 18–19, 61, 94, 216; and pessimism, 174–175; and queer child's relationship to parents, 228
AIDS/HIV, 28, 173
alienation, 85, 111, 114, 131, 149; constitutive alienation as one of many forms, 91; and Edelman–Berlant dialogue, 135–142; and silence, 218; Žižek and, 218. *See also* Other, the; traumatized/wounded subjects
Allen, Amy, 153, 155
Althusser, Louis, 126
American exceptionalism, 30–31, 37

Antigone, 46–47, 54, 56, 69, 109; Butler and, 108–109; Edelman and, 91; Eng and, 182; Lacan and, 46–47, 54, 109, 111; and relationality, 54, 80, 91, 108–109; and subjective destitution, 96
antinormativity, 4, 7, 37–43, 89, 152–157; as new norm, 97, 152–154, 157. *See also* negativity; opting out
antisocial strand of queer theory, 3–5; bridging the antisocial-social divide, 6–7, 127, 130–168 (*see also* Huffer, Lynne); and Edelman–Muñoz debate, 88–90; Edelman's formulation of antisocial thesis, 87–100; and forms of negativity, 131 (*see also* negativity); Lacan and, 4, 5, 80–81, 88, 91–100; Muñoz on, 6, 125, 142; promotion by white gay men, 6, 87–90, 125–126, 142; and theories of performativity, 159–161. *See also* Bersani, Leo; death drive; Edelman, Lee; Halperin, David
Arab Spring, 231
Are the Lips a Grave? (Huffer), 130, 133, 150, 157, 162
Aristotle, 46
Asian Americans, 183–184, 186
assemblage, 32–33

Athanasiou, Athena, 47
autonomy, 9, 137, 144, 159; Antigone and,
46, 56; Butler and, 56–58, 82, 89, 106,
119–120; and desires, 70, 72, 102; female
autonomy, 189–190, 192; Kristeva and,
70, 72; Lacan and, 46, 56, 72, 96; and
relationality, 58, 82, 106; and silence,
218; and white gay men, 186; Žižek and,
44–45, 50. *See also* defiance; freedom
Aviance, Kevin, 172

bad feelings, 2, 5–6, 9, 169–213, 216;
Ahmed's analysis of pessimism,
174–175; Bersani's ethical arguments,
10, 209–210, 212; and biopolitical
control, 5, 9–10, 196–204; Brown's
argument about women in Western
vs. non-Western cultures, 198–202;
Cvetkovich's analysis of depression and
trauma, 196–197; and Dean's impersonal
ethics, 208–212; depoliticizing effect
of, 195–196; and encounters between
self and real/"inhuman" aspects of
the other, 205–213; Eng's analysis of
racial melancholia, 9, 180, 182–185,
192; Halberstam's "shadow feminism,"
188–192; hyperbolic rhetoric of, 9–10,
194–207; Lacan and, 204–208; Love's
analysis, 9, 176–179, 192; and Muñoz's
queer utopianism, 169–175, 179–180;
and optimism, 175; prescriptive vs.
descriptive rhetoric, 192–193; Ruti's
critique of fetishization of, 9–10, 194–
207; as source of profit for neoliberal
capitalism, 193–194. *See also* affect
theory; depression; grief; melancholia;
negativity; pessimism; shame;
traumatized/wounded subjects
Badiou, Alain, 54, 94, 105, 112, 194
Barthes, Roland, 105
Bataille, Georges, 120
Benhabib, Seyla, 153, 154
Benjamin, Walter, 35, 47
Berlant, Lauren, 6, 129, 130, 135–142, 169,
208; and cruel optimism, 16–18, 61, 94,
134–136, 176; dialogue with Edelman, 9,
93, 130, 135–142

Bersani, Leo, 3, 41, 138; ethical arguments,
10, 209–210, 212; Lacanian perspective,
4, 80
biopolitics, 5, 48, 196–204; Brown and, 198–
202; Foucault and, 9–10, 22–25, 165, 197–
198; Kipnis and, 24–25; Lacan and, 63,
66; Marcuse and, 66; and marriage, 16,
22–27; and pornography, 62; and "rights,"
201–203; and rights-based models of
justice, 152–154; and women, 198–202
Birth of Biopolitics, The (Foucault), 197–198
Bloch, Ernst, 170, 171
*Bodies That Matter: On the Discursive
Limits of "Sex"* (Butler), 47
Bollas, Christopher, 122
Bouazizi, Mohammed, 231
*Bright-Sided: How Positive Thinking is
Undermining America* (Ehrenreich), 2
Brown, Wendy, 31, 150–151, 198–202
Butler, Judith, 4, 44–59, 107–109, 175–176;
and agency, 40–41, 49–50, 56, 86, 117;
antipathy for the (autonomous) subject,
57–59, 119–120; and autonomy, 58, 82,
89, 106, 119–120; and cruel optimism,
17; and desire, 83–84, 86; Edelman's
critique, 107–109; ethics of precarity,
57, 119, 159, 195, 206–207; Foucauldian-
Butlerian reverse discourse, 159–162,
177–178; Foucault and, 40; and gay
marriage, 13; and grieving, 219; Holland's
critique, 148; Huffer's critique, 144–145,
159–160; Lacan and, 4, 48–54, 65–67;
and Lacanian-Žižekian perspective,
49–55; and power, 40–42, 83–84, 86, 153;
reading of Antigone, 108–109; recent
theories, 57, 81–82, 159; and relationality,
54–59, 81–82, 94, 106; Ruti's critique,
40–42, 57, 81–82, 94, 117; Sedgwick and,
134; and subject's investment in their
oppression (subject as subjected), 54, 57,
92; Žižek and, 44–45, 48–50, 54, 65, 67

capitalism. *See* neoliberal capitalism
castration, 66
Chaplin, Charlie, 172
children: Edelman and, 27–28, 90–91, 93,
106–107, 110, 143; and impulse to repair,

Edelman–Muñoz debate, 88–90; and forms of negativity, 131. *See also* affect theory; Ahmed, Sara; Berlant, Lauren; Cvetkovich, Ann

socialism, 198

social order: and convergence of antisocial and social strands of queer theory, 7; and critique of homonormativity, 13–37; ideals of success, achievement, and productivity as route to happiness, 2–3, 16, 59–61, 175; and imperative to enjoy, 25–26; and Marxist theories of solidarity, 217; and misogyny, 188; and pleasure, 28–29; and religion and secularism, 200–201; and sexuality, 22–24, 83–84; and silence, 218–220; social restrictions on desire, 101–102; structural forces (poverty, racism, etc.), 5, 16, 131, 137, 139–142, 153; and trauma, 196–204; valorization of nuclear family, 7, 67; Western values, 59–61. *See also* biopolitics; gay marriage; happiness scripts; justice; Law of the Other; marriage; morality of the master; neoliberal capitalism; Other, the; service of goods

Spivak, Gayatri, 29, 188–190

Split Decisions: How and Why to Take a Break from Feminism (Halley), 148–149

structural forces (poverty, racism, etc.), 5, 16, 131, 137, 139–142, 153. *See also* circumstantial traumas

subject, the, 72–78; antipathy toward the sovereign subject/idealization of nonsovereignty, 9, 38–39, 57–59, 89, 119, 144–47, 149–52, 158, 176, 203–204 (*see also* Butler, Judith; Edelman, Lee; Huffer, Lynne); Berlant and, 135–138; Butler and, 41, 49–50, 56–59, 63, 82, 92, 119–120, 145; and constitutive and circumstantial lack (*see under* traumatized/wounded subjects); decentered by desire, 105–106; deprivileged subjects/subjects leading precarious lives, 9, 57, 58–59, 125–126, 142, 158 (*see also* traumatized/wounded subjects); destiny of (*see* destiny); dissociation from Other's desire (*see*

under Lacanian psychoanalysis); Edelman and, 9, 92, 96, 97, 119, 131–132, 135–138; and ethical dilemmas, 9, 58–59; and failure, 35–37; Halberstam's (straight, male) humanist subject, 190; Holland and, 147–149; Huffer and, 119, 142–147, 157–158; and interpellation, 49–50; Klein and, 134; Lacan and, 42–43, 50–56, 59, 63, 67, 91, 227; and memory, 150–151; and performance principle, 60; posthumanist subject, 127–128; and poststructuralism, 121–122, 126–128; and real life, 150–151 (*see also* traumatized/wounded subjects); rebirth of, 176, 179; Ruti on, 145–146, 150, 152 (*see also critiques of specific theorists*); Santner and, 122–123; and signifier, 119; silent subject, 215–233; subject formation and repression, 9, 52, 65, 67, 70, 72, 76, 169; subjective singularity, 123–125; and "subjectless" critique, 33–34; submission to language as precondition of subjectivity, 227; Žižek and, 49–50. *See also* desubjectivization; psyche; queer subjects; self-destruction; traumatized/wounded subjects; white gay male subjects

subjective destitution, 95–96. *See also* Lacanian ethical act

suffering, 17–20, 131, 179, 195, 207. *See also* cruel optimism; traumatized/wounded subjects

suicide bombers, 29–34, 206–207

surplus-repression, 61–62, 64, 70–71, 75, 76, 98

television, 22, 194

Terrorist Assemblages: Homonationalism in Queer Times (Puar), 29–34

terrorists, 29–34, 231

Thing, the, 72–78, 86, 97–99, 101, 117; and circumstantial and constitutive lack, 132; and creation of objects, 114–115; and defiance, 77; "the dignity of the Thing," 77–78, 223; and distinction between the object cause of desire and the object of desire, 222–223; and Eng's